Village Vets

Vets

CALVING STRAPS AND ZOMBIE CATS

Also available

Village Vets
by
Anthony Bennett & James Carroll
with Mark Whittaker

Village Vets

CALVING STRAPS AND ZOMBIE CATS

Anthony Bennett & James Carroll
with Mark Whittaker

ABC
Books

The ABC 'Wave' device is a trademark of the
Australian Broadcasting Corporation and is used
under licence by HarperCollins*Publishers* Australia.

First published in Australia in 2016
by HarperCollins*Publishers* Australia Pty Limited
ABN 36 009 913 517
harpercollins.com.au

HarperCollins*Publishers*
Level 13, 201 Elizabeth Street, Sydney NSW 2000, Australia
Unit D1, 63 Apollo Drive, Rosedale, Auckland 0632, New Zealand
A 53, Sector 57, Noida, UP, India
1 London Bridge Street, London, SE1 9GF, United Kingdom
2 Bloor Street East, 20th floor, Toronto, Ontario M4W 1A8, Canada
195 Broadway, New York NY 10007, USA

National Library of Australia Cataloguing-in-Publication entry:

Village vets 2 : calving straps and zombie cats / Anthony Bennett and
James Carroll with Mark Whittaker.
  ISBN: 978 0 7333 3419 1 (paperback)
  ISBN: 978 1 4607 0491 2 (ebook)
  Bennett, Anthony.
  Carroll, James.
  Veterinarians – New South Wales – Berry – Biography.
  Veterinary medicine – New South Wales – Berry.
  Country life – New South Wales – Berry.
  Other Creators/Contributors:
  Carroll, James, author.
  Whittaker, Mark, author.
636.089092

Cover design by HarperCollins Design Studio
Cover images by shutterstock.com
Typeset in Baskerville MT by Kelli Lonergan
Printed and bound in Australia by Griffin Press
The papers used by HarperCollins in the manufacture of this book
are a natural, recyclable product made from wood grown in sustainable
plantation forests. The fibre source and manufacturing processes meet
recognised international environmental standards, and carry certification.

Thank you to our families and the vets, vet nurses and animals who have taught us so much along the way.

THE STORY SO FAR

Anthony Bennett and James Carroll met on their first day of university, bonding during orientation week over their mutual love of the student lifestyle. They forged a friendship on the basis of shared experiences during the hard slog of five years at university – from slaving over late-night study, borrowing notes from missed lectures and helping to organise the social calendar of the veterinary faculty. After those years they went their separate ways. Anthony joined the clinic in Berry, on the south coast of New South Wales while James went north to Barraba, in northern New South Wales where he spent a few years having great adventures and learning the trade. Anthony stayed in Berry (who wouldn't want to live there?) but James was bitten by the travel bug, taking the well-worn path to the UK and experiencing his own version of James Herriott's *All Creatures Great and Small* for the next four years. After meeting his wife, Ronnie, while travelling, James came to a crossroads where it was time to get a real haircut and a real job, and he and Ronnie ended up back in Australia. While they settled initially in Sydney, the opportunity came up for a move to Berry with Anthony's business partner, Geoff Manning, approaching retirement. After a lot of thought, James and Ronnie found it hard to come up with reasons why they shouldn't move to one of the most idyllic bits of the world.

PROLOGUE
CYCLONE RODNEY

James

Hi, I'm Rodney Richmond, TV producer.' Short in stature and bristling with energy, Rodney burst into the clinic like an exuberant Staffie, startling the little old lady sitting in the waiting room with her cat cage on her lap. 'I'm going to make a show about these guys.' He gesticulated grandly back towards us. We'd only met him a minute earlier on this Saturday afternoon, nearing closing time. He'd greeted all the staff, and now he was making his way through the clients, working the room, telling everyone who he was and what he was going to do. He must have noticed the concerned look that was creeping across Mrs Ellis's face because he put his hand on her shoulder.

'Don't worry, love, you're in the clear. We're not filming today. But come back in a few weeks and I'll make you famous.'

Rodney was a whirlwind with designer stubble, and we were about to be sucked into his vortex. We weren't in Kansas any more.

Anthony and I had only been working together at our veterinary practice in Berry for about five months but we often joked about making a television show. One of us would get back to the clinic, perhaps covered in the poo of some large animal, and say, 'Oh mate, you shoulda seen what happened …' We'd be cacking ourselves immediately. The stories always seemed to include a lot of 'and thens'.

We'd howl some more. 'And then it's turned around and charged right at me.'

'… I've got the syringe in one hand, the cat in the other, and then …'

'What would you do for a video camera in those moments.'

The words, 'This would make such good television', were said more than once, always as a throwaway line, but with just that hint of seriousness. We knew it *would* make great entertainment. We were so busy managing the relentless chaos of an expanding practice, however, that it was never going to be more than a daydream.

And then one weekend Anthony went to a dinner party. At the end of a busy Monday he and I were perched in the cage room on stools watching a Border Collie come to from the anaesthetic after she had had a caesarean – tiny little pups cooing for attention and warmth and their first sustenance – when Anthony turned to me and said, 'Mate, have you ever really thought about this TV thing?'

'Well, yeah, but not really.'

Anthony and I like to dream big, but I wasn't sure where this was going.

'I was out to dinner on the weekend and I was telling a few stories when one of my friends said her friend's brother is starting his own TV production company and they're looking for ideas. She said they should do a show about us. I know it was just dinner-party talk, but I've thought about it a bit and I reckon we should have a look at it. I've just been talking to her again and she's rung him up and he apparently thinks it's a good idea. What do you reckon?'

'We joke about it often enough, but yeah, I reckon it's got legs. We should have a chat.'

So Anthony got back onto the brother-of-a-friend-of-a-friend network and organised for this bloke to come down. And here he was, just days later, going on about how we were going to make a show when we'd only just met. We ushered him out the back and sat him on the old treatment table where we'd normally see our patients.

'That thing you're sitting on used to be a post-mortem table for humans,' I said.

'Now it's where we send our jokes that die,' Anthony said. 'A lot of James's one-liners have been dissected right where you're sitting.'

Rodney cracked a smile before getting down to business.

'Right, so there's two of you. That wasn't on my radar. Vet shows usually only have the one dude. All right. That works. That's a point of difference. Okay, so what do you guys do? Do you see cows?'

'Yeah, we see cows pretty much every day,' Anthony said.

'What sort of things happen to cows?'

'Well, they get sick. We do a lot of calvings. Sometimes caesareans.' Anthony told him a few caesarean stories and he was flabbergasted.

'You do caesareans while they're standing up? Awake? At the farm? This is unbelievable. We need to film this.'

Anthony and I don't need an excuse to tell a yarn, so we probably trotted out just about every single one in the repertoire. Rodney was getting more and more worked up with each one.

'This is fantastic. This is freaking amazing. We've got to make this. And we've got you two taking the piss out of each other the whole time. This is brilliant. You two can play off each other and the fact you're mates. It'll give us some variety and a different angle. We'll have like a bromance.' He paused for a moment. 'Yeah, a bromance.' He raised his arms like Moses in the 1950s blockbuster. He had seen the way and it was two blokes with animals.

We hadn't seen the vision quite so clearly at that point. We just looked on, perplexed.

'What about alpacas?' he said. 'Do you see alpacas?'

'Yeah, we were out chasing one around a paddock yesterday,' I told him. 'Couldn't catch it. They're slippery buggers.'

'That's brilliant. People freaking love alpacas. We've gotta get some freaking alpacas in this show …' He paused before resuming with a fresh resolve. Now he was Noah with a checklist. 'I want alpacas. I want donkeys. I want cows. Horses. Dogs and cats. Rabbits. What about rabbits? We need rabbits.'

'Yeah, mate. We see them all the time. It's what we do,' Anthony explained.

'This is freaking brilliant. This will work. This will be a show. I'll sort it out. My mate and I. We're starting a TV production company. We'll come and film a pilot and it's gunna rock.'

Rodney said goodbye, the tornado passed, and we were left to clean up all the mental debris.

'Wow. That guy's enthusiastic.' said Anthony.

Rodney called a week or so later. 'Yep, yep, I'm really keen. I'm all over this. Couple of little problems. One, it turns out my business partner who was providing all the funds has dropped out. And by dropped out, I mean I think he's in a bit of froth and bubble and has dropped off the face of the Earth. Bit of a problem but don't you worry about that. I'm all over this. This has got legs, mate. I'll fund it myself if I have to. I think this is freaking great. I've only got 20K to put into it, but that's enough to make a pilot. We've had a few other ideas floating around, but yours is the best. I'm gunna make that pilot.'

'So to be clear here Rodney, you've got no job,' Anthony said. 'You've got $20,000, and you're going to come down for three days and spend it all making a pilot with us. That's your plan?'

'Yep. Totally. It's gunna be great, isn't it.'

We weren't sure exactly what we were dealing with. We knew Rodney had producer credits for *Domestic Blitz*, *Wheel of Fortune*, *The Footy Show* and a bunch of other things, but it wasn't like he'd ever troubled the scorers at the Logies. At least he had skin in the game, as they say in the business pages.

'What's going to happen next?' Anthony said.

'I'm coming next week with a soundo and a camera guy. I've got the best camera guy you'll ever meet. I'll have to find a soundo. What are your busiest days?'

'Monday and Tuesday.'

'Great. We'll come down next Sunday and film Monday and Tuesday. Maybe a bit into Wednesday. Perfect. I'll call you later.' And with that he was gone.

Rodney arrived on the Saturday of our work Christmas party at Anthony's house. It was late in the afternoon when he parked his black BMW X5 at an awkward angle across the drive. It was the sort of park that said the owner of this car doesn't necessarily play by the rules.

'I'm here,' he burst in, going around and introducing himself to everyone in the room again. He was in great form – a complete mess, but still bright and chirpy. 'Mate, I went to the *Australia's Next Top Model* Christmas party on Thursday night and I've been partying ever since. Haven't slept yet.'

Wearing his customary flanno and shorts, blue boot guards over his Blundstone boots, he was like the Loony Tunes Tasmanian Devil whirling in. He made an obvious impression on everyone, stayed for two beers, and whirled out again in the direction of the nearest motel. He needed to get some sleep.

At this stage, I had a ten-day-old baby, Charlie. My life had changed forever. I was supposedly on paternity leave, but I'd only had three days off. Work was ridiculously busy. I was coming in to help. Charlie wasn't feeding. He'd lost a heap of weight. I'd slept less than Rodney.

On the Sunday, the crew turned up and we did a little filming around the clinic. We had a few people we knew with pets that had little problems come in so we could film them. Skin problems and things like that. Rodney seemed well refreshed and keen to go.

'Where are we gunna get the alpacas?' he kept asking.

'It's cool,' Anthony said. 'If we don't get 'em by Tuesday, we'll go and get some on Wednesday. Don't worry. Plenty will happen.'

The crew followed us around on Monday. Wayne the soundo was a quiet guy. Rodney was his hyperactive self and soon it became obvious to us that this show was a little different from Rodney's earlier shows. We certainly weren't *The Footy Show*. Scott Barnett the cameraman was a legend. He provided the direction and would pull us aside and tell us what to do.

'We'll reshoot this,' he'd say. 'We need another angle here.' He did a fantastic job of explaining to us how things would work and putting us at ease.

Rodney got a busy couple of days. A lot happened: sick dogs, snakes, horses, cows to artificially inseminate. No alpacas, though. So we organised to go out and drench some for a client who we knew had a drenching due. That made Rodney happy.

We filmed enough to make a mini-version of a TV show and we were all happy with what we got. On that last night, we had a barbecue with the crew and they all seemed to think the show had a good chance of getting up, but they stressed that in the world of television, nothing was certain till the thing actually went to air.

I was on call and feeling pretty dead to the world around midnight when my phone rang. One of our regular clients, Max McCarthy, rang to say his beloved cat, Alan, had been hit by a car.

'He was sitting out the front on the fence like he always does and I went to get him in to put him to bed. He saw a possum and scurried after it, straight under a car that was going way too fast. The bastard didn't even stop!' Max was a mess. 'He's dying! He's dying!'

'Okay, rush him in and I'll meet you at the clinic,' I said, already moving towards the door to get the process started.

'I don't have a car.' Max was frantic.

'Don't worry. I'll grab you and Alan on the way past.'

I knew where Alan lived because he was a bit of a local legend. He was a tiny ginger cat who lived on a corner near a popular café. He'd sit on a brick pillar in the fence and let the patrons pat him on the way past. His diminutive size made him look like a kitten and endeared him even more to all the passers-by.

I jumped in the car and drove at a pace that approached the limits of what might be considered legal. In these cases, time is of the essence.

When I arrived Max was cradling Alan and crying. Alan looked like someone who knew how serious the situation was. I quickly checked him over. His heart rate was through the roof, his breathing shallow, rapid but clear. His gums were sheet white indicating that he was in shock and close to death, his abdomen extremely sore and swollen. Despite my best efforts not to hurt him or really even move him, there was the unmistakeable crunchiness of broken bones in his hind limbs and pelvis. This assessment only took seconds, and with urgency I helped Max, still cradling Alan, into the front seat of the car.

'Let's go,' was all I said, knowing there was nothing that could be done for him there. He was bad and might not make it, and I conveyed this to Max who nodded and showed that he knew, even if his heart didn't want to accept it.

On the way, I called Anthony to get some help.

'Alan McCarthy has been hit by a car and he's in a bad way. Can you swing by and pick up Rex on the way? I'm pretty sure we'll need to do a blood transfusion.'

Rex was my cat, an overweight tabby who was a regular blood donor.

'Should I bring the camera crew?'

'I don't care. You just need to get into the clinic to give me a hand as soon as you can.'

I asked Max if he minded having a film crew and he mumbled no, he didn't care. We were really only focussed on Alan.

When we arrived at the clinic, I jumped out, flung open the clinic door and leapt into action. Very quickly Alan was getting oxygen support and I had an IV catheter in him and fluids flowing. The catheter went in easy, which was a big relief because sometimes it's nigh on impossible to get them in with cats in shock after such serious trauma. Alan was limp and fairly lifeless, with shallow, rapid breaths. He only made a small yowling noise when we moved him and upset his severely damaged hindquarters. Most of the damage seemed to be to his abdomen and pelvis.

Anthony arrived carrying Rex under his arm. Rex looked a little confused, like he wasn't sure why his evening nap had been interrupted. He'd come in on Anthony's front seat. There'd been no time to find a cage but we put him in one now, with a little sedation snuck into him to make the blood collection easier. I shot Anthony a look that said, 'Geez, am I glad to see you, thanks, and this is bad,' all in one. It's a big relief to have another person on board helping with such a touch-and-go case. The crew arrived a few minutes after Anthony and set up quickly to capture the moment.

We fired up the X-ray and ultrasound machines, and got the IV fluids flowing, trying to replace the volume of blood that was seemingly being lost into Alan's swelling abdomen. Anthony collected blood from Rex while I recruited members of the crew to help me get the diagnostics done to assess the situation with a bit more clarity. Having all hands on deck was a great help in this case, though the crew were busy trying to capture the action and not get in shot at the same time.

The X-ray technique used in these cases is not the most accurate. It is aimed at getting the most information with the least stress on the patient. We call it a Cat-o-gram and it involves quickly plonking the cat on the X-ray plate and X-raying the whole animal, a luxury we don't get in the larger patients. As expected though, the view wasn't great. Alan's lungs looked okay and his diaphragm was intact – great news. But further back there appeared to be big problems. His pelvis was in pieces and both his femurs were broken. All of these things were bad, but the worst part was that the abdomen appeared all white on the X-ray – a sign that it was filling with fluid. Judging by how pale he was, this fluid was almost definitely blood.

We raced Alan back out, shaved up one side of his body and had a look with the ultrasound. Big, black swirls of fluid were evident where there should have been white tissue. This was all very worrying. Alan was clearly struggling, with his heart going so fast the beats could barely be counted. Max was shell-shocked and as we hadn't asked him to leave, he hung around out the back of the clinic. While he stayed back, he had a good view into the surgery because in our haste we had left the door wide open.

Time was of the absolute essence and we got lucky – Alan's blood type matched Rex's. Even if it hadn't, we would have had no choice but to administer it and hope there was no reaction. Dogs are a little easier to treat in this kind of scenario as they can have one blood transfusion safely without you needing to know the two blood types are a match. Anthony already had Rex on the table and was collecting the blood, while I double-checked his maths on how much blood we could take safely from Rex and how much we thought we needed for Alan. Doing maths at this time of night under this sort of pressure is never easy and it helps to double check. While the blood was being collected, we weighed it to accurately measure how much we had. I wanted to collect every drop we safely could from Rex. Luckily, he was big and Alan was very small. Hopefully, our luck would hold. Rex went back to bed feeling woozy. He too had given his all.

The normally crystal-clear fluid lines turned bright red as the blood transfusion started to flow. We had it going in as fast as we dared. We also had pain relief, antibiotics and oxygen flowing into Alan, trying to give him every chance as he clung precariously to life. We thought we saw him start to stabilise, but the bleeding in his abdomen was clearly getting worse, and all this was happening fast, way too fast for my liking.

'He's bleeding out, mate,' Anthony said, as for the first time we had a moment to pause and assess. My memory would blank out everything else that was going on with Max and the crew. I just remember Anthony's ashen face, his hopeless expression. We were losing. We both knew what the other option was but it wasn't something we wanted to do. I went to speak to Max.

'We've given him blood and we'll give him more, but he's just continuing to bleed. We're losing him because we're losing blood too fast and we can't stabilise him medically. He's on death's door.'

'Is there anything else we can do?' Max asked, taking on the gravity of the situation.

'Our only other option is to open him up and try to find where the bleeding is coming from and stop it. It's risky but it's our only option. His chances are poor. I can't put a figure on it but I'd say that without it he will bleed out. With the operation, I don't like his chances but I think they're better than without it.'

'We've got to try,' Max said.

I nodded and went back inside. Max followed me. He stroked Alan on the forehead before returning outside.

We added a whiff of anaesthetic to the oxygen that Alan was receiving and placed a tube down into his lungs. The monitoring machines told us that things were bad, and we had no option but to plough on. We had called Kahlia, one of our vet nurses, and got her out of bed to fetch us another blood donor as we prepped for surgery. The pace was frenetic. The crew was capturing the action as well as helping prep Alan for surgery with the producer holding things for us and fetching things that we were able to point him towards.

As soon as we opened Alan up, we saw problems everywhere. We sucked blood out of the cavity as quickly as we could. Once Kahlia arrived and prepped up, we had her start preparing to do an auto transfusion, pumping Alan's own lost blood back into his veins. It's an extremely uncommon procedure but we needed to think outside the box. As we made our way around Alan's insides, we were finding sources of bleeding and tying them off. Anthony held the spleen to stem the flow from there while I removed a section of bleeding liver. But as we turned our attention to the other side of the liver, the haemorrhage continued. The whole liver was mush and the blood poured from everywhere. The more we looked, the more problems we found. We sucked and scooped, patched and stitched as fast as our gloved and bloodied fingers could go. The blood just kept coming. I can only imagine that this is what human trauma surgeons go through. It was hard to believe that a cat that size had that much blood in it. As we worked to stem the flow, we could feel Alan slipping away under the anaesthetic. There was an awful, hopeless, sinking feeling as the monitoring machines started to tell us what we could already see in front of us – Alan was dying. The scene was horrific but we pushed on a while longer until we had to step back, shattered, to acknowledge that he was gone. There was blood everywhere, but no longer any pulse.

Stepping away brought home the full, awful scene in front of us. There was so much blood. Everybody was deeply affected: us, the crew, but especially Max. He was inconsolable. Losing Alan devastated Anthony and me. I hadn't dealt with Alan that much previously, but Anthony had known him since he was a kitten and knew Max well.

I got home from the operation about 3 a.m. My wife, Ronnie, was just putting Charlie back to bed. It was one of those wonderful rare occasions when he went straight to sleep and slept for hours. I, on the other hand, couldn't stop thinking about the night's events. Losing a patient on the table like that hits you hard. It had only happened to me a couple of times in my career. There was a feeling of failure at having tried everything and still lost the patient. I just lay in bed and worried about everything. The operation, the pilot, Max. He was so upset. Was there anything I could have done differently? Done better? It seemed to me that the show wasn't viable. We couldn't have a crew following us into these awful situations.

I'd barely drifted off to sleep when Charlie woke at dawn and it was time to get stuck into another day. One of the first things we did was buy a condolence card for Max and take it around to his place. We often send a card or flowers when clients lose a pet, but it wasn't very common for us to take it around in person. But things were so emotional; we felt it best to do it that way so we could talk about anything that needed discussing. We told the film crew to stay away. We offered our condolences as best we could.

We knew we'd made a mistake the night before in not sending Max home. We'd been so preoccupied with saving Alan's life that we'd let him hang around in the background. I didn't know how much he had seen because my focus had been entirely in the belly of that dying cat, but it was clear he'd been traumatised by the experience.

We tried talking him through what we'd done but we didn't feel like we made any headway. And then he hit us with it.

'Look, I just wish the TV guys weren't there,' he said. 'It felt like they were intruding on me and distracting you.'

I felt sick to the stomach. I knew that it wouldn't have mattered if Alan had been taken to the fanciest of university hospitals and seen by the world's greatest surgeon, he was never going to have made it. But perceptions are very important in such situations and it was easy to see how someone could come away from the experience with Max's feelings. Somebody out in the waiting room getting glimpses of the camera lights, the talk and the blood might have felt it was all too much. I know I couldn't have done anything more to save Alan. It was all there on film. We didn't do anything wrong but Max was devastated.

Rodney and the crew went back to Sydney to do whatever those guys do. Summer passed and we didn't hear from them.

I was deflated by the whole experience. Every time I thought about the pilot, I thought about losing a patient on the table. It was tainted in my mind. I chalked it up as a lesson learned and was happy to leave it all behind me. An interesting flirtation that was never meant to be.

TOM SHARP'S TRIPLETS

Anthony

Tom Sharp called, which was unusual. He was a very competent and hands-on dairy farmer who must have been doing it for forty years. He rarely needed us because he could do most things himself. Trish took the call and the tone of her voice told it all. Trish was a trained dairy farmer from western Victoria and had actually worked for Tom for six years when she first moved to NSW to marry her husband Kev. So when Trish put the call through to me, saying Tom had a calving to do, I knew there must be a good reason.

'I just can't make head or tail of it,' he said. 'I can feel multiple sets of legs but I can't find a head. I don't know what's going on. I think it could be twins.'

Twins are rare. Less than one per cent of calves. I thought his diagnosis was a little presumptuous. *He can probably just feel a back leg and a front leg*, I thought to myself. If you grab them and start to pull, nothing happens.

'Okay,' I said, 'No worries. I'll come straight out.'

Modern cattle are not bred for twinning. The gestation and calving knock the cow around, and then the calves drink twice the amount of milk and still end up small. Sheep and goats handle it better.

'Hey, James,' I called out. 'Why don't you come with me to this calving? It'll be a good chance for you to meet Tom Sharp, one of our more prominent citizens. He's just about the loveliest man alive. You can't help but smile when you're around him.'

'Yeah, no worries. I'm just finishing this spay.'

'I'm heading home that way too,' Geoff said. 'I've got to talk to Tom about something so I'll swing by with you.'

At this stage the clinic consisted of myself, James and Geoff Manning as the vets and Kahlia and Trish as our nurses. Along with our base in Berry, we had a consulting room at Kangaroo Valley. The business was growing at a tremendous pace and we were all flat out. There was a lot going on – new equipment, new ideas, new people. Trish was our most experienced nurse and a really dependable character. She had worked a few different jobs, not least of all on a fair few dairy farms, so she knew what she was talking about when she dealt with the farmers. Kahlia was much younger and had grown up caring for injured wildlife. We were lucky to have such great nurses. It really is a case of the people who make your business.

James had already bought Geoff's share of the business but Geoff had agreed to stay on to help with the transition. It allowed James to come out with me to get his bearings and be introduced to the clients.

It was great to have a new partner and mate along for the ride. The only thing tempering the enjoyment was the thought of, 'What the hell is going to happen when Geoff goes?' James and I were totally reliant on this business for our livelihood, and having a stalwart of the practice retire could really have an impact. James and I had been through lots of tricky situations together, like live horse anatomy practical exams and car breakdowns in the middle of nowhere, but how would we work together? It was in the back of my mind that James had been doing only small animal practice for the last five years and a large part of our caseload, probably approaching 50 per cent, was cattle and horses. Did that mean that I would be stuck doing all that work? Would James remember how to do a caesarean section and dig out a hoof abscess in a horse? More importantly, would the clients believe that he knew what he was doing?

We arrived at Tom's farm, which was one of the smallest surviving dairies – and probably the prettiest –in the district. We drove up the avenue of grand old trees, past the lily-filled pond, to find Tom at the yards with his son Andy and their worker Craig. With the three of us arriving, there was suddenly quite an entourage for the huge black and white cow who stood forlornly in the crush. Normally, at such events, there's a farmer and the vet and that's it. And half the time the farmer goes off to do something else. They're busy people.

This time it was like a social gathering as James was introduced around and everybody had a good old yack while I got on with the job, getting my gear out of the ute. The calving was incidental to the main business of talking. I put my hand into the cow and found, as I suspected, that one hoof was facing upwards and one facing downwards. *This is simple*, I thought. It meant that a front leg and a back leg were trying to come out at the same time.

'I think I know what's happening,' I announced, but stopped talking when I realised none of them were listening. Their backs were turned to me, and they were absorbed in the local gossip.

I pushed the calf's back leg in to get it out of the way. I ran my hand down the front leg until I found the chest, then moved across the chest. The other front leg had to be there somewhere. I found it and brought it forward. *Now, where's the head?* I thought. I found that, moved it round into position then got the ropes on the calf's front legs which felt big and strong. I had the calving jack there, so I rigged it up and slowly worked the calf out. Big dairy calves like this one can weigh forty to fifty kilograms so the jack makes it a lot easier. While it's important that the final journey through the birth canal take no longer than necessary, you also don't want to rush it. That can cause tears and all sorts of problems for the mother. So I used the jack like a fishing rod, pulling back and down with the rod, then reeling in with the lever. Pull back, crank, pull back, crank.

The boys barely paused in their conversation to see this magnificent new creature introduced to the world.

'It's a heifer,' I announced.

Tom looked around. 'That's a nice big calf,' he said, before being reabsorbed into the gabfest.

'That's all right,' I said to myself. 'Don't mind me. I'll just get on with the work.'

I thought I'd better check for tears or spares, knowing that spares – meaning twins – were highly unlikely in this case given the size of the calf. So I put my hand back in and it went straight to a leg.

'There's another one in here,' I called out. 'Lucky I checked.' It's seen as the height of veterinary embarrassment to do a calving and return to the clinic only to be called back to pull out a second calf that's been missed. It has happened. But not to me. Yet.

'I hope you don't charge double for twins,' Tom said.

'Second one is free,' Geoff said. 'Hell, you can have the whole lot for free since I'm retiring next month.'

My announcement that there was a second calf got the attention of the entourage to such an extent that they spun around ninety degrees and were now standing side-on to me, but they went straight back to their chatter and left me to the business of getting it out.

The second calf was further inside the cow, so I needed to reach in to the end of my shoulder to get the ropes on its legs. Getting the slip knot over the hoof and tightened above the ankle is always a tough assignment. You're working blind and everything's slippery. To complicate matters further, the calf is alive, so as soon as you grab the feet it reflexively pulls away. There's not enough room to put two hands in, so you can't hold the leg with one while putting the rope on with the other. You put the slip knot over your fingers, then you have to work it off your fingers and over the hoof, and then slide it up the calf's leg before you can put tension on it.

All this is quite routine, but it was made more difficult in this case by the depth of the calf inside the cow. I got the rope on, though, and pulled the calf. I might have even heard an appreciative 'Whoa' from the gallery as this one came out almost as large as the first – the size of a large suitcase. Forty kilograms. Alive. A heifer. Happy farmer. Females are worth a lot more to dairy farmers than bulls.

'Well, I guess I better check for more,' I said, jokingly.

'Where do you think she's hiding it?' someone said.

There was no way another calf could fit in there. They were both so large it was already an extraordinary performance from the cow. I put my hand in right up to the shoulder, feeling for tears in the uterus. I couldn't feel anything but the cavity was so huge I thought I'd better stand on the rail of the yard to get a bit more reach. This being an unusual calving, I thought there was an added risk of rips.

If my fingers went into a cleft, it would mean trouble. If the tear goes all the way through you can feel intestines. That's a nightmare. You have to stitch up that tear inside the cow, completely blind, trying to tie knots one-handed. You've got a long, sharp needle. You stab yourself fifty times and inevitably do a bad job. So while I was intently feeling for a tear, I was desperately hoping I wouldn't find one. My hand inched around the uterine wall, feeling the smoothness like a wet sleeping bag interspersed with regular rough bits which are the cow versions of placentas. It was all good, until, right down at the full extent of my fingertips, I felt something hard.

It couldn't be.

It was.

Another set of feet.

'There's another one in here,' I said.

'Yeah, right.'

'No kidding. I'm dead serious. There's one down there and it's one hell of a long way in. I can barely reach it. I don't know how we're gunna get it out.'

That got the gallery's attention. They came in closer and faced me directly. The conversation ceased. Of all the combined cattle experience in that shed – and it was about 100 years – Geoff was the only one who'd ever seen triplets before.

The cow had a contraction, moving the calf back towards me enough for me to get a hold of a leg. There was a possibility that if we just walked away, the cow might be able to deliver it herself, but the uterus by this stage was fatigued from all the pushing and pulling and manipulation. So I had to make sure the calf was delivered safely.

She was a brilliant cow. There was no jumping around or carrying on like some do. She didn't have unnecessary contractions. She didn't wee or poo down the front of my apron. The annoying cows seem to know to do all of these things. (And who can blame them?) But it was like this one sensed she needed help and we were in this together.

After a lot of fiddling, I got the ropes on and started pulling. The mum gave it a bit more of a push and the calf came into the birth canal. I could feel that this one was smaller. It wasn't long and sleek like it should have been but gnarled up and crooked. It had been squashed in the uterus underneath two big calves for months so its joints were a little knuckled over and frozen from not having been able to move for all that time. Its elbows and wrists were stiff which made it more difficult to get out. But its two big sisters had paved the way so there was a pretty spacious birth canal and, wouldn't you know, it was another girl.

Tom was building up his herd numbers at that time so he was ecstatic about the situation.

The fact they were all heifers was vitally important too. If just one of them had been a bull calf, then the heifers would all have been rendered infertile. What happens is that when they're developing in the uterus, the bull's testosterone crosses over into the heifer causing her to be born with no uterus or ovaries. They're called freemartins. Whenever you get a bull-heifer pair, the heifer will almost always be a freemartin – unbreedable and hence unmilkable.

I didn't check for quadruplets. There was no way. And even if there was another one in there, I wouldn't have been able to reach it.

Over coming weeks, the smaller calf's joints freed up and her growth rate picked up so that she gained on her sisters. All three of them ended up as productive cows in the dairy and went on to have sets of twins themselves.

STAFFIE ELBOW

James

The Staffie was a Sherman tank of a dog. He was the bubbliest, most pleased-to-see-you creature you could hope to meet. We'd received a call from the owners saying that he'd come off a quad bike and was busted up. But my first impression when I arrived at the property, after the long, winding road over Berry Mountain and down into Kangaroo Valley, was of a happy pooch who used his whole body to wag his tail. Staffies can be like blokes though. They'll get hit by a bus and dust themselves off and say, 'No, no, I'm okay. It'll take something bigger than that to worry me.' But then they'll get a little bug and be the whingiest, whiniest sooks in the animal kingdom.

So even though he looked fine as I approached from the ute, I knew it could be more serious than it appeared. He didn't run to meet me. He just stood there at the feet of his owners, tail wagging, tongue out.

Casting my eyes around at the rusted, red-tin roof on the unpainted weatherboard farmhouse, I gathered that the owners probably wouldn't have splashed out on a veterinary house call unless it was really needed.

The couple introduced themselves as Trent and Trudy.

'And this is Diesel,' Trent said.

'What happened to you, big feller?' I asked the dog.

Trent answered for him. 'He was on the quaddie with me. I was going at a good speed but that was okay, he's used to that. It was when I started to slow, he jumped off before I'd stopped and took a tumble. I heard a yelp and saw this big cloud of dust. He's just walked straight out of the cloud limping on his front left leg.'

'Yeah, okay. He's looking pretty good now,' I said.

'Yeah, he is, but normally he'd never show any pain so we think it's pretty serious.' Trent walked a few metres off to the side. 'C'mon, Diesel. Here boy.'

Diesel rushed towards his master and I could see he was limping on one of his front legs, but it was by no means obvious. I knelt down and ran my hand up the limb, which was hard to do with Diesel giving my face a tongue bath. He barely flinched as I felt around a very swollen elbow. When I tried to bend the limb, however, Diesel pulled it away sharply.

'I think something is seriously wrong,' I said, 'but I can't tell you what. The best thing we can do is X-ray the leg to see what we're dealing with.'

They went off and had a bit of a discussion. They came back agreeing that I should take Diesel back to the clinic in Berry. Our Kangaroo Valley facility was a consulting room open for two hours a day and not technically a clinic. All the gear for complex procedures was back at Berry.

So I loaded Diesel into the ute and he perked up like this was the greatest thing he'd done since the last time he had a ride in a ute. His tongue hung out and his tail wagged with the full-body motion for the entire twenty-five-minute drive. When I got him out of the car he smiled at me with that full-body smile. I led him into the clinic, got him sedated straight off and put him on the X-ray table.

The pictures came back and the result was clear-cut so I rang Trudy straight away. 'He's broken the pointy bit off the end of his elbow,' I said. 'It's quite a significant chunk that we can see floating around out there.'

'Okay, what can we do?' she said.

'Well, because of where it is – out on the elbow where the tendons attach – it's going to get pulled around and moved. So we can't just put a cast or a splint on it. The chunk is part of the joint so it's imperative that it gets fixed properly, otherwise Diesel's not going to be able to walk.'

I could hear their hearts sinking through Trudy's phone. 'So what do you need to do and how much is it going to cost?' she asked. 'Because the most we're going to be able to spend is 800 bucks. We can't afford anything more than that.'

'Well, it needs an operation. That bone has got to be fixed back in place, and the best person to do it would be an orthopaedic specialist because this looks like a difficult procedure. Unfortunately, that's going to be a long way out of your price range. But maybe Anthony and I could do it for that.'

Anthony and I share the same positive mindset. We don't look at a problem and say, 'Oh, that's a bit hard. We're not going to do it.' If a client can't afford to get a specialist, we'll have a crack. We'd never claim to be as skilled as the experts, but I knew if I didn't try, Diesel didn't have much of a future. This is an important learning tool as well – you can only learn by doing these sorts of things and once you've got your base surgical skill down pat it's really important to keep moving forwards. But the real benefit is in giving the dog a great outcome it otherwise couldn't get.

I spoke to a veterinary orthopaedic surgeon friend of ours, Eugene Buffa. I'd watched the gregarious South African operate on numerous occasions and it was always a delight to watch his nimble skills and his great depth of knowledge. He gave us a bit of advice and it's amazing how a few words from someone who is an absolute expert can impart the reassurance that you need. And it's equally wonderful how the experts in our profession make the time to help you like that. Before operating, we decided to rest Diesel for thirty-six hours and give him some painkillers and anti-inflammatories to get the swelling down. Now that the big feller was in hospital with a bandage on his leg, it was like he'd received permission to feel the pain in a mega man-flu dose. He was one sick puppy.

We had the surgery pencilled in for late the following afternoon, so we got in at 6 a.m. the next day in order to get through our workload and make sure we had time to do the operation. We had some horses and cows to visit in the morning so Anthony went out and did those. I stayed in the clinic where sick pooches and cats needing vaccinations and all the other things that filled our days, like computer crashes and tradesmen's visits, kept piling up. By the time Anthony returned around lunchtime, I'd admitted a bunch of spays and castrates and a few sick animals that required further investigations, like a vomiting dog that needed X-rays and ultrasounds.

The practice had run on three vets for years before Anthony and Geoff dropped it back to two. When I'd arrived a few months earlier, we were very busy even when all three of us were on deck. A few months later I bought Geoff's share of the practice and Anthony and I bought more equipment and offered more services. We were doing cool stuff – offering ultrasounds, CT, MRI and a lot more medical and surgical procedures that weren't previously on offer in the area – but were surprised at just how much more work that generated. We were busier than the one-armed paper boy.

Our usual practice was that we'd leave the complicated jobs like Diesel till the end of the day so that both of us could do them. You need the extra set of hands to hold limbs while you drill and you need the extra set of brains for that instant second opinion. We'd both done a fair bit of orthopaedics by this stage of our careers, but every operation is different depending on how the fracture sits. Having another head to bounce off is important.

As the afternoon wore on, we ploughed through the work so that we could get Diesel on the table and we were starting to see clear air ahead of us when a call came through for a difficult calving in Foxground.

'Okay, we'll do Diesel as soon as I get back,' I said.

'Let us know when you're on the way and I can start getting him prepped up,' Anthony said.

I did the calving and when I got in the car and called Anthony, he couldn't talk because he was doing a calving over in Kangaroo Valley.

'All right, I'll start prepping Diesel when I get back,' I said.

Almost as soon as I arrived, however, I heard the front door open and saw another Staffie come waddling through with a young couple in their twenties. This one was darker brown with a white patch under its chin. I went out and introduced myself to the owners.

Noah Cummings was a solidly built young bloke in Hi-Viz, with long black hair and a few days' growth. I'd already come across the Cummings family in my short time in town. They were salt-of-the-earth people who worked in earthmoving and construction. They were 'old Berry', part of the constellation of families that remained separate from the more lah-di-dah blow-ins from Sydney. The same went for Noah's girlfriend, Pia Graham, a petite woman in stretch jeans. Her family had been dotted through the hills since forever and had clung to their land despite the skyrocketing value of the real estate.

'This is Harriet,' Noah said, introducing the Staffie. 'She's a bit crook. She's vomiting and won't eat.'

'So what happened to her?' I asked as I led them into the consult room.

'Nothing that we know of. She's just been vomiting, vomiting. Won't eat. And she normally eats a lot.'

I lifted Harriet's lip and saw she was a bit dehydrated. She was a bright, happy dog. And she was still trying to be bright and happy despite whatever it was that was going on with her. She looked at me with sunken eyes and a big doggie smile. Dogs have no self-pity. She wagged her tail because she knew she should be excited to be here, yet she could barely lift her head off the table and the odd groan escaped her mouth. Like she'd had a big night on the tiles and somebody had dragged her out of bed at dawn to go for a run. 'Yeah, I'll be fine, I'll be fine. Oh god, I feel terrible,' I could almost hear her saying.

I took her temperature and it was raging. I felt her tummy and she reacted sharply. It was clearly very painful.

'So what do you feed the dog?' I asked.

'We give her a bowl of dry biscuits in the morning and half a can of tinned food at night.'

'Have you fed her anything out of the ordinary in the last couple of days?'

Pia and Noah looked at each other. You can tell when people are weighing up whether to tell the truth, a sanitised version of it or perhaps a complete untruth. Their faces flickered.

'Uhhhhh, well …' I suspected I was about to get the sanitised version. 'She ate some fat. There was a bit of sheep fat and she ate some.'

'Oh, okay. How much?'

'A bit.'

'Uh-huh,' I said, an eyebrow raised. It was almost amusing because I could tell there was something significant they were not divulging. 'How much fat exactly?'

'We butchered some sheep,' Noah said.

'Oh, yeah, okay. How many sheep?'

'Three.'

'And you gave her some of the fat?'

'Yep.'

'And were they fat sheep?' I asked, my brow arching.

'Yep. Real fat.' Noah's pride took over momentarily. 'We really finished 'em up well. They were massive. Really good.'

'Were you slicing it off and throwing it to her?'

'Nah, hardly at all. We threw it all into buckets and she got into that.'

'Well, I'm pretty sure I know what's happened here,' I said. 'I think she's got pancreatitis.'

Pancreatitis – inflammation of the pancreas – can occur for a number of reasons. In this case the cause was an extremely fatty meal, but it can be a change of diet or gastroenteritis that can trigger the inflammation. I explained that at the lower end of the scale an inflamed pancreas in dogs wasn't such a big issue. 'But I'm pretty worried that Harriet's going to be at the bad end of the scale.'

Thirty per cent of humans who get acute pancreatitis die. The actor Ashton Kutcher got it when he was preparing to play the role of Apple founder Steve Jobs. Jobs was a fruitarian for much of his life so Kutcher decided to eat nothing but fruit for a whole month. He was rushed to hospital with acute pancreatitis two days before shooting began and was lucky to survive. It's a serious condition. In dogs, too much fat is the main cause. Dogs often get it more mildly than humans do, but not this case, I suspected.

So I told Noah and Pia that I thought Harriett had this condition called necrotising pancreatitis – right up the very bad end of the scale. I explained that one of the pancreas's many functions was to produce a digestive enzyme. The enzyme remains inactive while in the pancreas but when the pancreas is damaged and gets inflamed, all the mechanisms go haywire. This digestive enzyme gets switched on and starts to digest the pancreas. Harriett's pancreas was, in effect, eating itself.

I sent them home and admitted Harriet into doggie hospital. I put her on a drip to start treating her with pain relief, anti-inflammatories and antibiotics to deal with any secondary infection of the abdominal wall and organs. I took some blood to test my hypothesis. The test we do involves mixing the blood with a liquid compound and putting the mixture into a receptacle that generates a chemical reaction. You wait ten minutes and if the test square goes darker than the control square, it means it's pancreatitis.

I took a sneak peek after just two minutes, and the test square was already black. It could not get any darker. It remains the most definitive test result I've ever seen. I sedated Harriet and took an X-ray to check that there weren't any foreign bodies hiding inside her but that was clear. I carried her great lump of a body over to our spiffy new ultrasound machine for a look at the problem. The pancreas is difficult to see on an ultrasound because it's a small organ that doesn't stand out from the other structures and organs around it except when it's inflamed.

'Quick,' I said to Anthony as he came through the door. 'Come and have a look at this one. It's a beauty. You won't miss this one.' Anthony was still learning to use the machine so he had a go. The fat around the pancreas was so inflamed it looked like someone had got a highlighter pen and kindly circled the organ for us. You could diagnose it riding past on a horse.

Anthony was ready to start the operation with Diesel, but I had a fair bit of work ahead of me to stabilise poor old Harriett. A couple more clients came through the door with some routine jobs and Anthony handled them. The work just never seemed to stop. The only solution we had for this treadmill was to work harder and longer. On this day, we cleared the decks at 5.20 p.m., but we still had Diesel looking at us from his cage with that eager expression.

We looked at each and looked at the book for tomorrow.

'This is ridiculous,' Anthony said. 'We could put Diesel off and say we're going to do him tomorrow, but we're just as busy then.'

'We should just get a coffee, put our heads down and do it now,' I said.

Us dashing down the street for a coffee, however, is usually a disaster. If you work in our profession in a small town, you're always running into clients. They all stop to say hello, you ask them how their dog or their cow is and they've usually got a question. A 'quick coffee' usually takes about an hour.

So we sent Kahlia to the café over the road and told her to hurry. It shut at 5.30 p.m. You know you're working too hard when you know the coffee deadline. While she was gone, we worked our way through the mental checklist of what we had to achieve. We made sure we had the equipment sterilised and ready to go. The practice was now closed so the phone got diverted to Anthony's mobile because he was on call. That's the other thing about having only two of you. You're on call more often and that phone becomes your nemesis.

Kahlia came bustling back through the door with three skinny flat whites. (I think I need to explain here that the streamlining of our work practices required that Anthony and I had to have the same coffee order. When new people come into the practice, we might indulge them for a day or two with their soy lattes with two sugars, but in the end, they either get the same order as us or they have to do the coffee run. Somewhere in there, Anthony converted the whole practice to skim milk despite the overwhelming scientific evidence that it will in fact make his butt bigger. I wasn't too happy about it. Even when I try to order two normal flat whites, the café staff still give me two skim flat whites because they know that's what the clinic gets. I've lost my autonomy. Basically we have become one person.)

Anyway, we downed our skinny flat whites, knocked Diesel out and shaved him with the cordless clippers. We wheeled him into the surgery and Anthony tied a lead to his leg and attached it to the light fitting hanging from the ceiling, lifting the leg clear off the table. This ensured that nothing was touching the leg so that when Kahlia did the preparation, using iodine and methylated spirits, she could do all the skin at once, not just one side and then have to turn it over.

Anthony and I were prepping for surgery, rubbing our arms and hands with iodine scrub to make sure we weren't going to contaminate the wound. If you get an infection in an orthopaedic operation, it's a disaster. We were going to be putting a screw into the bone and if the site for that got infected, it would be almost impossible to fix it without removing the screw. You're supposed to scrub for ten minutes – every surface of your arms and fingers – in a very methodical fashion that is ingrained into you at uni. For smaller procedures your attention to detail can waver, but when you're doing orthopaedics, you've got to be fastidious. Even though we'd be putting gloves over our hands, you still wash your bare hands so that you can handle the gloves and so that you are sterile beneath the gloves in case they get nicked. When you're not scrubbing, you're always holding your hands up so the bacteria can't come down your arms onto your hands.

That done, we turned off the taps with our elbows, put on hats, masks, gowns and gloves and got stuck into it. We covered the leg so the only part of the dog left visible to us was the point of the elbow poking through a small window in the green drapes. This little 12-centimetre by 12-centimetre square was to be our turf for the next few hours. On the other side of the table, Kahlia could see under the drape to make sure that Diesel was doing okay with the anaesthetic.

We do a lot of operations in the abdomen and also the knees, so at those places you know the landmarks. You know where to cut and how firmly. But when an animal breaks a leg in a funny spot, it requires more thought. You study the X-rays, read the textbooks and consult with specialists. After all that consideration, Anthony made the cut near the point of the elbow and curved it around with the scalpel, exposing the bone at the point. That was the easy part. When you're approaching joints, you also have to pull away the muscular attachments to get access. If you cut the wrong thing, you might fix the bone but destroy the joint. You have to be careful yet bold, because unless you cut in far enough to see what you're doing, you can't do anything.

As he cut through the subcutaneous tissues, I wobbled the leg around a little and the fragment was obvious to see. It was a chunk about a centimetre-and-a-half by a centimetre, broken off at an angle so that the bone was like a wafer of marble chipped off the main block. Our challenge was to stick this funny little wafer back on. The specialist orthopaedic surgeon had advised us to screw it in. Orthopaedics is a lot like carpentry. You've got drills and screwdrivers. You hammer and chisel. However, it's easy to replace a piece of four-by-two if you stuff up a DIY job, but if you break a dog's leg, that's kind of it for the dog's leg.

Anthony put the knife down. I could see a different approach so I picked it up and had a go. When we operate, the scalpel is like a speaking conch. Only one person can go at a time, but if you pick it up it's yours to use. So I cut away then hesitated.

'Just cut it,' Anthony said. 'It'll be okay.'

In the couple of months since we'd been working together, we'd found we operated well as a team. We were on the same wavelength and the more we operated, the more we intuitively knew what the other was doing. It's like when you're sawing timber with someone who knows how to do it. They hold the timber in the appropriate way while you cut. If the person has no idea about the force you're about to exert on that wood and the angle on which it will be applied, they're hopeless at holding it for you.

In this case, as we delved into the joint, we saw the bleeding and the trauma – the swelling. Despite studying X-rays and consulting with experts, the real thing never looks exactly how you expect. So having another person there who you trust is important.

I picked up our little 10.8-volt Makita drill housed inside a special sheath to make it sterile, and drilled a hole into the main part of the bone. I changed bits and drilled a slightly larger hole into the wafer. We didn't want the screw biting into the wafer and spinning it while we tried to attach it. I put the wafer hard up onto the bone so that the holes aligned, put the screw in place and turned the little medical hex-head screwdriver.

The point of the screw slid off the hole and into the broken part of the bone. Because we were operating on the point of the elbow, the angles weren't simple. Where you'd normally drill a piece of wood at 90 degrees, this was more like 70 degrees. When I put the screw in again and started to turn it, once again it slid off the bone. I just could not get that little sucker to bite into the hole. I had a couple more tries over about fifteen minutes, and then I handed it over to Anthony. 'You try. I can't do it.'

It was 7.45 p.m. when Anthony took the screwdriver. He tried and failed. Tried and failed. Frustration grew. We'd been at work almost fourteen hours. The swear jar got suspended from overuse. We tried different screws. We drilled at a different angle. We just could not get that screw in the hole. Then Anthony's phone rang.

Kahlia, at Diesel's head doing the anaesthetic, was the only one not sterile so she answered. I could hear an angry voice even though she didn't have it on speakerphone. Kahlia apologised profusely to the angry voice. It was disconcerting when trying to concentrate on a frustrating procedure.

'Anthony, Gavin Chapple wants to know when you're coming to his calving and why nobody has gotten back to him,' Kahlia said.

'What calving?'

'He said he left a message at about three.'

'I know nothing about it.'

As it turned out, Gavin had rung that afternoon and when asked to leave a message, had just said, 'Get Anthony to give me a call.'

Gavin was a city-based farmer who'd got the message about the sick cow from a caretaker who'd seen her and put her in the yards. Gavin had about fifty or sixty head in a well-run enterprise. He'd owned the property for twenty years so even though he was an absentee farmer, he was more knowledgeable than a lot of hobby farmers. Unfortunately, he wanted only to speak to Anthony because Geoff wasn't there any more and he didn't know me. Farmers are as a rule suspicious of newcomers – if they've got a question they don't want to speak to any old person, they want to speak to someone they know and trust. Often they didn't want to talk to me because I was the new guy. It was no use railing against it. Stomping your foot is only going to make things worse – it just takes time.

The message was written in the book but when Anthony got back from the valley faced with a mountain of tasks, the message with no further information had been shuffled to the bottom of the priority list. Gavin was upset. And we were upset that the message hadn't gotten through. Anthony had driven past Gavin's farm on his way back from the valley.

'Tell him I am very, very sorry. We're in the middle of an operation but I'll be out there as soon as we've finished.'

We had to refocus on Diesel's elbow, but our hopes had fallen. This screw was never going to go in.

'We'll give it one more go,' Anthony said. 'If it doesn't work, we're going to have to admit defeat. I've really got to get going to Gavin's place.'

Failure meant Diesel was never going to be able to use the leg properly again and was likely to suffer severe arthritis. So we steeled ourselves for one final effort. Anthony held the leg and pinned the fracture down with a pair of bone holders – pointy forceps that pierce the bone on either side and hold it down. I gently angled the fifteen -millimetre screw back into the elbow, gave it a turn and almost couldn't believe it when the screw didn't slide out. I turned again and felt the thread bite into bone. Gotcha! I turned some more, careful now that I didn't go too hard and crush the bone. If I stripped out the thread, it would be game over. The fragment was so small there was only room for one screw.

Anthony released the bone holders and to our enormous relief, not only did it hold, but the fracture line came together perfectly, like successfully gluing a broken vase back together. Anthony bent the elbow and the clunkiness that had been there was gone. It moved just as an elbow should.

We took a brief moment to pat ourselves on the back for being ever so clever – and for not giving up. We stitched Diesel up, and put a very strong bandage over the top to immobilise the wound as much as it was possible to immobilise a crazy Staffie.

Kahlia turned off the anaesthetics and we woke Diesel up. He roused in the classic Staffie way: howling and yowling the house down until he woke a little more, so we put him to bed on some strong painkillers. It was 9 p.m. when Anthony made a move to leave.

'All right, I'll go and do that calving now then,' he said.

'Mate, I'll come with you,' I said. 'This guy's awake enough now. Kahlia can stay with him while she cleans up.'

'Nah, I'll be right.'

'What if you get there and it's a disaster and there's no one there, the cow's aggro. It's gunna be really dangerous alone with a cow at night. Let's get some chocolate bars and we'll just keep going.'

So we got into the ute and drove back to the valley. It felt North Queensland kind of balmy as we got out of the car about 9.30 p.m. I gathered from the fancy gates and the nice driveway that it was a nice house with a nice set of yards but everything was in darkness and there was no one around. Anthony pointed the ute at the yards to use the headlights for illumination and there we saw one very sick cow. There was another cow with it which the farmhand had thoughtfully put in to keep her calm. Cows don't like to be alone.

A stench of death wafted across the yard on the still night air. That made diagnosis simple. She clearly had a dead calf inside her which had been dead for a long time.

'What's the temperament of the cows like here?' I asked.

'They're really quiet,' Anthony said. 'They're used to people working with them.'

'Good.'

As we approached, however, the cow snorted and scraped her front leg like a bull preparing to charge a bullfighter. The toxins from a rotting calf can get into a cow's bloodstream and into the brain and make them delusional. I would have loved to know what was going on inside her head, but all we could see was that she seemed to see us as the manifestation of all evil. She huffed and snorted and bellowed. She rolled her front shoulder into the dirt and tossed up dust which is one of the things they do to display imminent aggression.

We got all the gates right leading into the crush, then climbed onto the horizontal planks of the yard fence to encourage her up the race. We waved long bits of polypipe, we whooped and hollered, but one thing for sure was that our feet weren't going to touch the ground in that yard.

She made the odd charge at our legs but her mind didn't seem completely in the game. Anyway, the circular yards were well designed with gates rotating around a centre pivot so we could close her into smaller and smaller spaces until her only option was to go up the race. Faced with this choice, she promptly attacked the gate, fell on the ground and attempted to die.

We stood on the rails for a moment, each doing our own internal risk assessments. *If I get down there, will she stand back up and go me? If she does, will I make it back over the rails? If I don't make it, do I have funeral insurance?*

Such deliberations are always brief. Perhaps Anthony got down first. It's hard to recall, but we both tentatively approached her. Anthony had a halter and he quickly got it over her head and tied it back around to her leg, rendering her immobile.

With the cow in a haze of toxic fever and delusion, I put my weight on her neck, holding her down while Anthony quickly got his hands inside her, had a feel around for the calf and got some straps on it. We took turns to pull out the rotting corpse. No matter how much I might have tried, there was no way to avoid getting covered in all the fetid juices.

Anthony, who was more covered in stink than I, put his hand back inside her.

'It doesn't look good,' he said. 'There's a huge tear in the uterus.' This explained the toxic fever, because all the foul death juices had been able to leak into her guts.

'I think she's had it,' I said.

'Yeah, she's got no hope.'

Anthony called Gavin on speakerphone and told him what we'd found.

'Ah, crap, that's a bummer,' I heard him say. 'We've been looking for her. We knew she was due to calve, but she'd gotten herself into a paddock that she shouldn't have been in and hidden herself away and when we found her she was pretty crazy already.'

'There's nothing that can be done for her,' Anthony said. 'She's going to die.'

'Okay, can you please put her to sleep.'

'Yeah, sure, but you'll have to make arrangements for her to get buried tomorrow.'

Anthony apologised profusely for not having got there earlier, but we were consoled by the fact that a few hours wouldn't have made any difference. This had been going on for a week by the smell of it, but it was still a regrettable situation. 'We won't charge you for the visit,' he said.

'Well, thank you for going out in the middle of the night and trying to sort it out.'

After euthanasing the cow, we took off the stinking overalls and got back into the car, crestfallen. We'd gone from the high of fixing Diesel and feeling on top of the surgical world with our intricate skills, to being covered in stinking, rotten summer-baked placenta, leaving a dead cow behind us. It was 10.30 p.m. We'd been at work for sixteen and a half hours. As I allowed myself to relax into the front seat, I felt the exhaustion suddenly overtake me in a wave of fatigue.

'What on earth is happening?' I mumbled, too tired to form the words properly. 'I didn't realise I'd signed up for this level of busy.'

'It's ridiculous. We've got to get another vet in.'

'We do.'

And thus are the big business decisions made, driving with the windows down to reduce the omnipresent stench, feeling every bit as tired and delusional as Gavin's poor cow.

The next day was just as busy. We still had Harriet the Staffie in hospital with her pancreatitis. The walk-ins kept walking in. We were so rushed it was hard to start the search for a new vet, but neither of us had kids at this point and so we just applied the same solution: work harder, work longer. And while the load was ludicrous, it was fresh and exciting and new. I'd forked out a lot of money to buy the business. Fear was driving me. Life was crazily busy and Ronnie and I had a baby on the way so it was about to get a whole lot busier. It wasn't such a bad problem to have.

A LOAD OF BULL

Anthony

The sound of the phone ringing shattered the relative silence and gave me a momentary shock. I should have been used to it by now. The blasted thing hadn't stopped ringing in the decade I'd been in Berry. As per usual, though, Trish was on to it and had answered within a ring and a half. Not long after, I sensed that sorry-to-bother-you-but-I-really-need-you feeling of a nurse over my shoulder. This wasn't so bad because I had my head buried in tedious paperwork, trying to get my billing done for the month so that we could send out some invoices and perhaps get paid for all of the work that we were doing.

'Yes, Trish, what can I do for you?'

'Sorry to bother you, AB, I know you are busy, but Nick Pfanner from Kangaroo Valley is on the phone and he really needs to speak to you.'

'What does he want?'

'It's something about a bull and a crush but I couldn't exactly understand what he was saying.'

'Well, I hope it's a bull in a crush. I don't want to deal with one loose in the paddock,' I said, taking the handset from Trish.

'Hello, Nick, what can I do for you?'

39

Nick was a contract farmer who operated a farm-management business with his mum and dad in Kangaroo Valley. Never having had the opportunity to buy a place of their own, they'd found a good living managing the farms of the wealthy absentee owners in the valley. Nick was quietly spoken and reserved. He mumbled most of what he said into his goatee.

'Hi, Anthony, sorry to bother you but I have got a problem with a bull.'

'Okay, mate, is it in the crush or loose in the paddock?'

'Well, a bit of both actually.'

'What do ya mean, mate?' I said.

'Well, we had this young limo bull in the yards to change his ear tag and he took issue with the process. The yards themselves are fairly temporary, if you know what I mean. More so now.'

'So what's the problem? How can I help? I don't feel like driving fifty ks to help you ear-tag a bull.'

'No, that's not the problem, you see.'

I didn't.

'He's torn the head bail clean off the race and now he's loose in the yards with the head bail attached.'

'Woo, that doesn't sound good,' I said, trying to visualise the scene. The head bail is the two-metre-long, gate-like contraption that's meant to catch the animal safely and securely by the neck, so that you can perform whatever procedures need doing.

'What's he doing?' I asked.

'He's trying to jump out of the yards.'

This is the type of situation that normally the stockman would manage themselves, but I knew they wouldn't have called if they could handle it alone.

'Crikey! I'll be right there. If he gets out, we're in big trouble,' I said.

'Yeah, that's what I reckon,' I heard Nick trail off as I tossed the phone to Trish. I headed for the back door and out to my ute. James, with his renowned elephant-like hearing, intercepted me on the way out wanting to know what the rush was. I told him and he offered to come and help.

'But I do have a thousand other things I would rather do,' he said, 'including shooting myself in both kneecaps.'

'Na, mate, don't worry. I'll call you if I can't handle it … So expect a call.' I jumped into my Hilux, tore around the tight driveway side of the building and headed out onto Queen Street, feeling a bit like Batman in a super-unstable Batmobile. I really didn't know what I was going to do when I got there. I didn't have a tool for this in my utility belt, but I knew I needed to get there fast for everyone's sake.

The trip over Berry Mountain to Kangaroo Valley on the narrow, winding road was a bit of a blur. My mind was racing and I actively had to slow down and breathe deeply. Luckily this was the Hilux's four-hundredth-plus trip and I think it pretty much knew the way.

Pulling up the long driveway, past the majestic country estate, gravel flew off the wheels and I suspected the smell coming from the clutch wouldn't have pleased my mechanic. I jumped out near the yards and found Nick sitting cautiously on the top pine rail. As I climbed up to join him, the bull startled and began to charge around. One thousand kilograms of roan-red muscle dragging around a few hundred more kilos of galvanised steel stuck around its shoulders. Every time he moved, his front hooves would scrape and bang the lower part of the structure and freak him out even more, resulting in more running, more scraping and more freaking.

'Holy crap, Nick, what are we going to do here?'

'Well, I figured if you could take care of the bull then I would take care of the gate,' he said, smirking in the direction of a cordless nine-inch angle grinder in his right hand.

'Oh, yeah. Great. Thanks, mate. How about you take care of the bull and I'll take care of the gate?'

''Cause I said it first,' he said, smiling.

I took a few moments to ponder how this was going to play out.

I'd been wary of bulls ever since my childhood. My parents had a small farm at Foxground, barely fifteen kilometres to the east of where I stood. Even though Dad was a doctor, he was a farmer in his heart so we spent all our weekends and holidays at the farm. We had a lovely, quiet herd of Poll Hereford cows. But if you've got cows, you need a bull.

Dad went to a local Hereford stud of some repute and they sold him a bull who they assured him was of a quiet disposition. He was named Corby, after a famously fair boxer, 'Gentleman Jim' Corbett. I remember the day he arrived on the property, the truck that delivered him swaying with his weight as he moved around inside. He came down the ramp and he was a beautiful creature with a great thick neck as wide as a chair, and a white head with twirls of curly hair. He was massive. Twice the size of the cows. He was ushered into his bull paddock where he proceeded to roam, bellowing and digging the ground up, which is bull talk for, 'I'm here, and you're all my girlfriends now.'

We all thought it was a great show, the way he pawed at the dirt, throwing it in the air behind him, rubbing his head in it, posturing like a bull straight out of a Spanish bull ring.

He did calm down and over the next several years Corby proved to be a great bull. He got the cows in calf and produced lovely offspring.

He stayed quiet and was easy to handle. He never caused any trouble down in his paddock near the road where he lived for most of the year. Nevertheless, my sister and I were told we must never go in this paddock.

One year, he had just finished his annual two-month visitation rights with the cows and Dad and I were moving him back to his own paddock. We got all of them into the yards and separated Corby off from the cows. We let the cows out and pushed them back into their paddock, then let him out with all the gates open straight back to his paddock. It was all straightforward and Corby trotted down the lane back to his domain, heading straight for the far corner which took him closest to where we'd just put the cows. Dad wanted to check one of the fences over the other side, so we walked over there, checked it, and were returning via a deep, dry creek bed full of bush rocks and long grass when, suddenly, Corby appeared at the top of the creek bank. He was snorting and bellowing and pawing at the ground. My first thought was, *Why is he here? The cows are over there.* It soon became clear that he was here because he wanted a piece of us. I knew enough to know we were in trouble. There were no trees to hide behind. No fences to roll under. We were stuck down in the creek where we couldn't even run because of the large rocks.

Corby was right back in that Spanish bull ring. But he didn't waste too much time on theatrics.

He charged. And as it turned out, he *could* run on those large rocks. He came belting down the bank. I was beside Dad and maybe just a little behind. There wasn't time to retreat even a single step. Each of us had a piece of thin cane in our hands with leather straps on the end. My grandfather had made them for shooing cows along. They were more for noise and sight than substance.

As Corby bore down on us, those canes were all we had. Dad's a good tennis player and he just took a big swing at the bull with the leather strap, hitting him across the nose. Corby hadn't had a chance to get up a full head of steam on the rocks and the blow on such a sensitive spot stunned him sufficiently to make him pause. Dad went for the same spot on his nose again with the strap and got him. That was enough to freak Corby out and sent him scurrying to the other end of the paddock.

I can still remember shaking with the adrenaline and disbelief about what we'd just survived. We went straight back to the house and Dad picked up the phone.

'Can you come and get my bull,' I heard him say. 'And bring a few men because I'm not going back in the paddock again. And if you don't feel comfortable doing that, can you get someone with a big gun to come and shoot him.'

A couple of days later, a few men arrived with bikes and a few dogs. Corby was a big pussycat for them and trotted down the fence, into the yards and onto the truck. He didn't so much as look at us.

After that, Dad decided to get Murray Greys, a breed known for their quiet disposition. All the Herefords left and the Murray Greys turned up. Nevertheless, he went and bought a really big gun because he figured if he was ever stranded up a tree, we'd need something powerful enough to shoot a bull. It was like a cannon this gun, a 6.5-millimetre Mauser. I remember Mum once shot it at a milk crate across the gully. She missed, but the flame came about a foot and a half out the barrel and where her bullet struck, it looked like someone had hit the ground with a pickaxe and scorched the grass with a blowtorch.

The gun never got used in anger, but I suspect if he'd had it the day that Corby went for us, Dad might have gone down and shot him. He was not in a good mood.

So Corby was front and centre in my consciousness as Nick and I figured out how we were going to handle this Limousin – a French breed which is in no way known for its quiet disposition.

Given that physical restraint hadn't worked, the only ace I had up my sleeve was chemical restraint, but the two usually go hand in hand – like, you keep your bull still in the crush and I will sedate him. This obviously wasn't going to happen here. 'We need to somehow get the bull to stand still for a few seconds,' I said. 'Then I can try to sneak up behind him and give him a sedative into the tail vein.'

Older cattle have a large vein called the coccygeal that runs reliably up the underside of their tail. With all the blood collecting that vets do, you get quite good at hitting the vein blind just by lifting the tail slightly and slipping the needle between the tail bones. The trouble was that usually, the bull would be secured by the bail, not wearing it like a necklace.

I ducked back to the car and grabbed a couple of sturdy climbing ropes, the ones that you never believed would lift a minibus. I also grabbed enough sedation to stun an elephant – and a big dose of courage – from the back of my truck.

I explained to Nick that if we could corner the bull, then I might be able to lasso each side of the head bail and tie the big feller into the corner. Nick agreed and dispatched himself to the other side of the yards where he started to gesticulate and holler. It worked pretty well. The bull charged and tried to climb out of the yards like it wanted to eat him.

I took my opportunity and threw a loop of rope over a protruding pole on my side of the crush. The bull was still too preoccupied with Nick to notice his predicament so I took my chances and threw a loop over the other side of the head bail. I then threw the end of the rope to

Nick, at which point we were both holding onto a bull-powered, land-based vet-ski.

'On the count of three we tie him to the yards as tightly as we can,' I said. 'Once he feels the strain he's going to go berserk. If the ropes hold, I'll wait for him to calm down and then jump in behind him.'

Nick nodded. 'Here goes nothing.'

In our line of work, sometimes fortune favours the bold. And sometimes you get a broken leg. Luckily in this case the bull stood still. I jumped in and time stood still too as I lifted the massive tail – almost as wide as my hand at the base – covered in crap. I found the vein on the first shot and pushed down on the plunger to inject the elephant-sized sedative.

I then bravely ran away and sat up on the yards with Nick to see what would happen. Sure enough, about sixty seconds later, the bull started to grunt and salivate, a sure sign that the sedative was kicking in.

'Leave him tied up until he goes down, mate. In case I need to give him more.'

'I don't think that will be necessary,' Nick said, as the huge beast collapsed.

'All right, Nick, the bail is all yours.'

He donned ear-muffs and gloves and set to work with the angle grinder. The sparks flew back in a beautiful golden arc as he frantically worked to destroy the head bails. But a few minutes into the cutting process a strange odour started to waft out, separate from that of hot steel. It was somewhere between the acrid stench of skin cancers being burnt off and Korean barbecue.

'Shit! Stop, Nick,' I yelled as loudly as I could across the sound of tearing metal, trying to breach Nick's ear-muffs. 'You're cooking him one spark at a time.'

I ran back to the car and grabbed a few pairs of overalls and a couple of towels. On the way back to the yards, I dunked them in the double-sided cement water trough near the gate.

'Pack those under your cut line. I think the wet material should be enough to protect him.'

'Rightio, mate, whatever you reckon. The bull's your responsibility remember.'

It worked well and gave Nick the opportunity to cut the remaining struts of the bail and prise it apart.

Like something from the pages of a vet student's textbook, the huge animal rose to its feet only minutes later, seemingly unharmed. He stumbled off in the direction of the gate and freedom.

'Leave him in here a while, Nick, and let him work off a bit of that sedative. I reckon he must have a stinker of a headache. But we've left it too late to give him any Panadol.'

I arrived back at the clinic feeling like a bit of an all-round legend. Trish and James crowded around and asked me to explain how I had managed it.

'Well, Trish, just like what's under my fingernails right now, it was bullshit.'

HARRIET LOSES HER OMENTUM

James

Harriet, the Staffie who'd eaten all that sheep fat, was back. We'd given her three days of intensive treatment and nursing to bring her back from the brink of death. We'd even had to reach for the big gun in the freezer: a pack of doggie plasma, the pale yellow liquid component of blood. It's as expensive as it is effective. It did the job a treat and Harriet was soon bouncing around in her cage, ready to go home. Her owners, Noah and Pia, had taken her away with the jolly assurances that she wouldn't be getting her big Staffie jaws around any more lumps of fat.

Yet here she was, just two days later, barely able to walk through the front door.

'She's vomiting again,' Noah said. 'But there's not much to chuck up because she hasn't eaten all day. She won't get off her bed.'

'Okay, you'd better bring her through and we'll have a look at her.'

It was like she'd got in the time capsule and gone back five days. She was as sick as she'd been on the first day of hospitalisation. So we pumped her full of antibiotics, pain relief and drugs to stop the vomiting. Her shaved abdomen got another spruce up with the clippers and we had another look at her with the ultrasound.

The lining of inflamed fat around the pancreas was still inflamed, but it looked like the highlighter pen had faded. What we saw, though, were little pockets of black inside those highlighted strips. Fluids show up as black, so we deduced that she had abscesses – big pus-filled infections – forming in the bright fatty inflammation.

We gave her some pain relief and sedation and got her up on the operating table. Guiding a needle in with the ultrasound, we sucked out those black spots, filling a syringe with about five millilitres of yellow fluid. A quick look under the microscope confirmed that it was pus. Yep. We had abscesses in there. The tissue surrounding the pancreas was infected. We sent it off to a lab to tell us what kind of infection we were dealing with.

But long before any results arrived, Harriet came good. She was such a robust nutter that the minute she felt a little better she started eating voraciously and seemed for all the world like she was fully recovered. 'I'll eat, I'm fine. Totally fine. Don't worry about me.'

We called Noah and Pia back again and I explained to them what we'd done.

'It all looks pretty right in there. I think we've fixed the problem so she's good to go. But you're going to have to come back at the very first sign that she might be slipping.'

They thanked us and walked out with Harriett's tail banging on the glass door on the way out.

Two days later, they were back. We did the same thing, checking more carefully on the ultrasound for every little hint of an infection to make sure we got it all. Once again, Harriett bounced right back following rehydration with the IV fluids and started inhaling her food. We'd spoken to a surgical specialist who'd warned us that the surgery to fix this infection was complicated and dangerous. So we'd spoken to a medical specialist looking for ways to treat it without surgery and all they could offer was exactly what we were already doing. So, when Harriett returned again a couple of days later, just as sick as before, we'd reached a point where 'complicated and dangerous' was better than where we were going, which was nowhere.

The owners agreed. So in we went. As we opened up the abdomen, our eyes made straight for the pancreas. It was inflamed, but it looked like it was getting better. The tissue around it, however, was dead – necrotic, as we say in the business. It explained why we kept getting the recurrences of abscesses and illness.

The abdominal cavity has a fatty netting layer called the omentum that arises from the back of the stomach and spreads out across the whole cavity like a spider's web. It's nature's Band-Aid in the abdomen. When there's infection or inflammation, it puts a patch over it. But in this case, all that fatty spider's web that had lit up like a highlighter pen when we'd first looked at it on the ultrasound had died and was now rotting Harriett from the inside.

We had to get it out of her, which was no simple matter. Each time we came to a bit of fat, we'd be asking, 'Can we take it? Should we take it? Let's have a look at the next bit.'

We worked our way around the entire abdomen, snipping bits of dead fat, leaving others. By the time we'd done a lap of the gut, we'd become emboldened by our initial success. 'Take it out,' was the call as we made our way around for the second lap. We ended up with a huge bowl of fat next to us. Perhaps not as big as the bucket of fat that got Harriett into all this strife in the first place, but sizeable nevertheless.

The abdomen, now stripped of its omentum, had gone from looking like a warzone to being completely naked. The organs, freed of the fat that gave them definition, looked like a toddler's toy box after a rushed clean up.

I stitched her up and we woke her. She might have put on the characteristic Staffie whinging yowl when she first regained consciousness, but she never looked back from there. She was cured and never had a recurrence. Those operations are the most rewarding. This was such a long case, with a dog that had licked death on the face. Yet the minute she woke up from the surgery, she threw away her proverbial crutches and turned straight back into a big, boofy Staffie ready for her next folly. And her next – low-fat – meal.

SERVO THE CAT

Anthony

Servo was a jet-black tom cat. He got the name because that's where the children of the Hodgetts family found him, at a service station, while waiting for the school bus. They took him home and did the whole please-please-please-can-we-keep-him thing.

The Hodgetts lived on a spectacular dairy farm, its emerald pastures scattered with cabbage palms, its red-roofed farmhouses providing views east to the Pacific Ocean which switched from blue to green to black depending on which way the wind was blowing. Their farm had been known to lose cows off the cliff into the ocean. It was a beautiful place, but dangerous if you were a cow stretching for that succulent morsel clinging a metre below the lip of the cliff. The kids brought the little black ball of fluff in to their mother, Jemima, who was originally from the city. She was open to the idea of keeping it. Their father, Greg, however, was far less keen. He was more the pragmatic farmer type. To him, cats were just things that peed in the dairy, scared the cows and made messes that had to be cleaned up.

Greg was out-voted.

Servo became a cherished member of the Hodgetts family. He received all the care and attention any cat could hope to get. He was brought in for his vaccinations, which is unheard of for dairy farmers' cats. He was wormed and had flea and tick products applied. He got a fancy collar, microchipping and all of the benefits that modern veterinary science could afford. He was even allowed inside the house – when Greg wasn't around. As far as Greg knew, Servo was an outside cat.

Older dairies will often have cats to keep the mice down because there's a lot of grain floating around. They'll kill the mice and rats which is good, but at the end of the day, dairies are food-producing factories so the more modern types have a bent against semi-feral animals roaming all over the equipment, weeing, fighting, mating and transacting all their secret cat business.

Servo was three years old and a well-established member of the Hodgetts family when one day he disappeared. Everyone was distraught. We received a call at the clinic saying, 'What can we do?' It was a redundant question. Everything that could have been done, such as putting signs up, ringing around the neighbours, putting it on Facebook, had already been done. There was nothing we, as vets, could do to make him come back. Their house wasn't far from the Princes Highway where thousands of cars, trucks and trailers thundered up and down four lanes of bitumen each day. Cats aren't terribly savvy about roads, especially farm cats. So I didn't hold out much hope of seeing Servo again. But about forty-eight hours after she'd first called us, Jemima rang again, this time with a rushed, adrenaline-fuelled voice.

'We've found Servo and he looks like he's dying. He can't walk and he seems to be in a lot of distress. We're bringing him in.'

Fifteen minutes later, Jemima came rushing through the door with Servo yowling in her arms and a couple of worried-looking kids at her feet. She brushed past me, straight out the back to the surgery. She knew her way around the clinic because she'd worked as a vet nurse for the two Geoffs for seven years before having kids.

We hurried them into a consult room where she laid Servo on the stainless-steel table. 'I found him dragging himself back through the paddocks,' she said. 'He just made it to the edge of the house yard. He couldn't stand and was kind of dragging himself like a commando, just using his front legs, and yowling at the top of his voice.'

I looked at Servo on the table and he clearly didn't have any function in his back legs. He was breathing with his mouth open, which in cats is a sign of extreme stress. I thought it could be tick paralysis. That would explain the symptoms. But I pondered Servo's howling when he came through the door. That said, 'I'm in a lot of pain,' more than it said, 'I'm distressed because my legs are paralysed'. There was more to this.

I sniffed him and smelt blood.

Cats' blood has a distinctive metallic odour. When someone brings in an injured cat there's usually a rank smell of urine mixed with faeces because the normally fastidious creature will lose control of its bodily functions when hurt. But even over the top of those two pungent aromas, which were there in full, I could pick up that strong metallic whiff of blood.

I couldn't see a wound – he'd probably licked it clean – but I knew there was a bigger problem there somewhere. It only took a few moments of moving his limbs about to find that he had a broken back leg, his left femur.

'How far do you think he might have dragged himself?' I asked.

'I could see his tracks through the dew in the long grass. He'd come right across the paddock where we'd put the cows overnight. Don't know how far though.'

'From the direction of the highway?'

'No. He was coming up from the valley.'

'What day did he first go missing?'

'Saturday.'

'Okay, it's now Wednesday. Looks like he might have been hit by a car and it's taken him four days to drag himself back. Is there any sort of road down there?'

'Yeah. But it's about a kilometre away.'

'Well, I think that's where he was hit. All right. We know he's got a broken leg and that's very painful. He may well have other broken body parts but at this point we need to provide him with strong painkillers and some sedation to treat his shock. He probably hasn't had anything to drink for four days so he'll be dehydrated. We need to get him on an IV drip to stabilise him and restore blood flow to his organs. Then we can worry about taking X-rays and finding out the extent of his injuries.'

Jemima nodded in agreement. 'Okay, do that,' she said. 'We need to understand what's wrong. And whatever it is, we want it fixed.'

That might seem like an obvious statement, but it's not always clear-cut. Veterinary bills add up and not everyone has the wherewithal to pay them. No matter how much they love their cats, if the money's not there, it's not there. You often get a response that's more like, 'Well, let's find out what's wrong and we'll think about what we'll do from there.' We have to be highly attuned to what the client wants because there is more than one way to cause offence. You don't want to project an attitude of 'this treatment will cost at least $5000 and if you're not prepared to pay that, well, you're not much of a person, are you'; nor do you want to imply 'you're a dairy farmer so you'll want the cat put down'.

So it was good when Jemima looked me straight in the eye and said, 'Fix the cat. There are no other options.'

We all knew where we stood. While this was going on, Jemima's son Tom had been visibly distressed, adding to the feeling of urgency about it all. He was clearly very attached to Servo.

We stabilised the cat, improved his blood pressure, provided pain relief and calmed him down. Several hours later, once he was settled, we anaesthetised him ready to X-ray his back end. Before I'd even got him under the X-ray though, I realised just by feeling him that there was more than one bone structure affected. His whole back end was wonky. Once we took the pictures, I saw that he had two broken femurs and a broken pelvis. This was a big deal. Four-legged animals can't survive on two legs, so we had to fix the whole back section. And beyond mobility, there was the problem of bodily functions. The pelvic injury could affect his urination and defecation. The damaged area of the pelvis was where the nerves that control the bladder and the rectum originate. If those nerves were damaged, he would not be able to poo or wee, and it would be curtains. Nothing could fix him.

I rang Jemima and told her the bad news. 'So now, before we go any further, we have to wait and see whether Servo has the ability to urinate and pass faeces,' I said. 'There's no point us fixing his legs and his pelvis, then finding out a week later he can't poo and wee. We'd have put him through a lot of distress and pain for nothing.'

It was a difficult conversation to have. People want the cat home. They want clear answers. Someone who's in an emotional state doesn't want to be told that it's going to be very difficult to fix, let alone 'we have to wait and see if it's even worthwhile trying'.

Servo was put in a hospital cage.

'Okay, big feller, you need to tell us you can do these things,' I told him.

He was on IV fluids so we knew there was plenty of fluid going into his body. But it was not as simple as looking for puddles of urine to see if the fluid was coming out. That could just be leakage. We checked Servo multiple times a day, feeling around his lower belly. When the bladder was full, we'd feel it like a water balloon in the abdomen.

If the bladder was full every time we checked, that would be a very bad sign. It meant that the cat was not emptying it at will. The process was further complicated by Servo's lack of mobility. He couldn't walk over to the litter tray to urinate, so even if he was not weeing regularly we still had to consider that he might be holding it in because he didn't want to go in an uncomfortable position where it was going to go all over him. Cats can be stubborn so it's not easy to figure out.

And complicating things even further, it was possible that he'd lost bladder function through minor nerve damage, in which case he could get it back after seven to ten days.

With the poo it was simpler. If we found faeces in the cage a day or two after the accident, we'd know that side of things was good.

So there was a lot of work that needed to be put into Servo before he was going to walk out of the clinic. Then there was the added task of managing the clients. Jemima and Greg and all the Hodgetts kids came in for a talk with James and me about where we'd go from here. I ran through all the options for Servo to be whole again. Both femurs would need fixing.

'The best way to do that would be for a specialist orthopaedic surgeon to operate, but if you can't afford that, James and I could also do it. We don't have the expertise to fix his pelvis, but the advice we've had from the surgeon is it will probably mend itself in six to eight weeks if he's left in a cage. You're going to be looking at about $3000. Whatever happens here,' I said, 'we have to fix at least one of Servo's legs. We can amputate one leg if need be. That's the cheapest solution, short of euthanasia.'

We have to give the client the full range of options, but through it all, the steely set of Jemima's jaw never faltered.

'That's great,' she said. 'We want you to fix both legs.'

'Are you flipping kidding?' Greg said. 'There's no flippin' way we're spending that much money on a cat. I'm not selling a cow to pay for a cat. No way. That's it.'

I certainly had sympathy for Greg's position. Everyone has different attachments and different outlooks on how things should be done. The kids were crying and Jemima was upset, looking to us for a solution.

'You've got to fix the cat. How can we do this?'

'We'll do our best,' James said.

'Could you say that the cat is a cow because then we can deduct it?' Jemima said. 'Say the bill is for a calving?'

'No, we can't do that. But is the cat used to exterminate rodents from the dairy?'

'All the time. He's a great ratter.'

'Well, you'll have to ask your accountant but, geez, sounds like he's a valid business expense to me.'

Greg still wasn't happy. 'Even if we deduct it, it's still too much for a cat. We'd buy ten new ones, vaccinated and chipped and bloody dewormed, for that.'

The Hodgetts family said their goodbyes, leaving us none the wiser about how we were to proceed with Servo.

But Jemima was soon back on the phone. 'What about if I bring some cash in? Can you take that off the bill so that Greg doesn't see how much it's costing?'

I said we could probably work something out.

We anticipated the operation was going to take about six hours to put Servo back together, plus a lot of nursing time and care in hospital. Just like Greg saying that he was not going to spend the money on the cat, we couldn't spend all our time on Servo for nothing either.

With a femur, the thigh bone, you can't just put a cast on it. It needs more direct intervention to hold it together. So our first option was to screw metal plates over the fractures. It was a long operation, but one we were getting increasingly accustomed to. We rang Jemima to tell her that all had gone well, so things were looking up.

Servo recovered well and even started to bear a little weight. Five days after the surgery, however, I came into the clinic to be told by Trish that something was wrong with him. He was stumbling around like he had two broken legs again. We got him on the X-ray table and had a look and sure enough, the screws had loosened and the plate had come away. The break was so bad the plate just hadn't been enough to secure it. Servo was back to square one.

I rang Jemima and told her the bad news. 'Sorry – we did our best but it didn't work. Don't worry. We won't charge for our time in that surgery, but we'll still have to charge for all the ongoing nursing care.'

Jemima seemed to take it on the chin. As a farmer, she was used to the certainty that the next disaster was always lurking just one storm, one drought, one disease away. That's not to say she wasn't upset. She was. And she was dealing with the double-pronged stress of having Greg totally opposed to what we were doing. 'What can we do from here?' she said.

'James and I have discussed it and we think we can pin it together,' I said.

'How does that work?'

'Well, you take the bone at the part where it has snapped and you run a pin up through the hollow where the marrow is until it hits the solid, knuckly bit. You drill the pin up through that solid bit until it comes all the way out through the other side and out through the skin of the rump.'

'Crikey that sounds pretty full on.'

'It is. So once that pin comes through, you pull it halfway through so the other end of the pin has disappeared up into the bone. You then switch the drill around so it's attached to the rump end of the pin. You get the bones nicely lined up and drive the pin back down into the bottom part of the broken femur. That sets the bone. You drill the pin into the hard bit at the knee. You have to be careful because you can come out through the knee and stuff up the joint.'

'Okay,' Jemima said, 'so long as I don't have to watch. Let's do it.'

So James and I did that and it all seemed to go very well. We thought we were pretty clever. Two young blokes in the early years of their careers embarking on such extensive surgery with minimal equipment and limited expertise. Everything looked great. The fractures were right. We could see on the X-ray that Servo's left leg looked perfect, while the right hadn't come together quite so well, but good enough, we thought. Servo was recovering, the wound was healing, but over coming days, he continued to fail in his attempts to walk.

'He should be able to bear some weight by now,' James said, about three days after the surgery. 'He seems to be collapsing badly on one of his legs.'

We observed Servo for a while in his cage.

'He's a trier, isn't he,' I said, as he kept struggling to get up.

'Well, I suppose any cat that's been abandoned as a kitten, that's dragged itself a kilometre with a broken pelvis and two broken femurs is going to earn the title of survivor,' James said.

'Well, Servo the Survivor seems to be going okay on his right leg, but it's the left that's giving way underneath him.'

'Wasn't the left the one that we thought we'd done perfectly?'

'It was. I think we're going to have to take another look at him. Something else is going on here.'

So we X-rayed him again and the leg looked fine, but while we had him on the table we had a bit of a feel around. It didn't take long to realise that the knee was bending in all the wrong directions. We'd been so focussed on the femurs we'd missed this other major problem. It was what we call a 'global knee', meaning it was stuffed everywhere. Just about all sixteen knee ligaments were busted. You could turn his leg around and move it in ways it should not move. It was a disaster and it would never get better.

We beat ourselves up over it, but not too badly. Ligament injury on top of pelvic and femoral fractures was an easy one to miss. It had only become obvious once we'd fixed up the primary problems.

At this point, Greg was out of the equation. He was being drip-fed the bare minimum information. He wasn't visiting. Jemima and the kids had been in almost every day in the ten days or so since they'd first brought Servo in. So when they came in that day, I broke the news to Jemima that they still only had a three-legged cat. And the one that he was relying on was the one that hadn't set quite so well. It would heal over time. But his bad knee was never going to be right. 'We can make it better with another operation,' I said, 'but he'll never have much movement in it again.'

Even Jemima, poor saintly Jemima, was losing patience. 'How long's this going to go on for? I appreciate what you guys are doing, but what if you find something else wrong after this? How many more things are we going to find?' By this stage, James and I had reached a tipping point. We couldn't *not* keep going. The Hodgetts family had made such an emotional investment and so had we. The only way was to keep pressing forward.

'We've come up with a plan,' James said to Jemima who gave a sceptical tilt of the head.

'Hmmmm.'

'We are basically going to make an internal brace for Servo's knee using a metal screw above and below the joint and joining them with an artificial ligament. It'll enable Servo to bend his knee a little bit, even if he can't do much else with it. Scar tissue will form over the brace which will ultimately stabilise the knee.' *We hope*, I thought to myself.

'Fellers, I appreciate all that you've done, but I don't know if it's right to keep going. Maybe it's time to consider putting him down.'

She was right, of course. But I found it hard to even consider.

'Euthanasia is an option,' I said. 'But we've come so far. If money is the concern then we are happy to do the surgery for free. We realise you've done everything you can. We're going to just do this and see what happens.'

The truth is that we didn't know if it would work. The one thing we did know was that if it didn't, Servo was out of gas. He was cactus.

We were in the middle of a major renovation and modernisation of the practice and the next day, I was going to the snow for a week's skiing. The only time we had to do it was at dawn the next day before I headed off.

'Okay, we'll convene here at 5 a.m. tomorrow,' James said.

'Yep. Just you and me. We can't ask any of the nurses to come in. Their overtime is going through the roof. They're totally overworked. We can't ask them to do any more.'

'Okay. See you then.'

Next morning, we opened up the practice to find that overnight a hole had been cut through a brick wall and the whole clinic was covered in dust. The renovations were being done at night to enable us to keep the clinic running and the builders had left it looking like it had snowed inside. The surgery resembled the peak of Mont Blanc. The only room that was spared the cement blizzard was one of the consult rooms.

So that's where we decided to do the operation. We wheeled in anaesthetic machines and all the equipment we'd need. It felt like a field hospital out of M*A*S*H. The table was the wrong height. For surgery, you want your table to be up high so you're not bending over your work, breathing all over it. Consult tables are designed lower so that yapping dogs aren't at face-licking height.

So we embarked on this elaborate surgery in a consult room with no nurse or anaesthetic technician. It was just the two of us in unknown territory, figuring it out as we went along. Neither of us had ever done this surgery before, but it all seemed to go okay. We stitched Servo up and I went over to grab a coffee while James stayed to watch Servo wake up.

He was just coming to when I got back.

'Mate, it's up to you now,' James said to the patient.

Almost immediately he seemed stronger. He carried on like nothing had happened. True to form, he tried to stand up immediately. He didn't quite make it but he looked better. He kept trying.

James rang Jemima with the news. She was happy, but not ecstatic. All the tension with Greg was making her life difficult.

'I need the cat home,' she said. 'I really appreciate all that you fellers have done but I think we've reached the end of the road. If he's going to die, we need to have him home. If that's the end of him, we'll call you out to put him down. How soon can we take him?'

'We've got to keep him under observation for at least twenty-four hours, so maybe you could take him tomorrow afternoon.'

I went off on my ski trip holding grave fears for Servo.

He'd been taken home long before I got back from the snow. Servo left our minds for a day or two. I don't think either of us dared to call with our usual follow-up enquiries. The new week began. About Tuesday curiosity got the better of us. We didn't really want to speak to Greg so James rang during afternoon milking. Everything about the price of the operations had been on the lowdown. Jemima had been scrimping and money had been turning up in dribs and drabs. I am pretty sure the kids and Greg were eating homebrand bread that week.

Jemima was really happy. 'He's trying to walk but he can't get up, though he's managing to move,' she told James. 'He's not messing in the house. He's getting to his litter tray. He's eating and drinking and he's loving the attention. He's become a house cat. Even Greg's giving him some attention. He's enjoying having a pet cat.'

Life went on. We didn't hear any more over following weeks and Servo slipped further from our minds until, six weeks later, I got a text from Jemima with a photograph attached.

It was Servo, high up in a tree, looking like a normal cat hunting a bird. 'The milk-tanker driver has admitted it was him that ran over the cat,' the text read. 'All good now.'

So given that he had been run over by a semi-trailer, endured three imperfect surgeries under less than ideal circumstances and been faced with an owner who wanted him put down, I think Servo might have just about used up his quota of lives. But he's a survivor and that's got to count for something.

CHARLIE

James

Ronnie and I were taking big steps – uprooting our lives to move to Berry, buying a business, finding places to live and stepping in to a new world where we knew no-one other than the people at the vet clinic. As though the end of 2012 wasn't busy enough, providence shone on us, and we were expecting our first baby at the end of November. Ronnie continued working in Sydney right up till late October, so we decided to have the baby in Wollongong which is roughly halfway between Berry and the city. That way it was not too far from either her work or home so wherever she was when she went into labour, it wouldn't be far to go to the hospital.

The scans showed that we were expecting a big baby and the doctor, therefore, didn't want to let Ronnie go over term. So, come the appointed day, we trooped up to the Gong to be induced. It still took almost forty-eight hours to get things going, leaving us stuck in hospital with nothing to do. I'm not very good at sitting still. Back in Berry, we were renovating the clinic. Anthony was there being run off his feet while I sat in a chair in a corner of a hospital room. Ronnie was sitting up in bed, equally bored, waiting for the action to begin.

I got on the phone and ordered some stock for the practice. I googled equipment supply places and bought new surgery tables and lighting. I bought cages and other equipment. The whole time, I was looking around me at the schmick hospital gear. *Wonder what that surgery light's worth? Wish we had one like that … Must have cost $100,000 just to fit out this room.*

It was ridiculous. I couldn't escape work even in a labour ward. And I was mentally stealing things from a hospital.

It took a while but the contractions started to get closer together. This was the signal that we were getting serious and it was time to switch on. As I tend to do, I flicked the switch and immediately became totally engrossed in the moment. Ronnie might have been better off if I'd stayed on the phone.

When the anaesthetist came in to give Ronnie an epidural, I watched him with fascination. I admired the precision of his technique and we got chatting about it. He went into some detail about his various landmarks and how he did it.

'So how do *you* do it?' he asked, knowing that I was a vet.

'Basically, you wipe the shit off the tail, put an eighteen-gauge needle into the spine, wait for a hiss of gas and inject.'

It was heartening that he did not take notes. Nor did he hand over the needle to give me a go.

The nurses found out I was a vet around this time too so they started asking me their animal-related questions. One of them had a dog which had suffered a GDV – gastric dilation and volvulus syndrome, a twisted-stomach condition that is often fatal in dogs – so she had lots of questions about that. Another one had a dog with a skin problem and then another had the most common question we get: 'My dog is barking all the time.'

'Okay, when does it bark?' I said, looking at Ronnie to wordlessly beg her patience.

'It only barks when I'm not there,' the nurse said. 'It's driving the neighbours crazy because I'm often here all night. It's probably yapping away right now.'

'Well, that's probably a separation anxiety. You should see a behaviourist about that. You know they're prescribing Prozac for that sort of thing now.'

As the birth progressed, I was the one who needed something for my anxiety. It was a classic case of a little bit of knowledge being a scary thing. During the birth, Ronnie was hooked up to all sorts of machines monitoring her and the baby. Ronnie was blissfully unaware of it all while I followed the graphs, interpreting the data. Whenever there was a change in baby's heartbeat, I'd worry myself silly.

The hospital was busy. The midwife was doing a double shift through the night. She was there for sixteen hours, stretched between three simultaneous births. She'd come in, give me instructions on what to watch for and be off again.

'Come and get me if anything changes,' she said, before bustling out again. I could see the graphs changing all the time. What exactly did she mean by 'changes'?

I hid my anxiety by cracking jokes. I was trying to be funny, yet remain deferential to Ronnie.

'I could've got this out by now. I might have a bit of gear in the car. Just get the straps on there and hook you up to the calving jack and we'd have this thing out.' Dangerous territory, I knew, but it didn't stop me from going there.

The woman I loved was going through this enormously difficult and somewhat dangerous ordeal. I worried about her and the little human life about to begin.

True to the predictions, the baby was big. The obstetrician, a short, stout fellow, applied about as much pressure through the suction cup to get it out as I do to pull a calf. It was a boy. Nine pounds ten. We named him Charlie.

'Well, he's already just about the biggest bloke in the room,' the obstetrician said. 'He's about as big a baby as I could get out of you, Ronnie, so don't have a bigger one next time.'

'I promise,' she said.

My initial feeling post-birth was one of relief, but then a sense of wonder as the powers of nature started to overwhelm me. I'd had this feeling many times before, standing in cold and wet cattle yards, with a slippery calf lying on the concrete, but now gazing at our little human, all warm and wrapped, I felt that sense of wonder stronger than ever. As parents-to-be we had found so much to fret over with the birthing process and so much concern over what might happen. But now with Charlie's safe arrival, we were through the looking glass and into the foreign world of parenthood. We'd read books and we'd both been around babies a lot, but now holding our beautiful baby boy, I couldn't help but feel an overwhelming sense of 'what do we do with this thing now?' Charlie didn't come with an accompanying manual, and who reads those things anyway, so like most new parents we were unleashed on the world of nappy aisles and sleep routines with a fair bit of new-parent anxiety attached.

The friendly nurses came back to me with a bunch of out-of-date medicines and some old instruments.

'Would you use these?' they asked.

'Sure.'

So while most first-time fathers leave hospital carrying shiny balloons, flowers and baby car seats they don't understand, I had all that plus forceps, antibiotics and a goodie bag of decommissioned equipment. I didn't get the surgery light though.

Once we were home, I had two weeks of paternity leave, but when you're running a business, the distinctions between work and the rest of your life can blur.

Geoff came in to help Anthony, but the business had already evolved so much that he was unfamiliar with some of the new equipment – we'd replaced the X-ray, ultrasound and anaesthetic machines in the first few months and that change was gathering pace. So I had to be there to lend a hand. Anthony would ring and ask me to pop in at some stage to help with x, y and z. Faced with the choice of going to work or staying with a constantly screaming baby, work started to sound very appealing. So I'd line up a string of jobs for Anthony and me to punch out together, go in for an hour or two then go home.

Moving to Berry had removed Ronnie from the support networks of family and friends that are so important when babies arrive. We were all mentally frayed and sleep deprived. Charlie had trouble feeding and that led to trouble sleeping and he didn't mind letting us know when he wasn't happy. And we were in a small house, so if he was screaming I couldn't take over and let Ronnie sleep because she could hear him from every corner of the place. There were nights where Ronnie hadn't slept for thirty-six hours so I'd take Charlie into the clinic with me and do paperwork through the night. He'd still be upset and I'd still spend a lot of time struggling to get him to sleep, but at least he was away from Ronnie to give her a couple of hours' respite.

It was a tough time, and sometimes I did wonder exactly what I had gotten myself into. But, no, I was never tempted to put Charlie in a cage. Nor give him a nice horse sedative. Not once.

As time went on things improved – we got help, amazing early childhood nurses got Charlie feeding, we found ways to get him to go to sleep, and the load became manageable. Work continued to get busier, and once I caught up on some sleep, I was able to make a decent contribution. I think I might still be owed a bit of paternity leave though.

A DOSE OF REALITY

Anthony

The unmistakable enthusiasm of Rodney Richmond came blasting down my phone. 'Boys, boys, I've finished the pilot. It's unbefrickinglievable. I'm gunna come down and show it to you. It's gunna knock your socks off.'

It was late February and we hadn't heard from Rodney for more than a month. The project had slipped from our minds and the prospect of it ever happening had dimmed. The bad taste left in our mouths from the aftermath of Alan's death was still there, but here was cyclone Rodney, category three, brightening everything up again.

'Mate, where can we show it to you? I want to put something on. Can we show it at the pub? I'll take you all out. We'll make a night of it. The world freaking premiere.'

We were back in his vortex where, when things happened, they happened quickly.

Rodney put on a shindig, drinks and food, for all our staff and our families in a little room called the Coach House at the back of the Berry pub. The whole thing had seemed so rushed and ad hoc, and with Rodney being new to the genre we couldn't see how he could make it work. Anyway, we had all our family and friends with us plus the best-tasting beer in the world, free beer, and if nothing else we were going to get a disc to add to our home movies. We were all in high spirits when it began, and from that moment, we were spellbound.

What we saw over those next few minutes changed all our lives. Seeing the interaction between ourselves, our patients and their owners – even at the most vulnerable moments – clearly struck a chord. Everyone, including me, was clearly affected. When I saw tears streaming down Trish's face, I knew that we had something special.

Dad came up to me soon after. 'Whoa, mate, you're onto something here. That was pretty impressive,' he said. James pulled me aside. 'Crikey, this bloke really does know what he's doing. It looked amazing. Did you see the looks on their faces? Everyone was crying.'

I allowed myself then to believe that maybe something would come of all this. Rodney, however, refused to be optimistic.

'I'm going to take it back to my mate Simon Steele at Screentime,' he said, 'and they'll decide whether or not they will option it. It's still very unlikely that it's ever going to happen.'

'How unlikely?' I said.

'You've got a five per cent chance of this show ever getting made.'

Anyway, Screentime – the company that had made the *Underbelly* series of crime dramas, plus the reality shows *Popstars* and *RBT* – optioned it quite early. This meant they had the right to try to get it up and running, to sell it to a network and move it forward. We were pleased about that because we suspected they had more of the skills required to walk into a network boardroom and talk the talk.

'If Rodney can do what he's done, then these guys are going to really make it happen,' I said to James.

The weeks passed, however, and we got no word from them. Nothing. The weeks turned to months. Still nothing. Not so much as a call. Our television dreams once again faded. Well, it had been fun and at least we had an amazing home movie to show the grandkids.

WHOLE LOT OF SHAKING GOING ON

James

It was a cold, windy, awful night. And my computer had just died. Even though it was almost dark and a Sunday, Harvey Norman was still open so I'd gone to Nowra to buy a new laptop. Nowra is only twenty minutes away from Berry, so it was not a problem to drive there while on call. I meandered through the computer aisles with a straightforward plan to get a small, cheap machine. But the more I moseyed, the more my mind was captivated by the powers of modern computing. *Wow, look at this. It converts into a tablet.* I walked out with a significantly larger credit card debt than intended. It was a little after 5 p.m. as I crossed the bleak, windswept car park, guilt-ridden that I'd spent so much money, but excited to start playing with my new toy.

I was exiting the roundabout at Bomaderry ('cholesterol corner', as we call it, because it features two prominent fast-food chains) when the phone rang.

'Berry Vet Clinic after hours, can I help you?'

'My dog's having a seizure. My dog's seizuring.' It was a distressed woman speaking in short, sharp sentences. 'Can you come?' she pleaded. 'Save him. He needs help. Oh my god we can't stop it … '

I tried to calm things down. 'That sounds like a real concern. You need to bring him in so we can hospitalise him. Can you bring the dog in?'

'No, we can't. He's too big. I can't lift him. And we've been drinking. We can't drive. How long's he going to be shaking like this for? It's totally crazy.'

'Seizures typically only last a couple of minutes,' I said. 'I'm sure it will stop soon. How long's he been seizuring for?'

'It'd be eight or nine minutes.'

'Okay. Anything more than five minutes is a big worry. Has he ever had this before?'

'No, never. Nothing even like it.'

'Can you describe exactly what you're seeing?'

'He's fitting, mate. He's biting himself and he's frothing at the mouth. He's thrashing about. He's broken the bloody table he's shaking that much. He's bitten me husband. '

It sounded pretty bad, but what I can do for a dog outside the clinic is very limited.

'Is there any way you can bring him in? I'm going to have to take him back to the clinic anyway.'

'No, there's absolutely no way we can do it.'

'Okay, where do you live?'

'Callala Beach.'

That was twenty kilometres away. Callala Beach is extremely close to our practice in Shoalhaven Heads. By road, however, it's a half-hour drive. At least having come to Nowra, I was closer than I would have been at Berry. These people weren't clients. We had no relationship with them whatsoever. They were geographically a long way out of our usual range for pets, though we often did cattle work in the area. They weren't even clients of the Bomaderry vets with whom we shared our on-call work. The woman said they'd only ever taken this dog to a vet once or twice before using a mobile vet. Mobile vets don't provide an out-of-hours service. That's why she'd called us.

'I can come, but you've got to realise this is going to be reasonably expensive by the time I drive out to you, pick the dog up, drive back, do all these things. And your dog sounds pretty unwell. It's going to run into quite a few hundred dollars.'

'That's not a problem. Not a problem. We've gotta do everything we can.'

You always worry when you raise the issue of money and they quickly dismiss the idea of it being a problem. The first thing that pops into your mind is: *Money's not a problem because you have no intention of giving me any.* But you have to suck it and see. And she seemed genuine. In the back of my mind I was keen to recoup some of the dough I'd just spent on the whiz-bang laptop when a cheaper one may have sufficed.

I had the windscreen wipers on full bore as I did a uey on the highway and headed south into the gale, following the owner's slightly incoherent directions to the front door. There, I was greeted by a late-middle-aged couple: a short woman in a bowls uniform who spoke fast with an urgent tone; a lanky husband with a slow, casual drawl despite the urgency that he was so clearly feeling about the dog. His beard and head were all shaved to the same length: about a number three all over.

His name was Dick Meadows and I'd later learn he was a war veteran. He didn't mind a drink to help himself forget the things he couldn't unsee. I believe that 'self-medication' is the modern expression for it. Dick had some tissues wrapped around his hand, with blood spots coming through.

They ushered me into a big room with a slate floor, a full-sized billiards table in the middle and a home bar in the corner. As if to add atmosphere, a thick plume of smoke hung over the green felt table and the low-hanging light, a product of the anxious cigarettes consumed before my arrival. The scene was a little reminiscent of pool dens in the back of clubs that I had frequented in my youth.

'The seizure stopped soon after I hung up from you,' the woman said. Her name was Gwen. She apologised for not being okay to drive. She explained there'd been a function at the football club. Gwen Meadows had been asked to entertain some honoured guests. She'd clearly taken that duty quite seriously.

'Lazarus is just over here,' she said, leading me around the billiards table to an enormous Great Dane approaching the size and weight of a miniature pony. The sort of dog that creates fear by his size alone.

Lazarus was in a 'postictal' state, the drowsy, disorientated condition that follows a fit. He was lying down, looking confused, as was his master.

'He's a cracking dog,' Dick said. 'Cracking dog. I can't believe it. I was worried about him swallowing his tongue so I stuck my hand in his mouth to grab it and he bit me. And he crushed my ring. Look.' Dick showed me a distorted gold ring on his finger; the ring was bent and broken. His hand was fairly battered and bruised too. 'I was trying to help him and he bit me. Can't believe it. He's a cracking dog.'

The idea that humans and dogs swallow their tongues while fitting is a bit of a myth. It can't actually happen. Sure, you do need to make sure their airways are open and they can breathe, but you don't need to stick your finger down to their tonsils to check their tongues.

'I think it's important I take him back to the clinic and check him out,' I said. 'I'll need to hospitalise and manage him.'

'Yeah, mate. Whatever you gotta do. He's a cracking dog. Cracking dog. Love him. Just a cracking dog. Love him, mate. Whatever needs doing, you do it.'

I needed to make sure he got proper attention because I could see that if Dick kept on self-medicating the way he was, he might not even notice another seizure. He'd lit up another Longbeach by this time and cracked a fresh can of Rivet beer.

'You want one? I got plenty,' he offered.

'No, I'm good thanks. Gotta work. Where's that beer from, though?' I asked.

'Aldi,' he said.

I drew up a syringe of drugs to calm Lazarus down and prevent another seizure. It was with some trepidation that I approached such an enormous dog with a pointy, ouchy implement, but the needle went in without a flinch.

Lazarus couldn't walk well, so I got Gwen to find me a towel and we put it under his back legs and helped him out to the car. Dick and I managed to lift him into the back of the ute and close him in. I was a little apprehensive about taking him with me because I didn't have a muzzle. I hadn't left home intending to do this job.

'How you going to get him out at the other end?' Dick asked.

'I'll get someone to give me a hand.'

'Nah, I'd better come with you,' he said. 'You'll need help. I'll give you a hand, mate. He's a cracking dog.'

But I figured if I took Dick with me, I was going to have to drive him home. So I decided to solve the problem of how to unload Lazarus when I got back to Berry. I thanked Dick, jumped in the car and drove off. Lazarus was so big that it was like having a horse shifting about in a float. He actually moved the car around when he got up to look out the window. That was a good sign though. He seemed to be physically well. I called Kahlia, to see if she was available to help.

She was waiting when I arrived. I opened the back of the ute and her jaw dropped, 'Gawd, look at the size of him. How are we going to move him?'

I went and got the stretcher. We coaxed him onto that, and strained under his weight till we got to the treatment room where we plonked him down in the middle of the floor. He was too big to get up on the table. We put an IV catheter in him, got some blood to test if he had anything else going on with him and did a full neurological exam, which was a bit of a challenge, particularly with a dog of that size. You start at the front and test all their reflexes up there: whether they blink when you touch them near the eye; whether they blink when you go to poke them in the eye; what their pupils do in response to light; whether they can hear you. Then you look at their ability to put their legs on the ground normally and whether they know where their legs are. That's very difficult in a sixty-kilogram Great Dane who's got a few drugs on board. It's hard to tell what's him and what's the drugs. Then you tap his elbows and knees with a patella hammer just like a human reflex test. Their leg should kick out normally. This all takes a long time and you've got to be systematic.

Notwithstanding the fact he was full of the drugs to stop him seizuring, his brain appeared pretty normal. One thing I did notice though was that he had unusual marks in his mouth. Scratches and bleeding which I assumed were not caused by Dick's hand.

'Maybe he's got into some sort of toxin or something that's set off the seizure,' I said. We tested the bloods and they were normal. We popped him into a cage with a drip and some medications and I called Dick and Gwen.

'Is there anything you think he could have got into in the backyard? Can you go and see if anything's disturbed?'

They got back to me and told me he'd chewed through a large electrical cable which made me think he'd been electrocuted, causing the seizure and the damage to his mouth.

'Mate, I swear it was off,' Dick said. 'The cable's in a shed with its own circuit breaker and the circuit breaker was off because we were doing work out there.' He sounded like he knew what he was talking about.

'Okay, so that ruins my theory. We'll have to come up with another explanation.'

They described the seizure again to me in words of such extremity that I couldn't help thinking they were exaggerating. He seemed stable now, so when I hung up I sent Kahlia home and I stayed to observe him. I was standing in the cage room when suddenly the whole room started shaking. It was like an earthquake – cages rattled, shelves clattered. Lazarus was having another fit. He was not shaking so much as thrashing. It was the most spectacularly violent seizure I'd seen. The metal of the cage bowed and constricted with every bodily contortion. He was lying on his side with his legs outstretched and with each contraction of the seizure, he would kick out and push, super violently. The metal of the cage expanded and bent around him. When Dick and Gwen had tried to explain, I hadn't understood. I really had to see it to appreciate its power. Luckily, I had IV fluids running and I'd taped the catheter down strongly with a loose line so it stayed on with all the flailing about. I raced over to get some medications and inject them from the safety of outside the bending, wobbling cage. Unlike Dick, I wasn't putting my hand anywhere near that mouth. I could hardly believe he'd got his hand close to Lazarus's mouth let alone inside it.

A small Pomeranian huddled in the corner of the cage opposite, looking thankful for the metal bars separating it from this violent beast. I'm sure the Pomeranian was making a mental note to avoid the big guy in the exercise yard tomorrow.

I injected a high dose of anti-convulsant which thankfully took effect quickly and which I hoped would hold him steady for the rest of the night. There was nothing left to do but bunker down and play with my new computer while I watched Lazarus through the night. He slept soundly, so I snuck back home and into bed before the roosters started crowing. Kahlia came in early to keep up the vigil. She was there when Lazarus woke up good as gold. He was completely unaffected. So, as soon as I got back in, I rang Dick and Gwen and arranged for them to come and get him.

'We've done the basic work up for epilepsy,' I explained, 'but epilepsy is a diagnosis of exclusion so you have to rule out everything else before you can say someone is epileptic. Epilepsy almost always starts between the age of one and seven. So he's the right age. It is by definition seizuring due to an unknown cause or seizuring due to an abnormality in the brain. We don't medicate animals that are epileptic unless they are having seizures that are longer than five minutes, they're having more than one seizure in a forty-eight-hour period or they're having frequent seizures.'

'I've had another look through the shed,' Dick said, 'and I found some tins that it looks like he might have got into. I can't even remember what I put in them. There's paint thinners and garden chemicals, all sorts of shit that he might have got into.'

'Okay, well any of those could potentially have been a toxic trigger for all this,' I said. 'So they might have caused it, or the seizures might be caused by epilepsy. I'd recommend starting him on some anti-epileptics. Alternatively, if it was merely a toxin, we may never see him seizure again. It could be a response to that.'

So Dick and Gwen decided they didn't want to try the epilepsy medications. They were satisfied that the seizures had started because of whatever it was Lazarus had gotten into in the shed. They were very thankful and appreciative. And they settled their bill promptly.

I never expected to see them again. But about three months later I was once again on call on a miserable night with a window-rattling westerly blowing when Dick called.

'Mate, Lazarus is doing it again. He's having another seizure.'

'Okay, can you bring him in?'

'Nah, Gwen's not here and I've been on the turps again.'

Knowing the violence of the seizures and now that I had a relationship with Gwen and Dick, I was more than happy to go and get him.

I figured I'd need help to get the dog. Anthony had gone home an hour or two earlier at the end of a long and busy week but I called him anyway.

'Mate, can you come and give me a hand? I need to get this dog.'

'Can't the owners just bring it in?'

'No … There's some issues there. I'll meet you at your place.'

He was not best pleased that we had to drive half an hour to do this for people he didn't know. I started to explain Dick to him and that didn't seem to assuage Anthony's mood of discontent.

Lazarus was no longer seizuring when we got there. We walked through the front door and all Anthony's anger evaporated once he saw Dick coming towards us with a big, open smile.

'I'm really sorry. Thanks for coming.' Dick's the epitome of … something that's hard to put your finger on. He's a lovely guy and it's hard not to feel disarmed by him. 'I couldn't drive 'cause I've been on the sauce. But it happened again and fair dinkum I reckon this one was worse than the last one. And the last one was like a bloody earthquake. Can I show you where it happened? You will not believe what he's done.'

Walking through the billiard den, Anthony pointed at the Rivets piled up and looked at me with a furrowed brow of confusion.

'Apparently you get it from Aldi,' I said.

That seemed to satisfy his curiosity.

We went out the back to a pile of smashed-up timber.

'He was here in his kennel when I heard him starting. I ran out and he was just friggin' destroying it. It went on for more than ten minutes. He just kept going and going and there was nothing I could do. I wasn't sticking my hand in his mouth this time.'

'That was a kennel?' Anthony asked. 'Wow!'

It looked like the Big Bad Wolf had huffed and puffed and blown it into a pile of splinters.

'Is this the first problem he's had since I saw you last?' I asked.

'Yeah, absolutely. He's been good as gold.'

Dick started regaling us with stories about Lazarus, but mostly he just said, 'Cracking dog. Cracking dog.' Hugging him and ruffling his shaggy dregs. 'I just love him … Mate, a thief got in the backyard once and all we found when we came home was a pair of jeans and a shoe with teeth marks in 'em stuck to the fence.'

'Cripes, you're lucky you didn't find a human with teeth marks in him,' I said.

'He'd probably already eaten him before you got back,' Anthony said with his trademark snorting nasal laugh. 'Just hung up the clothes after he'd finished his meal.'

'Okay, Dick, do you want us to hospitalise him and look after him?' I said.

'Yes. Yes, that's what we want.'

So Anthony and I chatted some more with Dick before taking Lazarus back to the clinic and following the same process as last time. I kept watch on him through the night but fortunately there were no further seizures.

We did a neurological exam on him the next day and it was all normal. There were no toxins. No chewed-up electrical cables this time. If his blood checked out normal too, it meant he was probably epileptic.

The next day Gwen called the clinic to find out what was going on. Anthony took the call and explained what we'd found; that we thought Lazarus was probably epileptic, but that because it's a diagnosis of exclusion, we couldn't say for certain without doing a lot of tests.

'What are those other tests?' Gwen asked. 'What else can we do to test him to make sure it's not something else?'

'Realistically,' Anthony said, 'the main tests left to do are an MRI, a spinal-fluid tap and some blood tests to look for certain protozoa or parasitic infections of his brain.'

'How much would those tests set us back?' Gwen asked.

'It's probably a bit over $2000 to almost conclusively say there's nothing else wrong with him,' Anthony said, certain that it would be out of their range. 'But he's probably epileptic, so the tests are most likely just going to confirm what we already think.'

'Okay, we'll do the tests,' Gwen said.

Anthony was taken aback. 'What? But it is probably just going to confirm what we already think. We can start the epilepsy treatment without them.'

'Yep, nah, we'll do them. I'll just tell Dick he's gotta cut back on his smokes for a while and we'll do the tests. Love that dog, and he means the world to Dick. He's Dick's soulmate and companion. Lazarus is the only bloody person Dick ever talks to about anything so we've got to look after him. We've got to sort him out. Get on with it. How soon can we start?'

I walked into the office as Anthony hung up the phone and he was clearly surprised. 'I can't believe this. You wouldn't think Gwen and Dick had the money to spend.'

'They probably don't.'

It really brought home to me that you can't judge a book by its cover. If we hadn't offered them those tests, that would have been negligent. As the vet, it's beholden on us to give people all their options. For us to decide that Lazarus shouldn't have an MRI because it was too expensive was not our call to make.

So we phoned around and the next afternoon we were able to go in for an MRI in a facility to the north of Berry. I can't say where. Anthony called an old family friend who he'd known all his life, Louie Sakhlas, and he cleared the way for us to take an animal into his human facility to test with his machine.

Louie didn't want our unorthodox plans to be official clinic business. 'You guys just tee it up with the radiographer,' he said. 'We don't want any money. Just pay the radiographers whatever they want to run the machine for you.'

A few years previously, Anthony had travelled with Louie for a week. He was an incredibly nice man as far as we could tell.

We met the radiographers in the carpark out the back of the clinic under the cover of darkness. We walked the great dog through the back door, and then put him under with a general anaesthetic. It took two of us to lift his huge bulk onto the gantry that slides in and out of an enormous magnetic coil. MRIs are a slow process. We just had to sit there for forty-five minutes while the radiographers went through all the images they needed to get. The thing that stood out most about it was the noise the machine made. The coil switching on and off sounded like a duck quacking – *whark, whark, whark.*

'Do you want to see if we can get that duck out of your machine for you?' Anthony asked the radiographer. 'It might work a bit quicker.'

He got some stern glances as he flashed his smile and launched into his trademark snorting giggle. But he didn't seem to win them over. This was not a comedy act.

On the wall near the console where the radiographers operated the machine, there was a giant red button. 'DO NOT TOUCH. Pressing this button will de-energise the magnet.' The whole time we were there, looking at this enormous button saying 'DO NOT TOUCH', we were like a couple of kids with ADHD and maybe a bit of ODD (oppositional defiance disorder). Every fibre in our beings just wanted to touch that big red button.

'So, you must have lots of people come in and press that button,' Anthony said.

'No. Not really.'

'What would we be up for if we pressed it?' I asked.

'Energising the magnet takes several days and uses thousands of dollars' worth of electricity. So quite a bit I'd say.'

'Well, why do they make the button so damned tempting then?'

The dog was deep in the guts of this million-dollar machine when, at about 9 p.m., long after everyone was meant to have gone home, Louie suddenly appeared out of his room behind the radiographer.

'Anthony,' he said. 'How are you? So great to see you.' He rushed over beaming and gave Anthony a warm handshake. He started asking all about what we were doing and was clearly fascinated by seeing a dog go under the scanner. He wanted to see the images. He was used to always looking at human X-rays with the head at the top, like we stand, but you look at dog X-rays with their heads on the side, like they stand. So we had a good, friendly talk about this, Louie's head tilted to the side trying to comprehend what he was seeing.

We got the images we needed and sent them to the radiologist, whose interpretation was that the dog was epileptic. That is, there was no other cause shown by the images. But they also showed quite a bit of damage from the seizures, demonstrating how violent and prolonged they'd been.

The other tests came back negative too, so we could now say with a degree of certainty that Lazarus was epileptic. He was one of the few cases of epilepsy that we'd taken to that extent. But we had a clear course of action now, so we started him on medications and since then he's been well-managed.

He's had the odd seizure and some complications. Six months after the MRI, Gwen went on holiday for a few weeks and Lazarus ate everything that Dick ate. Hamburgers, pizzas, the whole lot. He stacked on eight kilos and got pancreatitis, but we got him through that potentially fatal condition.

The epilepsy medications are extremely expensive in a dog that large because you just need more of them. He's ten times the weight of a Jack Russell in good nick. It was a huge and onerous task for Dick and Gwen to look after him.

I don't think Dick cut back on the Longbeaches too much. He probably needed to cut back on a few other things as well. But he listened to our advice for Lazarus far more attentively than he did the doctor's advice about himself. Lazarus has done well. He is a cracking dog. It's a real joy to have him in the clinic. Everybody in the waiting room gets taken aback by his size but he is a lovely animal. When we get blood from him and ultrasound him, we do all the procedures on the floor and he just wants to lie on you and cuddle you. A cracking dog indeed, though I still wouldn't want to be the bloke who tries to rob his house.

A LITTLE PIECE OF DROOPY

Anthony

'Never buy an associate a car.' This was one of the many pearls of wisdom passed down to me by my former bosses, the two Geoffs. If only I'd taken this advice to heart when we came to employ our own staff.

I started my career with a maroon Mitsubishi Magna that had been my grandfather's car, before my sister and I shared it through uni. In my head I thought I'd start work, get a few pay packets then buy myself a ute or four-wheel-drive. I investigated some options but they all cost so much. Or at least the ones that were respectable enough to take to work. I took my time looking around and figuring out the market. By the time I was ready to make a move, I'd been a vet for four or five months and realised that the Magna was doing the job well enough so I decided I might as well stick with it.

Vet cars have a unique smell and it wasn't long before the Magna acquired this stench too. As a vet you become acclimatised to it, but when someone else gets in the passenger seat, there's always a strange face, a moment's hesitation, before their hand reaches casually for the window button. And mine goes to the air conditioning. I remember dropping friends home after our regular tennis game on a Monday night. They got in my car and did the funny look, the embarrassed reach for the window. The following week when I offered to take them again, they said it was a nice night and they'd walk. Same thing the week after that, except it was blowing a gale and freezing cold. 'Thanks anyway Anthony. We love walking in the rain.'

'But you don't even have an umbrella.'

Packing the boot was like playing Tetris, stacking the shapes into perfect lines to get it all in. And like a video gamer, I got better and faster the more I did it. The only time it was a hassle was during calvings because I always put the calving jack at the very back of the boot so I'd have to get everything out to get to it. The good thing about a sedan, though, was that you could generally keep the nasty smells isolated to the boot. I was vigilant about keeping the car clean inside and out to keep the pongs at bay. And to tell the truth, I didn't think it smelt too bad ... but it did. That vet-car smell is as dogged as death and taxes.

One major contributor to the olfactory decline of the Magna was a farm dog from Kangaroo Valley called Droopy. He was a Labrador that I'd picked up to bring back to the clinic to be desexed. As we came over the mountain with Droopy contentedly in the Magna's back seat, I suddenly smelt the most putrid odour I'd ever encountered – and as a young country vet I'd smelt a few things already. I turned around to see that Droopy had vomited on the back of my seat and on the inside of the window, where I could see it dribbling into the window recess.

'What the crap have you eaten? I told them to fast you.'

I later learned that his owners had diligently followed my instructions to not let him eat anything before the operation, but he'd taken matters into his own hands and gone over to where there'd been a calving a week or two previously and helped himself to a rotten placenta. He'd washed it down with hosed-out milk from the dairy. I didn't know that at the time. I only knew that it was beyond foul. As soon as I pulled in at the clinic, I tore my seat cover off and threw it in the bin. I saw that the vomit was also on my seatbelt.

Droopy turned out to be a pain the entire time he was in the clinic. He wasn't used to being inside. As soon as he woke up after the operation, he barked incessantly. I realised that when he was at home he was usually tied up outside so I took him out and tied him up round the back of the clinic figuring he'd be more comfortable there. I found a spot with shade and water and it seemed to do the trick. He stopped barking and I stopped thinking about him.

An hour later, I thought I'd better check that he was okay. I stuck my head out the back door and couldn't quite work out what I was seeing. The chain was going horizontal from the wall of the building it was tied to, straight through the window of my car. *How does that work? And where is Droopy?*

I rushed over to investigate and saw that Droopy had taken it upon himself to hop into the driver's window, which I'd left open to air out some of his foulness. He was happily sitting on the front seat, chest out, as if he was driving the car. He'd been good enough to scratch the door getting in. As I looked in, I saw that he had not, in fact, vomited all the placenta and milk up the first time. Some had clearly stayed in his belly, been rushed through to the bowels and been evacuated as a digestive emergency in an enormous diarrhoea poo all over the front seat of my car. My protective seat cover was, of course, in the bin. So Droopy's doo doo was all over the cloth seat. I 'placed' the dog out of the car, wishing I'd had an ejector seat installed because I certainly would have preferred never to have seen that seat again.

Despite my best efforts to scrub the Magna clean, a little piece of Droopy stayed with me for the rest of the time I owned it, contributing to my driving home alone after tennis.

I could never work out why the two Geoffs, my two bosses, wouldn't stump up for a car for me. Surely, I thought, they could purchase a cheap ute, put a sign on it and away we'd go. They could tax deduct it all and they wouldn't have to pay me seventy-five cents a kilometre in mileage.

Years later I asked Geoff Manning why they wouldn't agree to buy me a car.

'You never buy associates cars,' he said. 'That's a lesson you need to learn.'

'Why?'

'Well, we once had a vet, Jason, working for us. We like him a lot and against our better judgement we thought we'd get him a car. Soon after, we sent him off on a pretty straightforward little job down at Jaspers Brush. It should have taken him forty minutes but he didn't come back for three hours. We were too busy to question him at the time, but my wife was at the clinic when Jason returned and after she saw him she asked me what was wrong with him. There was nothing wrong with him as far as I knew but Pauline said he looked terrible, as pale as a ghost. She prodded me to ask Jason what was wrong. Jason confessed that he'd had a bit of an accident. He was heading to the job and he got to a level crossing and he wasn't concentrating. A train hit the front of the car, spinning it around and jamming it between the signal post and the train. It was a long freight train which proceeded to *click-click, click-click* through the level crossing, tearing the driver's side to pieces. Jason jumped from the driver's side to the passenger side but was wedged in by the signal post and he couldn't open the door.

'So he had to sit there while the train tore his new car to pieces,' Geoff said. 'And that explained the vacant expression on his face. And that's why we don't buy cars for associates.'

When I bought into the business a few years later, the Magna was on its last legs so I used the opportunity to buy a Mitsubishi Triton ute.

Then when James bought in, he just used his Holden Barina for the first six months. That got a lot of laughter from the farmers – at least we think that's what they were laughing at – so he went out and bought a Hilux ute and I got one too to keep things fair.

This brings us to my old Triton and our new associate.

Just to backtrack a little.

Since the crazy, stinking day we'd vowed to get another vet in to work for us, we'd advertised for an experienced vet, but over the following six months had failed to find a single experienced mixed-practice vet who wanted a job.

Through all this time, we'd had a steady stream of students coming through the practice on their month-long practical rotations in their final year. Every vet student has to do a month at a mixed practice – that is a practice that services both large animals (cattle, horses and other livestock) and small animals (typically pets). Most of those students don't want to end up doing mixed practice, but around this time we got a young bloke called Bryden Krebs who was one of the rare students who actually wanted to live in the country and work on cows, sheep and horses.

Before he even arrived, Bryden told us that he had a job lined up in Cooma and Jindabyne. So he was off limits. But on the day he started his student rotation, he told us the Cooma position had fallen through.

'Could I throw my hat in the ring for this job? I know you're looking for someone with experience but I'd just like to put it out there that I'm up for giving it a go,' Bryden said.

'Well, you're here for a month. Let's look at it as a month-long job interview. If we're happy with you at the end, we'll probably take you on.'

He was stoked about that. Bryden did his month and we found him to be diligent and willing to listen and learn. He graduated soon after and came straight back to start work for us. His wife's family was from the area. She'd told him he could work wherever he wanted but in five years' time she wanted to end up somewhere back on the south coast near her family. So for him it was a dream come true. He'd walked into the dream job in a dream area.

Because he was our first employee, we held his hand a lot. Maybe we were like 'helicopter parents', hovering over him, making sure he was all right. But he was very capable and cautious and his arrival coincided with our getting the new Hiluxes, so I handed over the keys to my older, but not that old, Triton.

A couple of months after Bryden had started working for us, I was working out the back of the clinic when I heard someone come through the door. My eyes went up to the security monitor where I saw a couple of enormous ten-gallon hats fill the screen. There's a strange phenomenon whereby the further south one travels in Australia, the smaller the farmers' hats get. The cattlemen in our area are rarely seen in wide-brimmed Akubras, most often getting about in baseball hats or little floppy cotton jobs that don't even warrant names. So I knew these guys were not from around here.

Trish phoned through. 'There's some people out the front who want to talk to you about castrating calves.'

I went out to find a man and a woman under the hats. And they did indeed look like they'd just walked in the door of the Birdsville pub – huge black ten-gallon hats, checked shirts tucked into Wrangler jeans tucked into fancy cowboy boots. Huge belt buckles. Their attire was near-identical except her checked shirt was bright pink.

'How ya goin'?' he said, with as broad an accent as you could get. 'The name's Slim. You blokes do cattle work, do yas?'

'Yeah, we do. What do you need done?'

'You castrate calves, do ya?'

'Yes. No problem at all. But most of our clients just put rings on them themselves.'

'Nah, we've let it go a bit far beyond that. Too big now.'

'Okay. Yes, you do have to surgically castrate them when they get too big. We can manage that.'

'You've done a few, have you?'

Slim continued asking a lot of questions. He knew all the cattle terminology like a ringer from the rangelands, but I couldn't quite figure him out. I had him pinned as running hundreds of head maybe somewhere out to the southwest of Nowra where the land is cheaper and the properties larger.

'What sort of facilities have you got?' I asked. 'Do you have a race and a crush?'

'Nah, nothing like that.'

'Okay, that makes it harder. We've done it before like that where we've lassoed them but it's not really ideal to do it that way. Especially if you've got to do a lot. How many have you got?'

'Just the one.'

'One?'

'Just one. His name's Nullarbor.'

There's a veterinary law that states that as soon as someone names a farm animal, its chances of dying during a surgical procedure are tripled. Despite this, I gave the job to Bryden. As it turned out, however, he'd never castrated a bull before as a vet. He'd done plenty of them on farm prac work, but doing them as a vet requires sedation, local anaesthetic and a generally higher standard of care.

'Okay, I'll come with you and you can see how I do it,' I said.

Slim had explained to us that there was a short cut to his place. If we cut across a small section of open scrub, it would take us to the end of his street, saving us fifteen minutes. I was driving in front, with Bryden following behind in the Triton. I drove over the gutter and up into an open area of weeds and scrub with a mound of raised earth about a metre high running down the middle. I drove around it and as I did so, curving to the right, I saw something out of the corner of my eye – it was the Triton just hanging on the crest of the mound, all four wheels off the ground, rocking on its axis. After an agonising couple of seconds the momentum or the weight of the engine tipped it forward and Bryden somehow managed to drive straight off in a plume of red dust.

Geoff's words of wisdom about why you don't buy associates cars came back to me.

We drove into Slim and Jane's property and it turned out to be just a suburban block backing onto a few acres that they leased for Nullarbor. I wanted to get out and tear strips off Bryden but I couldn't because the clients were standing there waiting for us. They were really nice people. It turned out they were both in the Navy and had grown up in Sydney. They just got into theme when dealing with their property. And Nullarbor fitted the theme as well, being a Brahman with the hump and the big floppy ears.

They had him on a halter and I sedated him and did the operation, somewhat nervously given that he had a name and a cowboy and cowgirl who loved him dearly. But it all went as smooth as the highway across the Nullarbor Plain. The ex-bull woke up two stone lighter and reclassified as a steer.

We said our goodbyes and as I didn't get the chance to take Bryden down over his driving folly then, I thought I might as well take my chance now with this chapter.

HOW TO SAY GOODBYE

James

The hardest part of being a vet is losing a patient. Sometimes no matter how hard you try, or how hard the animal fights, it just isn't enough and you have to let them go. Death is an unfortunate part of our job. You have to deal with your own emotions while helping guide the clients through the process as they deal with the intensity of their own reactions. It's something you never completely get used to. Over time, you do get better at it, though, and better at understanding what people need. A big part of it is telling them to do whatever the hell they want to do. If they want to hold their pet while it's put to sleep, that's fine. If they don't want to be there, that's okay, too. If they want to sit with them afterwards, that's not a problem. Some people will be emotional wrecks, bawling and wailing. I've had people throw themselves on the ground and collapse while others maintain a brick-wall of silence. Every client will react differently and part of our job is to allow them to grieve as they need to.

Margaret and Barry were a lovely couple. In a Noah's Ark-like crusade, they'd accumulated a lot of different animals in the brief time since they'd moved down from Sydney's Upper North Shore. Barry, a retired solicitor, was a slightly built, frail gent in his late sixties, with thin, grey hair sparsely populating the top of his cranium. Margaret, with her thick, black curly hair, was more like a retired hippie.

They'd bought a thirty-acre block about two kilometres out of town and populated it with a few cows, a couple of sheep, some alpacas, chickens, ducks, geese, a dog and two cats. They were thinking of squeezing pigs and a few guinea fowl onto the Ark as well. Their story was a typical Berry tale. Because the cost of land is so high, people who move here and buy a block are usually wealthy. Many of them are nearing the end of their working lives and have managed to accumulate enough assets to buy in. That demographic forms a large part of our clientele. They are a good type of client to have. They tend to be interesting people. They've done a lot of things in their lives and they're usually switched-on operators with a good story to tell. They're often also way out of their depth, trying to figure out what they've gotten themselves into. But unashamedly so: 'I know nothing. Help me.' We're not up against preconceived ideas about what needs doing, but sometimes we're up against unrealistic expectations about outcomes. They don't want their animals to die.

Fortunately, Margaret and Barry were realistic about the economics of their place. It's often hard for us when people spend upwards of a million dollars on a block of land and think they're going to make their living off it, only to be faced with the reality that they can run a maximum of twelve cows, so the best they could possibly do would be to make $12,000 a year. And even that requires all twelve cows to have calves and for all twelve calves to grow fast and strong, which requires good rain and few visits from us. And cattle prices also need to be high. It's amazing how many people chase a dream without getting a calculator out.

As the vet, you can feel like the bearer of bad news when you start breaking this down for people. I'm sure the real estate agents don't do it. The look on people's faces when you tell them can be somewhat deflated. Barry and Margaret, however, were well aware of the numbers. Their farm was purely a hobby, but like a lot of people who've been successful, they didn't do things half-heartedly. While they were going to have a Noah's Ark, they were going to understand each creature and immerse themselves in the job.

When one of their four alpacas fell pregnant, it caused much excitement. It was a big, happy event for them: the first birth on their farm.

Alpacas have got some funky names. An entire male is called a macho, the female is a hembra, the castrated male is a dull old wether, and since a baby is called a cria, pronounced CREE-a, the birth process is called a creation.

Margaret called their new cria Steve. All had gone well with his birth but about two months after the creation, little Steve suddenly become unwell. They called me on the Sunday of the Australia Day long weekend. The traffic in Berry was horrendous so it took fifteen minutes to cover the journey to their property when it would normally take five. Little Steve was lying still in the paddock when I got there. His mum was being protective, not wanting the other alpacas to come near. So just getting in to look at Steve was shaping up as a challenge.

When they're cranky, alpacas' ears go back, they stomp their feet and they try to head-butt you. If all that fails, they go to total war and unleash the spit – smelly, green gobs of gut grass. When I arrived, the mother was harassing the other alpacas who were all interested in what was happening. She was herding them away, spitting and head-butting. I approached with Barry and Margaret and, curiously, the hembra seemed more at ease with them than with her herd mates. But she still stood at attention, ears back, making guttural noises and threatening to spit at me as I approached. Barry, showing great courage, grabbed her and held her, enabling Margaret and I to get in and have a look at Steve.

He was in a bad way. He was pale, dehydrated and twitching, like there was something going wrong in his brain. The first thing you think about with sick alpacas around Berry is barbers pole worm. It gets its name from its resemblance to one of those old-fashioned spiral poles outside a barbershop. The blood coils its way through the worm's translucent white gut, giving it a distinctive appearance. The worms thrive in the moist, mild conditions. They hit goats, sheep and alpacas hard. Around these parts, it's barbers pole until you prove otherwise. But Steve wasn't presenting like victims of barbers pole worm typically did. They're usually weak, lethargic and anaemic, but not as dehydrated as Steve was and not showing neurological symptoms. The twitching was quite strange, like he was almost seizuring without going into a full epileptic episode.

Steve was at an age where he was starting to eat grass and explore the world, crossing over from his mum's protection to being exposed to all sorts of things. Very sick animals all present the same. They're dying. There was a list as long as your arm of conditions he could be suffering from – tetanus, blackleg, and pulpy kidney were a few early standouts. He had a lot of chest noise, so pneumonia was also a possibility.

I gave Margaret and Barry some options. We could hospitalise Steve and treat him intensively. We could try less intensive treatment and leave him on the property. Or we could put him to sleep.

'I think we'll want to do everything possible to save him,' Barry said, looking across to Margaret.

She nodded through worried eyes. 'Yes, everything we can do.'

'Okay, the best shot we've got is to get this guy back to the clinic and get him on IV fluids and figure out what's going on.' I gave Steve a little

Valium to calm him down and steady his twitching. I started to clear the back of my ute to put him in there, but Margaret came up to me.

'No. No. We'll bring him with us in the Range Rover. It's got air-con.'

I jumped in my car and we drove hard down the country lane for the first few hundred metres. Given Steve's dehydration, every minute could count. We turned right onto the Princes Highway and proceeded to crawl with the public holiday traffic for fifteen minutes over the last two kilometres into Berry. I was sure Margaret and Barry would be combusting with the stress of not having a siren on the roof. It was frustrating but at least Steve had the air-conditioning in the Range Rover. It was a very hot day.

We finally arrived at the clinic and carried Steve through to the treatment table. I got an IV catheter in, which allowed us to start running IV fluids immediately. I put Steve on the ultrasound table and with Margaret helping to restrain him, I used the ultrasound to guide a needle into his bladder to take some urine. It was dramatically discoloured, like diluted Ribena, which spelt bad news for Steve.

'I'm pretty sure he's been bitten by a snake,' I said. 'Your options are to put him on a drip and see if he can ride it out; give him anti-venom, which is going to cost you $900; or we can put him to sleep.' They were still keen to push on and so I gave Steve the vial of anti-venom and some steroids. I sent Barry and Margaret on their way and set up the cria in the shower.

Our clinic shower doesn't get used much for human washing any more. The shower cubicle opens into what used to be the laundry but has since been retrofitted as an X-ray room, with a special lead-lined door to prevent dangerous radiation from seeping into the clinic. The door has a small viewing window through which we can monitor the anaesthetised animals during the procedures. Occasionally, Anthony will jog to work and have a shower. I urge him to put paper over the window so as not to shock the poor nurses if they happen to glance in.

We've also put a baby gate on the shower cubicle so we can use it as a small pen for larger sick animals. We hospitalise smaller goats, sheep, alpacas and calves quite frequently. Small calves often get scours and dehydrate quite badly. A fantastic way to treat them is to put them on IV fluids in hospital. We put a mat on the shower floor so that their runny poo passes straight through and down the drain.

We joke about starting our own group within the Australian Veterinary Association. They already have the small-animals group, the cattle vets and the horse vets. We want to start the large animal companion medicine group. That way we can have conferences and talk about new and innovative ways to use your shower. The baby gate itself is worth a paper.

So we got Steve in behind the baby gate and I hooked him up to IV fluids, but unfortunately it was all too much for him. Despite all we'd done, he went into cardiac arrest and died about an hour after Margaret and Barry left.

It's a hard phone call to have to make to people who are so committed. Unfortunately, when your pets walk around in long grassy paddocks where snakes live, these things happen.

They were very upset. All that excitement and grand future they had mapped out had disappeared. Barry said they'd call back in an hour or two. I guess they wanted some time to process it.

Margaret called back. 'Is it possible we could bury Steve back at our place?'

'Absolutely. That's fine.'

'Okay, Barry's going to get our neighbour to come over with the backhoe and dig the hole, so if you could bring him out in a couple of hours that would be greatly appreciated.'

'I'll wrap Steve up and bring him out there at 5 p.m.'

I dutifully wrapped Steve's body in a heavy-duty blanket and continued on with my day. Then I put him in the back of the car and once again braved the traffic.

Just as people mourn the loss of their animals in different ways, so too can the burial part can be equally varied.

When I was working at Manilla in northern NSW, I treated a white horse with melanoma. The horse, Leanne, was old and in some distress. It was time to end her pain. The owner was a deaf woman by the name of Gillian Mercer with whom I conversed by way of pen and paper as I didn't know sign language. And she agreed, with a great deal of reluctance, that putting Leanne down was the best course to take.

She asked if we could organise a burial. 'I need to be there for ceremony,' she wrote.

'Okay,' I replied with my thumbs in the air. 'We will do it tomorrow. I will put Leanne to sleep and we'll bury her there.'

When I arrived at the paddock the next day, the excavator driver, Greg Paton – who was a good mate of mine and buried a lot of horses for me – looked at me as if to say, 'You're in for a bit of a challenge here, mate.'

Leanne was wrapped in white robes that Gillian had run up specifically for this purpose. Death robes. She had rosary beads around her neck. A lot of them. So many that they made it difficult to access her neck for the purpose of euthanasia. I had to peel the robes and the beads out of the way. Meanwhile, Gillian was drawing a picture with stick figures of humans and a horse and a needle. I took a look at it and deduced that she was trying to convince Greg to dig a hole with a gentle incline into it so we could walk Leanne into the hole and I could then inject her while standing in the hole.

I took the paper from her and wrote, 'No'. Even if we could have coaxed the horse into its own grave, there was no way I was getting into a dirt box with it. Writing as fast as I could, I scribbled, 'Me in six foot hole with 500 kg horse too dangerous. Leanne will fall. Might fall on me.'

Farmers are a pragmatic lot and they will often say, 'Here's the hole. Can you kill it so that it falls in?' They don't want the fuss of dragging the horse in. But this wasn't pragmatism. This was a serious ceremony that Gillian had planned.

I made a sorry face. Greg was over to the side not quite knowing where to look.

'Greg is very gentle,' I wrote. 'He will pick up Leanne very softly and place her in the hole. A very skilled and sensitive excavator driver.' This might sound like I was being a bit smart, but it was true. Greg's wife had many horses, so he was experienced in dealing with the emotions involved in horse euthanasia. It wasn't uncommon to see a little tear from under his safety sunglasses. I knew he absolutely hated this job, but, at the same time, there was no one better.

Gillian reluctantly agreed. 'But you have to say a prayer.'

I punched out my best version of 'Our Father', which I probably hadn't said for a few years because my church attendance had wavered in my teens and early twenties.

After I said 'Amen', Gillian started scribbling again.

'Now we have to put the teddy bears and the photos in the hole.'

'Ah, yes, the teddy bears.' Maybe I'd been blocking them from my consciousness but I hadn't paid the five bears much attention since my arrival on the scene. They were lined up off to the side along with a couple of photos of them with Leanne; Leanne as a foal; Leanne with various dogs; Leanne with Gillian. Now it appeared the bears were going to the afterlife with their playmate.

After I'd got everything neatly, and somewhat artistically, placed in the hole, it was time to put poor Leanne out of her suffering. I heaved up her ghostly robes and jangled the rosary beads out of the way. I injected the green dream into her jugular and Leanne fell to the ground within seconds. It was nice and gentle. Gillian wanted me to pronounce her dead by writing it on a piece of paper.

So I did that.

It was a bizarre experience but there was no right or wrong way to do it. Our job is to do the right thing by the horse and to help the owners cope and manage their grief process. I was satisfied I'd done both.

And Greg did a wonderful job placing Leanne in her grave ever so gently.

I couldn't help thinking of Leanne and Gillian when I arrived at Margaret and Barry's place later that afternoon. I drove straight out to the paddock where they'd told me they'd be and I could smell the incense before I'd turned the engine off. They'd decided to bury Steve under the tree where he was born. They saw a nice symmetry in this and I too thought it was apt. Margaret had candles burning which was interesting because it was a hot summer's day. Thankfully, they were in glass containers to minimise bushfire risk. The incense was burning in a Hindu- or Buddhist-like offering at the foot of a photo of Steve at the moment of his birth. The photo also helpfully enabled them to pinpoint the right spot for the grave, right down to its east–west alignment, the way he'd been facing at his creation.

Unfortunately, the neighbour had bailed on helping Barry dig the hole. Barry had a bad back so it was going to be Easter before he got down deep enough to bury a guinea pig. Wisely, he'd bored into the ground with a post-hole digger to soften it, but still he was struggling to make an impact on the loose earth. Faced with a bloke pushing seventy with a bad back trying to dig a hole, there was really only one thing for it, which was to run … no, it was to dig the hole myself. But I don't want other clients to get any ideas here.

'Leave it to me. I'll have a go,' I said.

'This is the right thing to do,' I said to myself as I threw my body into the job at hand. About thirty seconds in, I regretted the decision as the sweat quickly accumulated on my brow. 'But it's the right thing to do,' I said again. And I kept saying it as I rediscovered muscles in my body long left dormant.

As the sweat on my brow turned to drips off my nose, I stopped saying it. 'If only there was a noble way out,' I started to say.

Despite the fact that vetting involves a lot of physical labour, our hands aren't hardened. We're often gloved. We deal with soft, gooey stuff. We don't have those callouses you need for hard labour. So I could feel the start of the blisters and aches and pains in my lower back and legs.

Given that Barry had put a post-hole digger in at each corner of the grave to break up the soil, the hole was largely a matter of chipping away at the remaining earth and getting it out. Digging the hole was a lot easier than it could have been. It was also a lot shallower than it could have been, and the rules are that having used a lethal injection of Lethabarb, I still owned the drug inside the dead animal. I was responsible for it and had to get it down far enough so that no dog could come along, dig up the carcass and poison itself. After about half an hour, we judged the hole to be sufficient.

So we placed Steve in it with his head in the right direction. We put food, photos and fibres of wool from his mother into the hole. We filled it with the lovely black soil and red clay that I had toiled so long to get out and it was actually very satisfying.

When people are that upset, and they're that bonded to an animal, the burial and whatever rituals they choose to perform are all cathartic. It's gratifying for us to be able to help them with the process.

I packed some stuff away. Margaret went and got some cold drinks from the house. When she returned, the three of us sat on the tray of the ute and cracked a nice cold Boags. We chatted and reflected on our blisters and on little Steve's brief life ... and our own.

'This time last year I was sitting by the pool at our home in Wahroonga and look at me now,' Barry said. 'Digging a hole on the Sunday afternoon of a long weekend.'

'No, we weren't,' Margaret broke in. 'We were on Graham's yacht on the harbour.'

'Yes, of course. What a great day.'

'But you wouldn't change a thing, would you?' I said.

'I think I'd rather be on the yacht actually.' Barry laughed. We all cracked up, because the suggestion he'd rather be on a yacht was so absurd. We all knew he was lying.

ONE SHEEP, TWO SHEEP ...
INFINITY SHEEP

Anthony

Xavier Montgomery was a well-spoken Englishman, bordering on posh. He'd bought fifty acres of rugged country up the mountain, where the paddocks are constantly under siege from the ever-encroaching rainforest. He had some cattle and he was keen to do the right thing by them and the land. He called us a lot in those early days. He was a city boy and while his accent and his appearance – thirtyish with a mop of eccentric black hair – had him marked as something of a dandy, he was an incredibly hard worker. He did the fences, built the yards, tended the livestock and was always keen to learn more. He was clearly a very intelligent guy. He'd moved in when I was a young vet starting out, and we'd grown together. I taught him a lot and I learnt a lot from him as we dealt with all the little problems that our new neighbourhood threw up. He was courteous and didn't waste your time. A good client.

There was no house on the property in those early years. He stayed in an old Viscount caravan with no running water and no power. He mentioned that he was planning a house, but first he wanted to get the farm going right. He built a chicken house and a barn and improved the fences.

We spent a lot of time together up on his mountain block, but I didn't know anything else about him. He often had mates down helping him, but I hadn't seen any sign of a partner on the scene.

After Xavier had run cattle for a couple of years, he added sheep and goats to his collection. They're not as well-suited as cattle to the high rainfall in our area. In the moist country, sheep can suffer foot problems and there's the blood-sucking barbers pole worm that can hit them hard. It was all very well to have dreams of raising organic sheep, but that's hard to do when you've got animals dying from these worms. He'd lost a few but he'd got his head around the need to worm them and so the whole operation was settling down into a steady routine and he was calling us less often.

One time, I called in to help with a calving and he told me that he was about to start building a house.

'Good on you. That'll be a bit more comfortable,' I said, visualising him at least with power and water and a nice warm fireplace.

Soon after I had this conversation, I went up to Sydney and was walking through Hyde Park with my then-girlfriend who had a magazine in her hand. I glanced at the cover. It was one of the racier, more gossipy publications. And there on the front cover, amidst all the Kardashians and the weight-loss tips and the wardrobe fails, was a familiar face with a gorgeous blonde on his arm.

'Oh my god! That's Xavier! What's he doing in a magazine? Who is he with?' My girlfriend explained that the blonde was a famous singer, actress and model. We'll call her 'Brigitta'.

'I've never heard of her,' I said. 'All I know is *that's* Xavier Montgomery who lives up on the mountain.'

'He must be her partner.'

I grabbed the magazine and looked more closely. It was a paparazzi photo. You could tell they didn't want to be photographed. The story was something about them trying to conceive and they were copping some trolling over the internet and from some morning radio boofheads. Xavier had gone off the deep end and now they were ducking for cover from all the hype.

When I thought about it, I realised I had heard of Brigitta before. I just hadn't been paying enough attention. But it was kind of shocking to realise that Xavier had this whole other life separate from his bucolic retreat up the hill. I found out later he was actually a prominent record producer and he'd met her through her singing.

Soon after the magazine cover, work began on their dream house. An angular, architect-designed geometry set of glass, concrete and corrugated iron soon rose out of the paddocks, and any remnants of the idea that Xavier was a battler trying to eke out a dream were soon put to rest.

By the time the place was finished, Brigitta was pregnant and Xavier told me the plan was for them to move down permanently to raise the child. They'd built a studio in the house so she could continue to record. Not that we ever spoke much about that sort of thing. Our conversation was largely confined to the animals and the farm.

A year or two on, it was an extremely hot day. The new fire alert of 'catastrophic' had been declared. I was at home on call, trying to think of ways to do as little as possible as the light shimmered outside. The phone rang. Of course. It was Xavier.

'Anthony, I'm awfully sorry to call on a day like today but I've got a problem with one of my sheep. It's collapsed. Looks like it's dying.'

My initial reaction was surprise that he was calling me. I thought we'd got him through this stage. It was almost certainly a worm infestation. So I began the standard list: 'Have a look at the colour of its gums, its vulva and its eyes and tell me what—'

'I've done that,' he broke in. 'They're all a nice, healthy pink. I don't understand it. It doesn't look anaemic at all.'

'Oh, okay, I guess I'd better come and have a look. I can't tell you over the phone.'

I drove up the mountain and it was even hotter at Xavier's place, nestled on the western slope of the escarpment, copping the full force of the sun and the oppressive drilling of the westerly wind.

He led me to the sheep which was lying down, barely conscious, panting, in the full sun.

'Quick, let's get it into the shade,' I said.

'How about the garage?'

'Great.'

Xavier disappeared and backed out an old ute and a Porsche. We carried the sheep inside where they had a gym set up with exercise bikes, dumbbells and mirrors. I started to examine the patient. She was in full wool, so she was overdue to be shorn and covered in burrs and spikes. I cut my hands as I buried them in the wool trying to get a pulse. Xavier was leaning over the top of me like an overprotective mother.

'Can you see what's wrong?'

Her heart rate was elevated. She was panting. I took her temperature: 42.5 degrees.

'Phew! That's hot, hot, hot. Where's she been?' I asked. 'She's really cooking.'

'She managed to separate herself from the flock and got herself into a paddock she wasn't meant to be in. No shade. I found her out there just before I called you.'

It seemed reasonable that this sheep was suffering heat stroke. It had got to a temperature where its cells were going to start to dissolve. Since the cells make up the muscles and the organs, when that happens it's all over.

But I continued the examination to see if there was some other underlying condition that had caused her to break off from the mob and lie down in the sun in the first place. Xavier was right. She wasn't anaemic – the go-to symptom for down sheep in our district, indicating barbers pole. I couldn't find anything else wrong with her.

'We need to get this sheep shorn,' I said, 'but we can't do that on a Saturday afternoon. And shearing now will only distress her more, which will increase her temperature and she'll die. Have you got a hose or a bucket? We can wet her down and get a fan on her.'

Xavier started running around looking for a fan and a bucket but he didn't seem able to get his hands on either as he criss-crossed the big garage and out the open doors to where the infinity pool above us cascaded over the edge into a return that was down at our level, all beautiful mosaic tiles and black marble pavers.

'Right, I've got an idea,' he said. He picked up the sheep and lifted her towards the infinity pool return.

I was almost in slow mo: 'Nooooo...'

But he was already committed, with forty kilograms of dirty wool and bones tumbling into the sixty-centimetre-deep return. As soon as the sheep's body entered the water, lanoline and sheep shit, burrs and mud floated out and formed an Exxon Valdez of gunk across the ornamental return, which immediately began to circulate it up into the main infinity pool.

Xavier went to pull her out. 'Is this bad for her?' he asked.

'No, it'll be good for her but it's going to make an awful mess of your pool. I just didn't want all the muck getting in. I don't think there's much to be gained from getting her out now though. You've already cleaned off the worst of the mess.'

Xavier looked back at the slick, looked at the sheep, and then looked at me. 'Don't tell Brigitta.'

The shock of the cold water had done nothing to raise the sheep out of its almost comatose state. It half-stood, half-floated, like a stunned mullet wearing a dirty, woolly jumper. Sheep aren't known for their love of swimming. If they get wet, they become so heavy they can't stand. The lanoline is a protective mechanism to stop that from happening, but dumping them in a chlorinated pool will cut through it. She just sat there and stared blankly into the middle distance for five minutes before awareness started to creep back into her brain. She began to look around with a bit of curiosity. You almost could read her mind: *I'm a sheep. What am I doing here? Where are my floaties?* She started to bleat, calling for her mates. She was definitely coming around, and just to prove the point, she plopped a stream of poo pellets into the water. At that point we figured she had recovered sufficient bodily function to warrant her immediate removal from her therapy pool.

'You'd really better not tell Brigitta now,' Xavier said. 'She won't swim for a month.'

It took the two of us to lift the sheep back out. She was three times heavier than when Xavier dunked her in. We carried and pulled her back into the garage. Xavier eventually did find a fan. He put it on and we shut the door, confident in the knowledge that she was going to make an even bigger mess in there, but at least she was going to live.

The country dream ended up not working for Xavier and Brigitta. It is so difficult for people juggling young children and careers to throw in isolation and the added workload of a farm. We were saddened when they moved back to the city. Reality rarely matches up with expectations, but I'm sure Xavier left a big piece of himself back there on the mountain and every time a paparazzo pops up in his face I'm sure I know where he'd rather be.

FOREIGN BODIES

James

The staff bonding session was going well. We'd all got into fancy dress and completed a ten-kilometre mud-themed challenge. After a quick shower we were gathering at the pub when Bryden's phone rang. He was on call so the clinic after-hours number was diverted to him. By the time he hung up, I was just arriving at the table with the first round of drinks.

'It's Leonard Luxford,' he said. 'Bruiser's got a bone stuck in his throat.'

We all looked at Bryden knowingly. 'We'll see you in ten minutes. Give him some anti-inflammatories and send him home.'

In the vast majority of suspected bone-in-throat cases, people rush their dog into the clinic and we find nothing in there at all. It's usually kennel cough, a condition like whooping cough.

When a dog really does have something stuck in its throat, it comes in almost comically standing there pointing at its throat with its paw, saying, 'Get this darn thing outta here!' There's drool everywhere, the dog paws at its face and throat. You could diagnose it from a low-flying aircraft. But the incidence of that is rare. People feed their dogs bones a lot less these days so it just doesn't happen so often.

Horses suffer from oesophageal obstruction too. Horse people have a great name for it – 'choke' – and it usually just means that the horse hasn't chewed its food properly. It's distressing for the owner to see their animal extending its neck in and out desperately trying to get something down with saliva flying everywhere. Out of the dozens of times I've been called out for this, however, there's only been a few where the horse was still choking by the time I got there. The horse can usually clear its throat itself.

So as Bryden headed off up the road to what we were all sure would be a false alarm, it brought to mind my favourite choking story from when I'd worked in the UK.

'Stop me if you've heard this before,' I told my assembled colleagues.

I don't know why Anthony tried to choke me at this point but I thought it important the staff hear how a bit of lateral thinking can often save the day.

In the UK they get a lot of choking cattle because they feed potatoes and other excess crops to their cows. I'd see these great piles of root vegetables the farmers couldn't sell, rising above the vast flatness of the Cambridgeshire fens where I worked for a few months. One day, I got a call from a farmer to see a cow that had swallowed an entire sweet potato without bothering with the niceties of forty chews per mouthful.

I went out and found the cow – a big red and white Holstein – in a state of distress, extending her neck back and forward, throwing her head around, spraying drool everywhere. There was no question of the diagnosis because I could feel the lump through the neck. The farmer tied her head to keep it still, while I gave her a little sedation, then got a gag between her back teeth to hold her mouth open so I could get in and have a look down the throat. But it was too far down to see, so I tentatively put my hand in and had a feel around.

The cow jacked up. She was getting stressed. Imagine if some stranger came along and put his hand down your throat. So I gave her more sedation and stuck my hand in a little further. I ended up having my entire arm down this cow's oesophagus. At the same time I had the farmer help by pushing the sweet potato upwards from the outside. There was no risk of it going any further down because the narrowest point of the oesophagus is where it enters the chest. And that's where it was stuck.

By the time I reached the lump, the cow's teeth were scratching into my armpit. If she moved her head suddenly, it would dislocate my shoulder. I was right down in there, fully committed. I could feel the sweet potato and could just about get my fingers around it, but the cow was producing so much saliva to lubricate this thing away, I couldn't get a grip. I tried getting my fingernails into it. I tried hooking a finger underneath. But I just couldn't do it. After about forty minutes, my hand was getting weak and I knew I just wasn't going to make it happen.

The only other option was surgery. The oesophagus, however, is not a good thing to operate on. You can't rest an oesophagus so healing is difficult, especially in a cow that's regurgitating all the time. And the farmer didn't want the expense of an operation.

I stood and looked at this poor sad-eyed cow.

'Look, I've got another idea,' I said. 'Do you have a corkscrew?'

'Yes, I think so,' he said.

'A T-bar corkscrew?'

'I don't drink, but I might have something there.'

He came back with a corkscrew with a big wooden handle. We cut the T-bar off and just left a little stub, not much wider than the actual corkscrew. I held it with my middle finger over the point to protect the throat and reached back down into the oesophagus until I hit the sweet potato. I threaded the corkscrew between my fingers and started turning it into the hard orange flesh of the vegetable. With my arm at full stretch and my body almost horizontal, every quarter turn was an effort, but I eventually got it in. I put my two fingers around the remaining T-bar and pulled.

The great big root started moving and once I got it going it came through easily.

The farmer looked at the enormous sweet potato and thought it was the best thing he'd ever seen. For him, it was an absolute miracle we'd got this thing out. In his mind, he'd just about written off the cow, which was worth a few thousand pounds.

'Oh laddie, you'd better keep that corkscrew in case you need it again,' he said.

'This isn't very common,' I said.

'Never mind, if it can happen once, it can happen again.' He insisted, so I hosed it off and dropped it into my kit. I gave the cow some anti-inflammatories and we let her go. She went outside and started eating immediately as if no stranger had had his arm down her gullet for the last hour.

So as we sat around the Berry pub awaiting Bryden's return, I told my rapt colleagues how I went back to that farm three weeks later to do herd health checks and preg-test some cows. There were twenty animals penned in the dairy waiting for me to look at them. I worked my way through them until one came along with no sign of anything wrong.

'What's the matter with this cow?' I asked.

'Well. you tell me. You're the vet,' he said with a cheeky grin.

I had a quick inspection but she seemed right as rain.

'Don't you recognise her? This is the one where you popped the cork. She's the most famous cow in the county now. I've been telling everyone about it.'

I looked around ready to acknowledge the professional acclaim of my colleagues when the phone rang. It was Bryden.

'What's up, mate?' I asked. 'Your lemon squash is getting flat.'

'I'm still here with Bruiser. He actually does have something stuck in his throat,' Bryden said. 'And it's really quite bad. I've anaesthetised him and had a look. There's an enormous bone stuck in the oesophagus.'

'Okay, I'll come and give you a hand.'

It crossed my mind to ask the bar staff for a corkscrew but figured it might not be so effective on bone. I walked the 300 metres back to clinic to find that Bryden had done all the right things. The Bull Terrier was out cold, lying on his chest, with his legs 'frog-legged' out the back to make him nice and stable. He had a tube down his windpipe for breathing and so that none of the saliva could go into his lungs. Bryden had suspended a dog lead around Bruiser's upper jaw and looped it up over the light support from the roof so we could hold his head up and his mouth open to give us good access. They don't teach that in vet school. You've got to learn that one on the job.

We gathered the equipment we'd need: various grippy, grabby, opening kinds of devices and very good lighting because it was going to be dark down where we were heading. I sat down on a saddle chair (it gives you good mobility, like you're standing while sitting) at the end of the table. I had my powerful miner's light on my head ready to go digging in. I got an endoscope – a fibre-optic tube with a light and a camera on the end – and stuck one end down the throat, then put my eye up to the other end. Easing it through, I came to a roadblock in the form of an enormous bone almost the size of my fist stuck in Bruiser's oesophagus at the level of the thoracic inlet, which is down next to the equivalent of the collarbone in a human. It's where the oesophagus narrows and was the exact same spot where the sweet potato had got stuck in the cow on the fens. The bone simply could not fit through.

My endoscope had a grabber attachment designed for precise little jobs, but this one called for something far more agricultural. There is a drawer in the clinic that we rarely open. Not surprisingly, it is called the Seldom-Used Instruments Drawer. And if you ever find yourself opening it to rustle through the jam-packed, disorganised contents, you know you're having an interesting day. It's chock full of weird stuff filed under the last-out, first-in system as determined by the law of the great vet Murphy, so what you're looking for is invariably at the back on the bottom. At last I got to an extremely long set of forceps. They're about forty-five centimetres long with a gentle curve in them. I have no idea what their name is. I call them the Big Long Grabby Forceps.

We had a student with us and she helped immobilise the dog's head. Bryden was pushing the bone from the outside of the neck trying to massage it forward to the mouth and I was operating down the oesophagus with the endoscope and the Big Long Grabby Forceps. Combined with the breathing tube, there was a lot of gear going down Bruiser's throat. I was glad he wasn't a Shih Tzu.

The big risk was damaging the oesophagus. People ask why we don't just cut the oesophagus open, and that is an option, but it's the last option. Just like with the cow, there are all sorts of problems with those wounds healing and if you scar the oesophagus the animal will have difficulty eating for the rest of its life. You can tell humans to chew properly and eat slowly while the wound is healing, but that doesn't work on dogs, particularly not ones prone to eating fist-sized bones.

I pulled while Bryden pushed. I couldn't get the Big Long Grabby Forceps around the bone, only on the end of it. I'd move it a few millimetres before it would slip away with all the lubrication from the hyper salivation. The time ticked by. The frustration grew. It took us about an hour to get the bone up far enough for me to see it without the camera. That allowed me more room and a better view to get the V-shaped biting bit on the end of the forceps into the bone. I pressed it together and ratcheted it down for the tightest grip possible. I went too far and bent the forceps, but at least I had a really good grip now. I pulled the bone further forward into the mouth but it was still stuck.

It had us all wondering how on earth Bruiser had swallowed this bone in the first place, because even now as it came up, it was still wedged tight.

We got some obstetrical lubricant, the sort you'd use in assisting a birth, and injected it around and behind the bone with a syringe. It was like a puzzle now. We had to manipulate the bone into a position where it could come through the last little bit. We got another set of clamps in there and pulled it around until, millimetre by millimetre, we turned it to the angle that we figured must have been the way it had gone in. After two hours of work, we were sweating. My arms were sore. The student's arms were almost falling off from holding the rope that held the dog's head still and Bryden's fingers were shot from massaging this thing up. It came out quite quickly in the end and we continued to be gobsmacked by how huge this thing was.

I handed it to Bryden.

'And that is why we don't feed bones to dogs. I think you better show that to the owners. Now I'm returning to the pub to put something more fluid down my throat.'

DON'T LOOK AT THE DRONE

Anthony

We had given up on the idea of a television show. Rodney told us that Screentime had shown it to the networks, but that was about all anyone was getting told. I tried calling Screentime myself but didn't get anywhere. So I let it go. We were proud of the pilot and had shown it to friends and family on disc. But that was it. It looked like Rodney had blown his money on a really good home movie for us.

It was exactly a year after we'd shot it, December 2013, that we learned that Foxtel looked like it might actually commission the show. The twist was that Screentime hadn't yet signed a contract with us. We'd said to Screentime from the beginning that we needed to see a deal in writing with plenty of notice so we could read it, digest it and modify it. But they hadn't yet sent a thing.

There were a few stumbling blocks in the negotiation and it struck us that the TV people were incredulous that we battled so hard to keep some degree of control over what went to air. We realised later that everyone they deal with is desperate to be on television. While we wanted it to happen, we were very aware that our main asset was our business. It would be there long after any show had disappeared, so we had to look after that first, and we were happy to walk away if the deal didn't protect the practice.

We talked with the Veterinary Practitioners Board, the Australian Veterinary Association and our insurer. We didn't know how the professional bodies would view it. I couldn't imagine they'd received calls like that very often. Perhaps one from Dr Harry Cooper back in the 1990s and one from Dr Chris Brown when *Bondi Vet* got going in 2009.

The two professional associations said the same thing. 'Be careful you don't do anything that could damage your professional reputation, and do not do anything for television that you wouldn't do in normal life.'

The insurer said as long as you're doing your job you're insured.

While all this was going on, we hadn't told our staff a thing. We hadn't wanted to talk it up before it happened. They were all wondering why we were sneaking out to our cars and talking on our phones with the air-conditioning up or in the office with the door closed. That wasn't our usual way.

As a deal with Foxtel became increasingly likely, we decided we'd invite Rodney to the office Christmas party again. The staff hadn't seen him for nine months and he wasn't quite as tired as at the previous year's bash, but he was still in good form. I stood and thanked the staff for their year's efforts.

'And it's probably pretty obvious to you all now with Rodney present that it looks like we are going to be filming a television show early next year and it's going to be called *Village Vets*. We hope you're all keen to be involved.'

There was a shocked silence, then a round of applause. Everybody was pretty chirpy and it was the main topic of conversation for the rest of the evening.

The show got greenlit on 22 December. It's a crazy industry.

Nothing happens for nine months, then a year's work gets done in two weeks.

Filming was set to begin at the Berry Show on the last weekend in January. When I thought of TV shows, I thought of vans and satellite dishes, wardrobe and make-up. But when the appointed day came, it was just three blokes – a producer, a soundo and a cameraman – who came bustling through the door with a camera and some sound equipment. The cameras were turned on and we were off. It was quiet. Not so much because the animals weren't coming in but because the staff stopped talking to us. There'd be a break in filming and one of them would approach us.

'Ian Rasmussen called at 9.30. He's got a calving and he needs help.'

'That was an hour ago. Why didn't you tell me?'

'You were filming.'

It quickly became obvious that things weren't working. At the end of that first day, we called a staff meeting and said that we needed everybody to be normal. If they needed to interrupt us, that was okay. The crew was making a show about vets treating animals and that's what happens in a vet clinic.

We needed to run the clinic first and foremost.

'Filming can be redone but a dead animal can't be,' we told the staff. 'The animal is the priority and the business comes second. Filming comes way down the line. You have to interrupt us if need be.'

The hardest part was clarifying everything to the clients. They would come through the door and there'd be the crew hanging around, a camera and microphone. We had to explain it every time a new person walked in. There'd be a waiver to sign if the camera touched on them at all, so there was a bit of client anxiety.

'Crikey, I'd have done my hair if I'd known.' That sort of thing. But only one client declined to be on the show – a dairy farmer who'd let a problem go a little longer than he should have and was worried that it would show him and his industry in a bad light.

The cameraman, Matt Bronger, was a really experienced and capable lensman, but he was also a livewire, just bouncing off the walls if there was nothing to do. He told us on the first day that he was an electrician by trade.

'If there's nothing to film and you guys need any electrical work done, I'd be more than happy to do it for you.'

'Well, actually there are a couple of things we wouldn't mind having done...'

He put lights in, hung picture frames, and just did general handyman work around the clinic.

Tim Vincent was the field producer and he had enormous energy too. He'd been in front of the camera for years on the kids' show *Totally Wild*, so he knew how it all worked. He was always ready to go at any time of the day or night. Those two would just keep shooting till the day was done. If that meant eighteen-hour shifts, they'd do it. We had other crew rotating through as well and they, quite rightly, stuck to their contracted ten paid hours a day. But that just wasn't enough to track us through our days' work.

'If you go home now, you're going to miss the end of the story.'

When Tim was on, that situation occurred less often because he worked so hard that the others just tended to follow. He looked like Gilligan from *Gilligan's Island*, always wearing a bucket hat and a big goofy smile, marking in his notebook what was happening when.

We filmed for several days before Tim told us that we had to do a formal interview where he'd get us to recount everything that had occurred in the last few days. He'd ask us questions about why we'd done something or what we were thinking when we did it.

I was the first to arrive at the outdoor studio they'd set up for the Q&A sessions with a beautiful background and lighting. While I was waiting to start, one of the crew, David, decided he was going to put a bit of make-up on me.

Oh god. What's going on here? I thought. *This is not what we signed up for. The veterinary association said don't do anything you wouldn't normally do.*

It was a hot day so I'd covered myself in sunscreen and was glistening like a disco ball. David needed to dull the shine. Just as he was doing so, James pulled up in his ute. He thought it was hilarious.

'Who's a pretty boy then?' he said, laughing.

He didn't think that through, though.

I did my interviews and James sat down. David came in with the powder puff to put make-up on his shining sunscreen face. I snapped off a couple of photos and had them off to all our uni mates before the first question had even been asked.

'And he said TV wouldn't change him,' I captioned the photos.

We filmed for nine weeks, over which time we came to get used to the peculiar demands of the industry. Like the repeated refrain: 'Don't look at the drone!' (That was difficult because those little beggars were less common then and to have one hovering just above your eyeline was hard to ignore.) Another demand was wardrobe. Lacking one of those big white vans parked outside the clinic, we had to supply our own. By way of background, let me tell you that vets wear striped and checked shirts. That's it. It's the uniform.

But Tim told us we could only wear block colours because checks and stripes strobed the camera. At the start of filming, James owned just one solid-coloured shirt and I had two.

We'd get to the interviews and they'd say, 'We need you to say something about that cow you operated on last week but because the rest of the interview about that was in a light-blue shirt with blue trousers and you're currently wearing a dark-blue shirt and cream trousers, we need you to change.'

It got so that we'd turn up to these interviews with every shirt we owned, some of which had been ruined during the filming process.

'We need that light blue one.'

'It's torn and it's got a dirty great bloodstain on it.'

We both ended up going out and buying a bunch of new shirts. We started calling ourselves Fifty Shades of Blue.

As time progressed everyone got in the groove of filming. The crew understood the ebb and flow of the clinic, when to back off and let things happen and when to ask questions. They were all fascinated and asked about all sorts of things that we considered routine. This was really important as when you're ensconced in an industry you tend to forget to think like an outsider, so their questions prompted us to remember who we were talking to. Quite a few of the crew fancied themselves as vet nurses too, and over the series got a great thrill out of helping to put bandages on and hold dogs for minor procedures like ultrasounds or taking blood – Tim always joked that he'd earnt his scrub shirt and was taking up vet nursing.

REX

James

Part of the show involved the crew following our lives outside work. So they'd film brief bits of the after-hours lives of our partners, families and staff. But I never expected my own pets to star in the show.

It was the Saturday of the district cricket association first grade grand final. I was the wicketkeeper, so I had excused myself from filming duties for that whole weekend. The film crew weren't interested in a cricket match because they'd already filmed our clinic taking on the Bomaderry clinic in a social game. Early in the week, there'd been a massive deluge, so by Wednesday, the cricket ground was underwater as Broughton Mill Creek burst its banks and crossed the highway. It had fined up by Thursday but we knew there was going to be no cricket played that weekend. Unfortunately, our opposition was more optimistic, so they made us turn up on Saturday to confirm that the ground was indeed not fit to play on. Then, rather than just abandon the game and allow us to head to the pub and celebrate on Saturday night, they made us turn up on the Sunday to once again be told at 10 a.m. that there was going to be no cricket. Because we'd finished first on the competition table, we were crowned champions.

We were at last able to start the celebration and did all the things you do in the case of a glorious victory, even an anticlimactic one. We hugged, we squirted sparkling wine at each other and we drank freely from the premiership cup – which tasted a lot like Silvo.

We then jumped on a bus to watch third grade who were playing their grand final on a synthetic wicket at Shoalhaven Heads. I was on the bus when Ronnie rang.

'There's a huge, black snake right outside Charlie's bedroom window.'

Charlie was now a bright and bouncing one-year-old who had overcome his initial feeding issues to tip the scale at over nine kilos. He loved animals already but we weren't keen on him getting anywhere near this particular creature!

'Crikey. Okay, I'll call Kahlia.'

So I rang Kahlia who is our resident expert snake catcher. I thought I'd better call the fellers from the show too. So I rang them and Rodney came out to get me.

Kahlia caught the snake – a nice big one. The boys got the footage and I was set to return to my celebrations. However, Ronnie told me that our cat, Rex, had been out in the yard with the snake and we worried that he might have been bitten. He looked completely unaffected. He was the same old over-affectionate-bordering-on-needy Rex. But I thought we'd better check just in case.

I took him to the clinic and tested him. He was okay. So we went and released the snake and I retired to the Berry Hotel where my mighty cricket team was gathering for the bash and to commiserate third grade on their defeat.

I had a few more beers but I just couldn't get Rex off my mind. I'm a worrier by nature, and this time I let my anxiety fixate on Rex.

What if he'd been bitten? Black-snake venom can be very slow acting. What if it hadn't shown up in my test because it hadn't taken effect yet? I couldn't bear the thought of losing him, we'd been on such a journey together – Rex, Ronnie and I.

When Ronnie and I were a new couple, living the life in the UK, I was working at a clinic in south London where the busiest part of our practice's working day was the nights because we covered the after-hours work for nineteen other clinics across south London. Because we were on call for the whole area, we got to know the police. Any animal emergencies at night had them calling us. The bobbies seemed keen to help injured animals. Not so quick if you were about to be stabbed, but very keen to help a distressed cat.

One day they turned up with a skinny, starving-to-death dog.

'We've had this one for a week,' the bobby said. 'A woman brought it in and said she'd found it wandering about like that. What sort of filthy animal'd do that to a dog?'

I examined the dog, all ribs and hips, eyes and skin. 'This dog has clearly been badly neglected,' I said. 'It's in a bad way, but you've had it for a week, so it's difficult for me to say what it was like a week ago. I don't think I can give you the declaration you need to be able to prosecute anybody.'

'Yeah, sorry. It's our fault. We got busy. We couldn't bring him in sooner and we didn't mind having him riding around with us in the car. We've been feeding him up. He looked a lot worse when we got him.'

I pulled out a very unpalatable worming tablet. The sort you normally have to hide in folds of meat for a dog to eat, but this one just went *woof* and devoured it off my hand.

Lovely dog but you had to watch your fingers when food was involved.

The police told me they'd already scanned the microchip in the dog and had phoned the registered owner. He'd told them he had given the dog away a year earlier to a woman named Sally Bruin. As it turned out, Sally Bruin was the name of the woman who'd brought the dog in, saying she'd found it wandering the streets.

So the police twigged to what had happened and were now looking to build a case to prosecute the woman. But my reluctance to give a declaration on the state of the dog, given that it had been in police custody for a week, put the kybosh on their plans. They didn't look too upset.

'We'll just go around and pay her a visit. Maybe put the fear of God into her.'

They said goodbye, and I didn't have to wait long to find out how they went. Within the hour they were back at the clinic with a cat cage.

'We went and said hello to one Sally Bruin,' the constable said. 'Gave her the spiel about how she had committed an offence in mistreating the pet and lo and behold we found these two cats wailing around the back.' He reached into the purple plastic cage. 'This one here's the worst of 'em.' And he pulled out the ugliest, baldest, skinniest cat I had seen.

'Okay, I might be able to make a declaration about this one,' I said.

I weighed the cat – a full-grown male with a large frame – and he was 1.9 kilograms. I'd expect an average cat of his size to be about five kilograms. All his hair was falling out, emphasising the bones jutting through the mottled skin.

I tested his blood and the results were horrendous. He was in multi-organ failure from starvation, but despite that, his character shone through.

The police prosecuted Sally Bruin for cruelty to animals and the cats were surrendered. I never had to go to court because she pleaded guilty and agreed not to keep pets for a certain number of years. When people starve animals like that, there's often a degree of mental illness involved, so I agreed that this outcome was for the best.

The clinic took over the care of the cats as a charity case. Their names were Henry and Anne, but when we used Henry's name he kind of glared and cowered at us so we renamed them Anna and Rex, as in anorexia.

Anna was in reasonably good condition. After a week, we were able to send her along for rehousing, but Rex needed a lot more care. He was so starved, his body couldn't handle food. If you gave him more than a teaspoon of it, he'd vomit it straight back up. At the same time, he was absolutely ravenous. I took a video of him where he saw me coming with the teaspoon and started clawing on the front of the cage and howling. I had to throw it in and slam the door because he was coming at me so hard. Not aggressive, but frighteningly overenthusiastic. He was starving to death and manic for nourishment. I've never seen an animal so besotted with food. Accordingly, the nurses wanted to help him so they kept feeding him too much so he kept on vomiting.

I had to lay down the law and forbid them from giving him anything.

'Just to be clear,' I said. 'From now on, I'm the only one that's allowed to feed Rex.' Every fifteen or twenty minutes I'd give him half a teaspoon of a special prescription cat food. In essence, it was chicken and rice. It was very bland but full of nutrition. I'd have to give it to him carefully because of his mania. And over the coming days he became obsessed with me because I was the food guy. And because the clinic was often quiet during the day, I'd let him out and he'd follow my every step, looking up at me with those enormous, hollow eyes, rubbing my legs with his bony hips.

'Are you going to feed me now? Look at me! Are you going to feed me now? Look at me!'

Rex was like a dog, which was kind of appropriate given his name. He was a real character who loved hanging out with humans: 'Hi, how's it going? Pat me. Love me. Feed me.'

I was minding him one night when we got a call for an emergency coming in. I walked up the stairs to our flat above the clinic and Rex followed. Ronnie's not much of a cat person. I, too, prefer the company of dogs, though I don't mind the felines. But this one was special.

'Here's Rex, that cat I've been telling you about,' I said. 'Can you look after him for an hour or two? I've got to go back down to do an operation.'

The night got busy and I ended up being gone for six hours. By the time I returned upstairs, Ronnie was asleep on the couch with Rex perched on her chest, asleep with a rattling great purr going on.

'I think we've found our cat.'

Dogs weren't an option in our tiny studio and we both craved having an animal. We had agreed that if we found the right cat we would take him in and eventually take him back to Australia. It looked like this was our guy.

Of course, when Ronnie woke up, she was covered in cat hair because Rex was still in a bad way, still almost bald, and what little hair he did have departed his body at a prodigious rate. So we put on our special worst clothes whenever we held him, and that way we didn't ruin every outfit we owned.

In the time that Ronnie and I had lived in London, we had renovated a flat and got ourselves a cat. This was clearly a serious relationship. Rex soon took up residence on the end of our bed. We couldn't separate him from us in that tiny place so we had a brown polar-fleece rug for his hair to fall out on. The sun would come up at 4.30 a.m. in the summer and I'd come back from on call and wake him. I'd just want a few hours' sleep before work started again, but he'd be rubbing my face, purring.

'You've woken me now. Come on. I'm awake. I'm awake. Playtime.'

'Get away.'

We had trained him to understand that if he stayed on the brown polar-fleece rug he would not get in trouble. So I'd be mumbling, 'Get back on brownie', aware that maybe we hadn't trained him up quite as well as we thought. And that would be it for sleep. I'd drive Ronnie to the station in the morning and Rex always insisted on coming in the car with us.

He was even more challenging to live with for the first three to four months because his gastro-intestinal system remained in disarray. It took his guts that long to calm down. In the meantime, sharing a six-metre by four-metre apartment with a cat suffering severe diarrhoea at 3 a.m. led to many shouts of, '!@#$%^&*(!@#$%)%^!'

It was so smelly you couldn't roll over and go back to sleep. At such moments Rex was definitely 'my cat' as opposed to 'our cat'. I'd have to get up and take the litter tray downstairs to empty it and bring up a fresh one. We couldn't possibly live with the smell.

Our kitchen was a tiny space, so small that the shelves where we kept our food didn't have doors on them because there wasn't enough room to actually be in the kitchen and open a door at the same time. Rex would get up in the middle of the night and get in there, pulling a whole swathe of groceries off the shelf with his paw, devouring anything he could chew. Whole loaves of bread, packet noodles, birthday-cake candles.

Even though we were feeding him a lot in small portions, he remained manic for food. Obsessed. When we returned to Australia, we put Rex into quarantine and they fed him well there too because he came out heavier and happier. We stayed at Ronnie's parents' apartment for a while and after we'd been there about three days, Rex scurried up a roof, traversed an exposed concrete beam and perched himself on a ledge about two bricks wide. In high winds. Three storeys above ground. He looked terrified as we all peered out into the dark, windy emptiness.

'Well, that wouldn't be a very good return on investment if he fell,' Ronnie's dad quipped gruffly while Rex's meek meows echoed back to us. After quite a tense standoff, with him ignoring our calls, and us discussing whether we should call the fire brigade, the obvious solution hit us. Fish. He came straight back for it as soon as we brought it out.

Rex survived the city and we brought him with us to Berry, and now here I was obsessing about him while nursing a beer which I should have been chugging back in celebration with my teammates.

While red-bellied black snakes aren't as poisonous as browns and tigers, you probably lose more animals from their bites because people don't realise their pet has been bitten. The slow-acting poison takes an insidious hold and then it can be really hard to beat. So I was always cautious about black-snake bites.

Bryden was the on-call vet that day, so I rang him up and some six hours after the initial call from Ronnie, I met up with him at the clinic, just a few minutes' walk down the road from the pub. Rex was still there in a cage and he was showing no sign of any problem. I knew I was being a bit over-concerned, but we took more blood and more urine anyway.

The snake-bite test is one where you are looking for the enzymes that come from the breakdown of tissue caused by the venom. And what do you know. Rex was ragingly positive, despite still having no symptoms.

I gave myself a little pat on the back and we treated Rex with the anti-venom and his test returned largely to normal.

He stayed in hospital thirty-six hours and he was fine. It was lucky. Lots of animals are bitten without their owner's realising it and they get much more profoundly affected.

After the episode went to air, people wrote in and said, 'You've staged that. You've faked it. Shame on you.'

Did they not notice that I'd just been celebrating a marvellous cricket victory in a slightly over-the-top fashion and the last place I wanted to be was on national television with my hat hair and droopy eyes, even if I was a bit loud and chatty.

The viewers would have seen a cat in his full 6.9 kilograms of pomp and glory. Mildly overweight with a pendulous gut, Rex was a striking contrast to the 1.9 kilograms of skeletal runtiness we first met. He's still hung up about food. If his bowl's empty, you can't sleep at night. He yowls and carries on. We have to feed him very low-energy food because he demands so much of it and is impossible to live with if he doesn't get it. A lot of our time together is spent with him trying to head-butt our faces. He's got a lot of love.

Ronnie and I always talk to Rex in a cockney accent. He's a big London geezer. We tease him about the cricket … except when England's winning, at which times we shunt him outside and don't let him near the telly.

JUST AN ORDINARY PRACTICE

Anthony

We thought that taking on Bryden would solve all our workload problems, but it didn't. We just kept getting busier and the business was expanding. We were doing a lot of work in the Shoalhaven Heads area and there was an opportunity to open a practice – much better than operating out of the back of our car. So before *Village Vets* started shooting, we took the plunge and decided to take on a fourth vet. But who to get?

We had a lot of great applicants and we narrowed them down to two standouts. In the end, we chose Hannah Belling, a new grad who had family ties to a farm in the area.

Historically, there has been a lot of prejudice against women in country vet practices. Most certainly, there are times when you need physical strength. Calvings are the obvious example. You reach in grabbing and pulling with every ounce of force you can muster. But we all know it is technique, not brute force, that gets most jobs done. And female vets often have better technique because brute force is out of the equation.

We went through the initial interview process on the phone, then arranged for Hannah to come down and meet us. It's a bit of a filtration process. If someone's not willing to make the drive from Sydney, they're probably not going to be that committed. So we were waiting for her to come but we didn't hear anything more from her. We'd spoken to her on Monday and it was now Saturday so it was starting to look like she'd been filtered out. Once again, however, we were busier than two mosquitoes at a nudist colony, and hardly had time to notice. We'd just opened our Shoalhaven Heads practice and were having an open day. James and I went out there to set up and we left Bryden manning the fort at Berry. We had a barbecue, a jumping castle, a petting zoo, the whole palaver to get the word out that we'd arrived.

A diminutive young woman turned up and said, 'Hi.'

'Hi, how you going?' I replied.

'Good, yeah, I just got in.'

'Yes, we've just opened up out here. Do you have any pets?'

'Yeah, I'm Hannah.'

We stopped turning sausages to look at her a little blankly.

'The vet. Hannah Belling. Didn't you get my message that I was coming today?'

'Yes,' I lied. 'Of course. Great to meet you. What are you like at chopping onions?'

'I'm okay.'

'Excellent. Can you get started on that sack over there?'

And that was the final vetting of Hannah. She chopped like a demon. It's always good to have little tasks for prospective new employees, but we don't usually make them cry.

We thought that taking Hannah on would solve all our problems. We were wrong.

We were suddenly running three clinics. And somehow four vets weren't quite enough. We felt like we had enough work for four and a half vets, but when the show was filming we needed an extra half on top of that.

So the decision to take on one more was precipitated by the filming of the show. We gambled that there was going to be a second season.

Chris Stott had been recommended to us by a friend in Kempsey, plus James's old boss in Barraba. He'd been to both their practices as a student. We made contact and he got right on the front foot.

'Why don't I come down on the weekend and meet you guys and get a feel for the place?' he said.

'Yeah, sure.'

So he turned up on the Friday afternoon. Wouldn't you know, we were incredibly busy.

'Hi, Chris. Good to meet you. Can you come through and hold this dog?'

He'd thought he was coming for a formal sit-down interview, maybe a coffee and a chat, but we just threw him into it and he got stuck in.

At the end of the day, he said, 'We didn't get much opportunity to chat. I'm hanging around for the weekend, so why don't I come back tomorrow morning and we can talk then?'

'Yep, great idea. We'll see you tomorrow at 9 a.m.'

Of course, the next morning in walked a dog that had swallowed a fishhook. The fishing line was still hanging out of its mouth. Chris was enrolled as the X-ray guy and phone answerer. We were very impressed with how he handled it all, but we were filming, so we got dragged off in another direction and we never actually got to have that chat, though Chris did manage to get himself into an episode of season one.

We'd seen enough, however. We thought he'd be a great fit with us. The following week, we had to drive up to my house to do some filming, so James and I put on the speakerphone and rang him to formalise the offer. It was a good deal, we thought, and jobs weren't that easy to come by. As we sat in my car on the hill in front of my place, James started to run through how the contract worked, what his duties were going to be and how much he was going to get paid. But as James went on, I detected a note of reservation in Chris's voice.

'Hold on a sec, James,' I said, 'before we go any further, Chris, do you even want the job?'

'Actually, I don't,' he said. We paused for a moment, a little surprised. 'Thanks for the offer,' Chris continued, 'but the whole thing with the filming and everything has put me off. I don't know that I want to walk into that for my first job. It all seems a bit hectic and I'm not that keen on having all my mistakes documented on national television.'

'Mate, we can shield you from that,' I said. 'No one has to be involved in the filming if they don't want to be. We'd be taking you on to be a vet and that's that.'

'Thanks, but just with all the chaos and everything, I don't think it's going to work for me.'

'Fair enough,' I said. 'I can understand that. Thanks for your time. We're pretty busy so we've got to keep going.'

It was better to know now than a few months down the track. It left us in a hole though because we were too busy to go headhunting. Just the prospect of beginning the search seemed daunting at that too-busy-to-scratch-ourselves time. About six hours after talking to Chris, however, I was driving back from Kangaroo Valley faster than normal. The guys were desperate to film a sunset and I was needed. I was going as quickly as I could on the narrow, steep road up the mountain. They wanted me in front of an old milk wagon on a dairy farm. They'd interviewed all the staff one by one at this site. The only one who hadn't done it was me. They needed it all to look the same. The sun was going down. The clock was ticking. As I threw the ute into the hairpins, the phone rang.

It was hard to even get a free hand to press the Bluetooth buttons.

'Hi, Anthony, it's Chris Stott again. Look, I've had a think about it, and I've changed my mind,' he said. 'And I reckon I'd be crazy to turn down an opportunity like this just because the filming's going on. If you guys would still consider me, I'd love to take the job.' So I gave him the spiel again about how the filming wasn't going to change anything and he didn't need to be on camera.

'I remember how it felt in that first six months out of uni, so we'll protect you. You can just be yourself and we'll be there to support you. We can shield you from the mayhem. It's not always as busy as the days you were here.'

I drove into the farm and everyone was in a mad flap to get the shoot done before they lost the light. But I was still on the phone to Chris.

'Everything will be okay. That day you were here was crazy. It's not always mental like that.'

The crew was yelling at me to run.

'Hang up the phone,' James screamed.

I gesticulated with my hands, palms down, for him to cool it. The cameraman ran up to me and started undoing my shirt, trying to change it while I was on the phone.

'No, it's always possible to take a step back. There's going to be times where we're going to have to help you through things, and don't worry, we'll be there to do that'

'Hang up the freaking phone. We'll call back. It can't be that important.'

'I'm really sorry, Chris, but as I was saying it will just be an ordinary vet practice. Nothing will change for you, buddy. You'll get all the support you need. Anyway, I've got to get going. It's been great talking and I look forward to seeing you down here.'

I hung up cranky. 'That was Chris, I was trying to …'

'We need this shot. Come on.'

Arrrrrgggggghhhhh.

There were two film crews of three people each. The first crew would work for three days straight, then the second crew would take over for four days. The following week, they'd swap. James and I, however, worked the full seven days, often doing sixteen hours, trying to manage everyone's expectations. Our longest day was eighteen hours in which we left the crew in the dust. I'm sure the continuity people noticed that our hair was greyer in the last episode than the first.

Filming, for the most part, though, went smoothly. Most people were generous with their time. They'd humour the crew and allow the producers to ask questions. They'd let the crew drive up and down their driveways multiple times for cutaway shots. They'd shake hands over and over, and repeat key sentences with the camera in a different spot. It was, nevertheless, difficult to manage the clients' expectations while fulfilling the demands of the show.

So we got to the final day and it had been a whirlwind. It was a life-shorteningly stressful nine weeks. We were exhausted, longing for it to be finished. On the very last job of the last day, Tim said he needed to do some final interviews to tidy up a few stories.

'I think we'll get you leaning on that gate over there,' he said. 'The light's perfect if we're quick.'

'But we've come out in overalls,' James said. 'Our civvies are back at the clinic.'

'Mate, I need you in that light blue shirt with the dark blue trousers.'

'Well, I've only got my shorts on underneath this and I don't feel like going all the way back to the clinic to get my gear.'

The three of us stood there in something of a fatigued Mexican standoff, until Stevie the cameraman piped up, 'I've got something in the car.' He went off to grab a shirt of his.

'Here, just take mine,' said Tim, stripping the light blue shirt off his back.

They came in close and just shot our top halves. I was standing there in pink shorts and a blue shirt while Tim was interviewing us shirtless. We ploughed through the interviews, shook hands, said our farewells, and the guys were gone. They were all keen to get back to their families. And that was it.

Having endured three blokes living in our pockets seven days a week for two and a half months, I'd longed for it to be over, yet when suddenly it was done, I found myself feeling sad. A little lost.

A month or so later they showed us a big batch of footage. If it was a story that was going to go for three minutes in the final cut, they'd show us twelve minutes' worth of footage. The vast bulk of it had already been edited out.

'This is all the footage we will use for this story,' the executive producer David Alrich said. 'So have a look and if there's anything you object to, write down the time codes and we'll delete it.'

They still had the opportunity to make us look like turkeys with some creative editing, but so long as the veterinary procedures were as they should be, we told them they could do whatever they liked. We only took out little things. Once, one of us was holding a needle and syringe in their mouth while juggling a few things. Another time, a dog under anaesthetic was being carried out from surgery with its head lolling a bit. There was nothing wrong with it, but it didn't look good. There was another case where a dog woke from an anaesthetic screaming awful doggie screams. This happens sometimes. They're not in pain because the anaesthetic's still working, but they're disorientated and scared and they respond by vocalising. We toned that down so it didn't look like the dog was in pain. There was little need to edit anything else. Knowing we had the ability to do that had made a big difference to us. The crew had known the deal and we had been able to relax while filming because we knew that if we made an inappropriate joke we could take it out later. Since we've been known to tell the odd inappropriate joke in the privacy of our own practice, it meant we weren't worried and could be normal.

Looking at those early shots, we were incredibly impressed by the job they'd done and how pretty they'd made the district look. We knew it was going to be well received so when it came time for the first episode to be aired, we invited everyone we knew to come down to the Berry pub to watch it. We thought we'd get thirty to fifty people but about one hundred and fifty showed up, plus the local members of parliament and the local media. It was quite glitzy.

We welcomed everybody and it was all going smoothly until the opening credits rolled. Apart from a few cat calls as our heads popped up on screen and some cheers as the drone shots swooped over the town, the room was silent. The television sound wasn't coming across the PA system. But the microphone was working, so I held the mic up to the TV in order to get some sound. James had a good idea and raced down to the clinic and got a drip stand and some Leucoplast tape. We rigged up the microphone to the top of the drip stand to broadcast the sound. For the rest of the screening of the series, that was how the sound was done.

We'd only planned to come to the pub for the first night, but the publican, Steve Fellows, saw a hundred and fifty people eating and drinking on a Thursday night and obviously had a burst of inspiration. He jumped up on stage immediately after the closing credits rolled and said, 'See you all next week.'

'Huh? What?'

But it was on and that proved to be one of the most enjoyable parts of the whole process: watching local people view the show, seeing people they knew, their street, themselves, their pets coming up on screen. It turned into a bit of a Thursday night tradition at the pub.

When we knew someone was going to be on that week, we'd let them know and we'd watch them sitting there waiting, waiting for their moment. Seeing the way they lit up along with all the people around them when their moment came, the ribbing and jokes, was one of the great pleasures of the whole thing. They'd often be shaking afterwards. Full of beans.

And if we ever got blasé about seeing ourselves on screen, we extracted a lot of excitement from the faces of our friends and clients.

FRANKIE THE DOG

James

Frankie looked like a Balinese street dog. He was one of the least attractive dogs in the district. A German Shepherd–Kelpie crossed with just about everything else. For all that, he was a friendly, affectionate dog, much loved by his owners, Valerie and Reg Malone, right down to his black-spotted tongue.

Frankie was an inquisitive, active fellow. He loved doing all the doggy things, especially chasing snakes. One day, he was yapping at the heels of a cow and Reg wanted him to come back. He called and whistled, but Frankie didn't follow instructions ... until *YELP!* He got zapped by an electric fence.

He yelped. And he ran. And ran. And he yelped. He bolted through a couple of fences, past the nearby wedding reception venue and through an old farm. It was like a Hairy Maclary book. And he was gone. Frankie Malone was on his own.

So Reg got in the car and started searching. He knocked on neighbours' doors and poked up through all the nearby lanes. Nothing. He scanned the side of the highway looking for a body. The weeks passed and he kept looking out, but over that time he realised that

Frankie was not coming back. He decided to go back to the pound to get another dog.

He found one called Magnus. Magnus, too, might have blended in nicely in the back streets of Denpasar. He shared Frankie's pedigree, but he was the bigger, brighter, bouncier model.

One of the pleasures of this job, and this area in particular, is that you're continually being surprised by the things people have done. Reg Malone was a lovely old bloke. He was passionate about his cows and he always kept his property neatly presented. It turned out he'd played the equivalent of English Premier League football for a London club back when it was called First Division. He walked strangely on his battered ankles as a legacy of that time. He'd come to Australia and risen to be a top executive at a major fast-food chain.

It was four weeks after Frankie had gone missing that Reg phoned us up.

'We've found Frankie, and he looks a bit Moby Dick. We're bringing him in.'

'Huh? Moby Dick?'

'He's sick. "Crook", if you want the Australian translation.'

'Okay, what's up with him?'

'Well, he's half-starved and he can't walk properly.'

'Okay, we're waiting for you.'

When they arrived minutes later, Frankie looked more than ever like his Balinese cousins, except he was being carried by his loving owner.

'What happened?' I asked.

'Tony Schofield just called me up to tell me he'd found him hiding under his house. He thought they had a giant rat. The last couple of days he'd started to hear a bit of movement under there. I reckon

Frankie might have got hit by a car or something and gone and hidden under there three weeks ago. He can hardly walk.'

'Okay, we'll check him out.'

I had a feel around and couldn't find any obvious broken bones, but it was clear something was wrong. I lifted Frankie over to the X-ray table and he was super light. All fur and hard, bony bumps.

I brought up the X-ray image on the computer screen. And there it was, plain to see. Frankie had broken his pelvis and healed it all by himself. It wasn't healed well, but it was healed enough that it was fixed in position. The pelvis is like a three-sided box. When it breaks, much like collapsing a cardboard box, it's got to give in at least three places, so pelvic fractures are almost never one break. Frankie's had collapsed very significantly, but because he'd kept himself still, the muscles had been enough to brace it and fuse it back together, albeit all skew-whiff. It seemed that it was only in the last few days that he'd started moving and making the noises that led Tony Schofield to him.

Frankie cocked his leg and did a big wee in the consult room. I was unusually enthusiastic about that. This was an important diagnostic event.

'Can he poo too?' I asked Reg.

'Yes, he did one before I put him in the car.'

'Well, if he can walk and poo and wee, I think he's going to be all right.'

Frankie was one tough hombre.

He went back to life as normal. He'd lost a bit of speed and size, though, and so was hardly in good shape to fight for his place in the pecking order against his new rival, Magnus. And Reg was worried about Frankie's habit of chasing snakes. If you take up snake fighting as a hobby, you're going to come second one day. Especially if you've lost a bit of speed.

And so it happened that six months after Frankie's miraculous reappearance and recovery, Reg was doing some work around the yards when Frankie ran off and started barking crazily. Reg followed him and found him in the hay shed, covered in blood, sniffing a dead red-bellied black snake.

Reg rushed him to the clinic as fast as his dodgy ankles would allow. Frankie was already in a bad way as they came through the doors of the clinic. He was quite out of it, vomiting, panting and having difficulty breathing. It was hard to know if the blood that was all over him was his own or that of the snake. It's usually the snake's. The puncture wounds left by Australian snakes are very small. Their teeth are minute. You rarely see the wounds. More often, you just see swelling.

Frankie's face was a little swollen, looking like an allergic reaction.

We whisked him out the back. Chris put an IV catheter in and gave him some anti-venom. There is no specific anti-venom for red-bellies but tiger snakes are a close relative and tiger anti-venom will do the job. The treatment costs between $900 and $1000 but Reg wanted everything possible done, so we gave Frankie a vial straightaway. Chris collected urine, gave Frankie oxygen and collected some blood.

One of the $64-milllion questions of veterinary science is: how much anti-venom is enough? There is no test, no scientific way of knowing how much to give, except that in most cases one vial is sufficient. I spoke to the guru on this topic, a vet from Tamworth, Peter Best, who's written a lot of papers on it. His view was that, at the end of the day, it was my call.

'If you think the animal needs another vial, it probably needs another vial,' he said.

So we got the urine results and the blood results back and the tests showed elevated levels of the enzymes indicating muscle tissue damage.

That was a bad sign, given he was already showing clinical signs of illness. At that point, you have to back your judgement.

'I think this is the dog that's going to benefit from a second vial.'

It was a difficult conversation to have because it was going to cost Reg an extra $1000. The total bill was already well over $1000 and to add $1000 onto that was a tough call when I was also saying, 'We're not sure that Frankie needs it. There's no scientific way of telling. All I've got is that I've seen a lot of snake bites and this one's really bad. If you have the money, spend it now.'

Reg was less hesitant about it than me. He was more than willing to pump as much in as I thought Frankie needed. So I gave him another vial. We hoped and we waited, watching Frankie constantly. He soon started vomiting a lot. So we had to manage his electrolytes and his clotting times. A quick measure of how much venom is in the system is to get a bit of blood and put it on a slide and see how long it takes to turn into a clot. Frankie's blood didn't clot at all. So that was another sign of how badly affected he was. We had to make sure he didn't bleed to death. And one of the most important treatments for snake bite is to just get the animal on IV fluids to help their organs while they deal with the insult of the venom.

Frankie remained stable over the first twenty-four hours, but on the second day he started to develop some worrying signs. His heart rate drifted higher, so we listened to it more and started hearing the odd abnormal beat. We began to monitor his ECG constantly. The occasional abnormal beat is okay but it started to get worse. He began throwing what we call ventricular premature contractions, or VPCs. That's where the heart muscle in the ventricle is so distressed by what's going on that it decides to beat independently of all the other heart muscles. It doesn't listen to the signals designed to hold the rhythm. It's like if you replaced Ringo Starr with me. Even the Beatles would lose the beat.

Seeing VPCs after a snake bite is not uncommon, but poor old Frankie was running them at fifteen or twenty in a row. He was just living on VPCs. His heart rate was extremely high. We needed to give him drugs to slow down his pulse and to decrease the likelihood of these VPCs occurring. By this stage, Frankie was very flat. He was not only affected by the snake bite, now his heart was shot as well. He was only able to lie on his side and when I walked into the room, he'd roll his eyeball upwards towards me. He tapped his tail against the stainless-steel frame of the cage like a good, happy dog should. But that was it.

Frankie had put some of the weight back on after his big starvation diet, but Reg had purposefully kept him lean because extra weight would put too much load on his wonky pelvis. So now he was lying there, still skinny, unable to eat, three days after the bite, and he was basically dying.

Reg came to visit and I carried Frankie out for him to see. As I explained the heart problems, Frankie started getting a little excited. He did his eye roll and his tail flick, but he also tried to lift his head. This was a bit too ambitious and he promptly fainted.

When a dog is fainting from arrhythmia, it is on the edge of death. I rushed Frankie back into the treatment room, hooked him up to the heart monitor and realised he was now running constant VPCs. I didn't see that we had much choice now but to start injecting the drug lignocaine to correct the rhythm of his heart. It's scary because only a few milligrams separates the therapeutic dose from the lethal dose. Lignocaine is most commonly used as a local anaesthetic, but it is also very good for decreasing the heart rate. I got out my clipboard and paper and started working out how much to give and what the maximum dose would be over a certain period if we needed to give him more. It was complicated and unfamiliar because it's not the sort of thing you do every day, but I got some numbers and I injected the first one and a half millilitres. Once it was in, my eyes went straight to the heart monitor but there was no change.

'Okay let's give him another one and a half,' I decided.

We gave him several more doses but his heart just wasn't slowing. We were pushing up towards the maximum dose when at last the pulses on the ECG slowed. There was a sigh of relief all round as we set the lignocaine up on the drip to begin a small, constant dose. But just as we got that up and running, he went into a string of VPCs and fainted again.

I expected he might die at any moment so there was nothing to lose. I upped the dose of lignocaine, taking him right to the maximum dose. But the monitor showed the heart was still flailing about like me on a drum kit.

All the arithmetic and the advice from a specialist and the readouts from the ECG were swirling through my head and eventually I got to a point where I concluded that the dog was going to die if I didn't just give it more. This ran the risk of slowing the heart to such an extent that it just stopped, but I felt I had no choice. We had to keep these arrhythmias at bay. So I gave it more. And more. I was like Scotty in *Star Trek*: 'She cannae take any more, Captain.' But the ship didn't shudder. Quite the opposite. It steadied and Frankie came through smoothly to the other side. He was, however, far from in the clear.

Aside from his heart problem, his wee was something akin to the colour of a pinot noir. His muscles and tissue were being destroyed by the venom and the red urine was the wash-up. His kidney and liver were okay. The IV fluids were keeping those under control, but his kidney enzymes were starting to creep up, indicating there could be a problem looming.

'This is bad, Reg,' I said. 'I don't know if we can save this dog. This is as bad as it gets in terms of side effects from snake bite. We've got to get this under control. And the best way I think we can do that is if we put his heart to sleep for the next three to four days, slow it right down and really hit it hard with drugs to try and control the heart rate and rhythm, and then when we've got that right, try to wean him off these drugs.'

'Well, if you think that's the way to go. That's the way we'll go,' Reg said.

So that's what we did. We put Frankie's heart to sleep with lignocaine, and we watched him.

The other thing that helps with heart arrhythmias is intravenous magnesium. The reason we hadn't already given it already was that there's also a risk it can just stop the heart in its tracks and kill the patient. But we'd got to the point now where we just had to try everything. I checked my maths four times to make sure I wasn't giving Frankie too much. The sums can be complicated. I was certain I'd got it right ... but still I worried. I drew up one millilitre or so out of a 500-millilitre bag intended for a cow and I put it into his IV solution, closing my eyes and holding my breath as I pushed down on the plunger.

'I hope he doesn't die as I'm giving him this.'

A crowd had gathered to watch the ECG while I injected. The clinic was as busy as all get out, with all the usual comings and goings, but for this moment, time stopped as the ECG continued on its unsteady way. There was great relief all round that we didn't kill him, and we even started to see a reduction in the rate of VPCs.

So now it was a matter of getting Frankie through the next three days. On that first day, I got Kahlia to just sit in the room with him and watch the ECG. I explained the wave forms: what a normal one looked like and what the abnormal ones looked like.

'If there are lots of abnormally shaped ones, you need to come and get me.'

I went out to do a consult, but I'd barely got past ushering a dog with itchy skin into the consult room when there was a knock at the door.

'It's Kahlia. The waves have all gone funny.'

I apologised to the dog's owner and left to inject more lignocaine. I watched for the ECG to steady, which it did, before I went back to the itchy dog. Five minutes later, *knock, knock*. It was Kahlia again. The ten-minute itchy-skin consult took half an hour.

The line-up of people in the waiting room grew. Anthony was out seeing a cow. Bryden was at the Shoalhaven Heads clinic. Hannah was at Kangaroo Valley. We were trying to run the day-to-day practice, but we had to prioritise the sickest animal. We overstaff the clinic all the time to give us the ability to deal with these issues, but still we were stretched.

I was speaking on the phone to specialists asking what else I could do. The take-home message I got from them was that if we could just steady the heart and keep him alive for three days, he'd have a decent shot at making it. It was reassuring to have that in the back of my head, because in that first twenty-four hours, it just seemed like he was certain to die.

Hannah watched him through the first part of the night and I came in early to find him still hanging in there. When I phoned Reg that morning to tell him Frankie was still alive, I could hear the raucous applause as Reg passed the news on to his wife.

Reg was a great client. He and his wife would cheer each morning as we told them Frankie was still with us. He loved that dog so much. He came to visit most days, and he'd call every day for an update. Reg was committed to saving the dog, but he also had realistic expectations.

'Reg, your bill is $3500 ... Reg, your bill is $4000 ...'

'That's fine. I don't care about the money. I just want you to save the dog.' At least I think that's what he said. And then he went on, 'You know, if Frankie does pull through this, we'll probably have to get him a new home, because he spends his whole life chasing snakes. There are so many snakes on my property, it's ridiculous. But we'll cross that bridge when we come to it.'

So here was Reg, with a bill heading towards $5000 for a dog he didn't intend to keep. 'Who's going to take him, I wonder,' Reg said. 'I mean, look at him. He looks like the back end of a bus.'

'Reg, if you can't find anyone, I'll take him.' I'd become very emotionally invested in Frankie, as had everyone else at the clinic. We'd all put in so much time and effort.

After a day of the super-duper intensive therapy, he seemed to come a little more under control. We were able to be more confident in our control of his heart. One vet might stay back doing paperwork so it would fall to them to check him until they left. Then whoever was on call would come in and check in the middle of the night. Then another vet would be coming in early to do paperwork and would see him then. When a patient is that sick, you either have everyone chipping in and helping with the monitoring, or you sacrifice one person for the next day and have them sit there all night.

After three days, Frankie was still alive and his heart was steady. We'd climbed Everest, but we still needed to get back down. We started weaning him off the lignocaine, dropping the dose steadily over the next forty-eight hours. He responded well in that his heart stayed in the normal zone but he was still lying flat most of the time. But then he started to improve and when I entered the room he might sit up and wag his tail more vigorously. We'd carry him outside to empty his bladder. Good dog. But we had to keep rolling him from side to side so he didn't get pressure sores. And all this time he kept on vomiting from the effects of the venom, so he was back to being the skinniest dog in Denpasar.

We had to get some nutrition into him. We gave him anti-vomiting drugs and fed him – half a teaspoon at a time – a soft, highly nutritious dog food designed for this sort of situation.

Frankie stayed with us for seventeen days before he could keep down enough food to enable him to go home.

It was a huge effort. He was certainly the sickest dog I've seen survive a snake bite. He could have died so many times along the way. Reg and Valerie were effusive in their praise for what a great job we'd done. It was a very rewarding case.

But, on the seventeenth day, when Reg came in to take Frankie home, Frankie started acting strangely towards Reg – this man who loved his dog so much that he was prepared to pay all that money even though he might have to be rehomed. Frankie didn't run to him when we let him out of the cage. He was standoffish and headed over to nuzzle Kahlia, then me.

'I think this dog likes you more than me,' Reg said, clearly taken aback that Frankie didn't love him any more. 'You'll have to take him.'

'No,' I said. 'I'm sure he's just finding his way.'

But I really was worried that Frankie had developed Stockholm Syndrome, where the victims of kidnap become bonded with their kidnappers. He'd become very attached to us. We were the guys who had fed him all this time. You can imagine how hungry he had been. Even though we only gave him miniscule servings, we were feeding him frequently. So he grew to crave our company and our half teaspoons of bland food.

'Well, I think he associates me with the snake bite because I was there with him when he was bitten,' Reg said.

Nevertheless, Reg took Frankie home and I visited them the next day.

Reg had built Frankie a special living area – his own wing of an undercover shed, so he couldn't over-exercise and chase snakes. Poor old Frankie was clearly unhappy that he was locked in this enclosure while Magnus, his competitor and arch-nemesis, was free to roam.

Imagine getting run over and starved and living under a house for three weeks and you come home only to find you've been replaced by another. Then you get bitten by a snake, taken to the edge of life and death and you find yourself coming home again, only to be stuck in prison while your enemy is out there chasing snakes to his heart's content.

'His whole mission in life now is to beat the crap out of Magnus,' Reg said.

I went into Frankie's new pad to check him out. But far from rushing up for a pat, he didn't want to have anything to do with me. His eyes, his retracted tail and ears, were all screaming at me: 'Don't you take me back to that terrible place.'

Reg was back as the centre of Frankie's universe. To this day, Reg still feeds Frankie three or four times a day because his stomach can't handle a big feed. He was soon allowed back outside and all would have been right with his world if he could have just dealt with Magnus.

And so ends the story of Frankie Malone, bitten by a snake, now safely back home.

OPEN ALL HOURS

Anthony

It was a busy Saturday morning – one of *those* mornings – when we got a call from a guy who wasn't a regular client. He said his dog was sick and had been vomiting. We didn't really have time to fit them in. I was between consults and managing operations and answering the phone. But it sounded serious so I figured we'd just have to make time.

'No problem,' I said. 'We can slot you in at 11.30.'

The dog sounded like it might need a lot of care and I wanted to do it while Trish was still there to help.

But the guy soon rang back and told Trish he couldn't come in. The car was broken down.

When she told me, I asked her to ring him back. 'Tell him I'll go and get the dog. It needs to come in now and not later.'

She reported back to me that the guy said he'd be in as soon as he got the car going. She said she'd tried to explain to him that that would be an after-hours visit and more expensive, but the guy insisted.

That put me offside. There's a perception with after-hours that you're at the clinic waiting to answer the phone at 2 a.m., ready to slide down the pole like a fireman and rush out to deal with whatever concern the client might have. The reality is, you work all day, you go home, you go to bed, you happily get up to handle emergencies, you go back to bed and try to sleep before fronting up for work next morning and doing a full day there.

So when there's a problem that can be dealt with in business hours, you want people to be reasonable and to come in when you're open.

I was just pulling into the carpark of the pub at 6 p.m., about to have dinner with a friend, when the guy rang back.

'Mate, got the car working. I've gotta bring Shultz in now. I'll see you there in ten minutes.'

I walked back up to the clinic and opened up not feeling favourably disposed towards this new client. An old red Ford Falcon, with one door a different colour from the rest, soon pulled into the car park. Two blokes got out, followed by a badly emaciated German Shepherd that was wobbly on its feet. I could see even before it had come through the door that it didn't have any muscle down its jutting spine. Its coat was sparse and dull. Its head hung low as they led it in.

I tried to keep it civil as I got them to put the dog on the scale. Twenty-three kilos. It should have been more like forty-five kilograms.

'How long's Shultz been vomiting for?' I asked.

'Only today.'

'Has he been eating?'

'Yeah, he's been right as rain till today.'

That was obviously a lie. The dog was in such poor condition it was clear that he had been sick for a long while. Either that or they weren't feeding him. As I sized them up, I concluded that anything was possible. They were probably in their early thirties. The stocky one had a round belly and no shoes. The tall, thin one had a pair of old blue trackies hanging loosely off him. Teeth were missing. The tattoos looked homemade.

'It's probably worms,' the taller one said. 'You reckon it could it be worms?'

'It's highly unlikely worms would cause this level of sickness,' I said. I wanted to say: 'The dog's starving to death and it's pretty obvious it's been like this for ages.' But while I suspected that this was an abuse case, I remained polite. They had sought veterinary attention, after all, and so they deserved the benefit of the doubt. 'But it is possible worms might be contributing to the problem,' I said. I gave the dog a worm tablet while the pair of them wandered around the clinic taking toys off the shelf. They gave one of the toys to Shultz. I thought it was a good thing that they cared enough to want to buy the dog a toy.

'Look guys, Shultz needs some serious long-term care and some serious investigation,' I said. 'This is not something I can solve at 6.30 on a Saturday night. We need to do blood tests. We'll probably need to take some X-rays and do an ultrasound and really investigate what's going on because there's something seriously wrong with your dog. And I feel it's probably a chronic issue. You need to bring him back on Monday and we'll investigate further.'

'Okay, that's good. We'll do that,' the tall one said.

'Now, I need to get your details,' I said, handing over a new-client form. The stocky one filled it in and handed it back as they went to leave.

'Excuse me. Before you go, I'll need you to fix me up for tonight.'

They patted down their pants. 'Oh, um, we don't have our wallets.'

'Well, you're going to have to fix me up somehow.'

'Don't see how.'

'You can't just come in and receive a service then leave. I don't know who you are. You're not a regular client.'

'How much is it?' the tall, thin one asked.

'With the two worming tablets, the dog toy and the after-hours consult fee, it's $140.'

'Bloody hell, that's just ridiculous.'

'Hold on a minute. I've come in on a Saturday night to see you after I've clearly asked you to come in earlier. We pleaded with you to come in at a more reasonable time when it would have been a lot cheaper. And you wouldn't do that. So what exactly is ridiculous? Is it the fact I've answered the phone and come in here to provide you with a service that you otherwise couldn't have received? And tried to help you? Or is it the price?'

If he'd answered 'the price', I might have been willing to negotiate. They clearly weren't men of means. But he didn't.

'No. It's ridiculous that you think that it's worth that much for an after-hours call.'

My blood was boiling now. I thought I'd been fair and reasonable, given them the benefit of the doubt.

'Get out of my clinic. Now!'

The short one stared at me momentarily, sizing me up. He then reached over and grabbed the form he'd just filled in with all his details. He scrunched it up, snatched the dog and they both took off and jumped in their car and hooned off up the road.

I took a deep breath and I smelt burnt rubber. *What just happened there?* Over coming days, I put the word out to other clinics nearby that if people fitting that description turned up, it was more likely a cruelty case than a veterinary case. But I never heard of them again. I asked around a bit and heard that they had moved to the area looking for work, but their go was to offer to do work, take money in advance, steal from the properties and move on.

You never know who is going to walk into your clinic. Somehow it's always the random calls that are the quirkiest.

One Saturday I answered the phone to hear a thick Aussie accent.

He didn't introduce himself, he just launched: 'Yeah, mate, I've got a problem with my cat. It's had a sex change and now it doesn't seem right. I'm really struggling to come to terms with it.'

My mates from uni seem to think my voicemail exists solely as a mechanism to wind me up: 'I've got a problem with my aardvark's snout. It's really smelly and I need you to come and tell me if it's safe to take it for a swim at the municipal pool.'

So I thought I'd hear out my sex-change caller to see if I could pick which mate it was. See what his punchline was.

'Right. Can you tell me what's wrong with this cat?'

'Yeah, yeah, it's had the sex-changer operation and it hasn't worked out too well. I think it's got a problem with its identity.'

'Oh, yeah, of course, it's had a sex change. Did you get its nails done as well? That can often help.'

'No.'

'Has it had problems with its implants? It might be able to join one of those class actions against the silicone implant manufacturers.'

'No, no, nothing like that,' my caller insisted. 'Mate, my cat's crook.'

He was sounding defensive and I still couldn't pick the voice. I started to get a sinking feeling.

'Who am I speaking to?'

'Greg Reilly.'

I didn't know the name. 'Now Greg, you say it's had a sex change. What are you talking about? We don't do sex changes in animals.'

'My cat, he couldn't piss so they chopped off his willy and gave him a vagina.'

Shivers! He's for real. 'Oh, right. Okay. Um. Well, bring him in.'

Male cats often get blockages at the end of the penis that stop them from urinating. There's a procedure for chronic cases where you bypass the penis by making an incision just below the anus and diverting the urethra to the new opening. It looks like a vagina but it definitely isn't one. And it certainly is not a sex-change operation.

The procedure does leave cats predisposed to urinary tract infections and I suspected that that was what we'd be looking at here.

When Greg came in he looked a little sheepish. 'I'm sorry about the way I spoke on the phone,' he said.

'Mate, I'm sorry for the way *I* spoke on the phone. I thought you were someone else geeing me up.'

'I just can't cope with the whole concept of what's been done to Muggles. I don't know how to explain it. I didn't mean to be rude.'

I prescribed antibiotics and explained that his cat was still very much a boy and there were no 'issues' of identity. He took it all in but seemed unconvinced.

I, however, had found a new 'wind-up' for the next time I got put through to my uni mates' voicemails.

WHEN BUGS CRY

James

When you walk onto any farm, you can tell how well it's run. As much as you may not think you make judgements on how clean it is, how organised, you do. One sunny spring morning I was called to a job at one of those very tight ships in which you could almost eat your dinner off the dairy floor.

The owner, Neville Caldwell, was a big, jovial feller who was always waiting for an opportunity to take the piss out of me or anyone else who came into his orbit.

He'd call up the clinic and when the nurse asked what was wrong, he'd say, 'Dunno. If I knew what was wrong with it I wouldn't be calling.'

That joke notwithstanding, it was always good fun out at Neville's place.

Well, almost always. This day I arrived at his spotless yards expecting the usual flurry of light-hearted insults. But Neville seemed a little quiet.

'What's the go?' I said.

'This cow is as crook as buggery. Won't eat. It's off its tucker. Dehydrated. Bloody show cow.'

'I didn't know you were into showing your cows, Nev.'

There was a suitable pause. 'I'm not. It's my girlfriend's. It's Lucy's absolute favourite cow. Belle Star08. Treats it like it was her baby.'

Lucy was also from a dairying family, but unlike Neville's family, hers went in for the whole show thing. She was used to petting and preening her favourites.

I looked at Belle Star08, a nicely framed black and white cow with her head drooped low. 'Geez, she does look crook.'

I gave her a pretty thorough examination, looking for signs of trouble, but all I could find was a total absence of gut noises. In cows, this isn't the acute emergency that it can be in horses, but it is still serious.

'She's off her food, eh?'

'Yep.'

'And she's not been passing much excrement?'

'None that I've seen,' Neville said. When he answered in such a straightforward way, I knew that something was very wrong. He'd never normally pass up the opportunity to have a banter and to throw some verbal excrement my way.

'I'm pretty worried that she's got rumenal shutdown,' I said. 'There's nothing going on in there. This is potentially fatal if we can't get it up and running again.'

'Yeah, of course it's something like that,' he said. 'We're getting married next week and I can tell you, if this cow carks it, there ain't going to be no honeymoon.'

'Right, okay, we'll get some stuff into her. I'll treat her with antibiotics and anti-inflammatories. We'll get some blood and take some rumenal fluid for testing.'

I pulled out a long, fat needle and jabbed it through the cow's skin. She hardly flinched as I pushed it through the abdominal wall and straight into the rumen. I pulled back, drawing up some brown liquid. I tested the pH level with the kit in the ute, and it was way too low, meaning the stomach was too acidic. That's a bad sign. The bugs in a cow's gut need a more neutral environment to live.

We think of a cow as eating grass and surviving on that, but what happens is that it eats grass to feed all the bacteria and protozoa living in the rumen. When the cow absorbs the contents of its gut, a large part of what it is consuming are those bugs. They are absolutely crucial to the cow's nutritional requirements so the cow's gut has to be a suitable habitat for vast numbers of micro-organisms. It is the be-all-and-end-all of the cow. And in this case, it was stuffed.

Her rumen must have suffered some sort of insult. She had probably eaten something she shouldn't have and it had destroyed the ecosystem.

I tried probiotics – a paste of good bacteria delivered to the cow in a caulking gun like you'd use for your Liquid Nails. And while I was trying to get the bacteria up and running in the rumen, I gave her an injection of antibiotic, lincomycin, which has the effect of making the small intestine contract more often. I hoped it would help get the whole digestive process started again. I also gave her another antibiotic jab to treat any infections in the abdomen. While on the one hand I was trying to encourage the bugs to grow in the rumen, on the other, I was trying to keep the bad ones under control in the abdomen. Fortunately, the rumen is like its own little ecosystem so if you jab the antibiotics into the animal's muscles, it doesn't affect what's happening in its giant, grass-fermenting vat.

I went back two days later and Belle Star08 was looking a little better. But there was no sign that the probiotics had done anything to bring her gut back to life.

'Neville, this is pretty serious now,' I told Neville. 'She might not make it to Saturday.'

The wedding was now a week away, and as the cow continued downhill, so too did his mood.

'Why does this thing have to decide to go and die the week of our wedding?' he said. 'It could die during the honeymoon. At least that way Lucy's not gunna know till we get back and she's already underground.'

For all of Neville's bravado, he was a softie. And also a little superstitious.

'She's gunna go and die the morning we get hitched, right when Lucy wants to be getting ready. She's gunna be in tears. "Will you take this man to be your lawful wedded husband?" "Boo Hoo." This is gunna be bad. That sort of thing happens, the whole marriage is on the skids from the start. Bloody show cows. Who'd want em?'

'Hmmmm,' I said.

'What are we gunna do?'

'Look, the only hope we've got is to go in and have a look to see if we can find something that's wrong, and then if we can't find anything, I'm going to have to do what they call a transfaunation, which basically means getting rumenal fluid from another cow and putting it into this cow. It's a transplant.'

'Right,' he said. I could see his mind ticking over. 'What do we need?'

'We need to get the rumenal fluid.'

'How do you do that?'

'Typically, you do it from a dead cow or you get it from an abattoir. Seeing as how it's the Easter long weekend so there's no abattoirs operating, and in the absence of knowing anyone with an otherwise healthy cow that's just dropped dead, we're going to need to get it from one of yours.'

He frowned.

'Don't worry, it's very low-risk for the donor cow. But I will have to operate. I've got to go into the donor's rumen to get the fluid out, then pump it into Belle Star.'

'Can't you just pump it out?'

'No, you couldn't get enough through the oesophagus. It's a fairly minor operation, but do you have any that you're looking to cull any time soon? Because we'd usually use one like that.'

In the really big dairies where they're feeding the cows a lot of grain, dead rumens can be a big problem. Eating grain lowers the pH which kills a lot of bugs. So they actually have donor cows with a permanent opening in their sides. The vet just comes along and scoops out what they need.

Neville didn't have a donor cow, but he did have one that had chronic mastitis which was going to be culled in coming weeks.

'Okay, you get her up and we'll come back tomorrow and do the operation.'

Anthony was just finishing up at the Easter Show by this point so I asked him to drop in on his way home to give me a hand. I wanted that second opinion. That second set of hands when you're searching for the needle in the haystack. Neville was a good client with a precious cow and an anxious bride. It didn't get more important than this.

First up, I wanted to open up Belle Star08 to see if there was anything going on inside her which we hadn't picked up on. So we did an exploratory laparotomy – a look-see in her abdomen. We were searching for a cancer, perhaps a liver abscess, an undetected twist in the stomach, or a bit of swallowed wire causing infection that might have stopped the rumen from moving. We opened up her abdomen and I had a feel around. I couldn't find anything so I asked Anthony to have a feel around too.

He couldn't come up with anything either, but just having him there to say, 'Mate, I can't find anything,' was really reassuring. So I sliced into Belle Star08's rumen and the first thing I noticed was the complete absence of unpleasantness.

A good healthy rumen is a bug factory. It is fetid and awful. A non-functional, sick rumen has the rather pleasant odour of soggy cut grass. The cow's rumen has been found to be one of the densest ecosystems of microbial activity anywhere in the world. When you go into a healthy cow to operate, the rotting fermenting mess contracts and rumbles. But this one sat there, inert, like a flaccid potato sack.

We both had a feel around in there, right up to our armpits in the soggy soup, seeking out a bit of wire or a nail or something that might have punctured the rumen. But nothing. We were hoping for the eureka moment. That wonderful instant when you reach in, pull out a bit of wire, toss it to the farmer and say, 'There's your problem.'

They call wire stuck in the cow 'hardware disease', which is a lot easier to remember than the proper name – traumatic reticuloperitonitis. A piece of wire can sit inside a cow for a long time without ill effect. The problems often arise in late pregnancy because the pressure the foetus puts on the rumen punctures the wire through the thick wall of the rumen and into the abdomen. Infection develops around that. But it often gets worse. The wire can go through the diaphragm – the barrier of lung-pumping muscle that separates the heart and lungs from the guts – and even perforate the heart.

It was a big problem in the past when hay used to be baled up with haywire. So it got diagnosed all the time when cows had mysterious tummy problems. But over the years because the value of cattle and the standard of vet science has gone up we do more of these exploratory surgeries. The result has been that we've found that it is actually quite rare for wire to be the cause of the illness.

But we were hoping it would be in this case. At least it's easy to fix once you've gone inside. However, we failed to find anything. The one consolation was that at least it confirmed my original diagnosis.

We hosed out the crush to clean up the mess and we changed into clean overalls before the donor cow came forward in the race. We shaved up the left-hand flank of the skinny old cow with mud up the back of her bony legs. If a purpose-built tool for extracting rumenal fluid has been invented, we must have missed the catalogue. We had to figure out a way of getting this stuff out of the rumen. We tried various methods, with limited success until we struck upon the idea of using an old antibiotic bottle. They come with a plastic case around the bottle for protection and this case was just the right size to get through the small incision into the rumen, cupped in my hand. I scooped up the fluid and brought it out, tipping it onto a towel stretched over a bucket so the solids were filtered out of the juice.

It took a lot of scooping for us to get the required three litres of the precious fluid. It's a seed population, like a giant probiotic but you need a lot of it to make a difference in the 180-litre stomach. Putting a little pill or some paste in there would never do the job. We stitched the donor up and gave her antibiotics and anti-inflammatories to cope with the operation and let her go into a little holding pen.

Our patient had endured an exploratory laparotomy, wide awake, only an hour or so earlier. So not surprisingly, she wasn't that willing to come anywhere near us standing there at the crush, but eventually we coaxed her in. We restrained her head, got the magic potion, put the tube down her rumen and used our big yabby pump-type contraption to pump this liquid down into her rumen. This treatment often kick-starts an amazing recovery and Belle Star08 perked up immediately.

So we packed up and went home. It had been a big job – two vets; two operations; two animals; many hours of our time on an Easter Monday– but it gave us the ability to say to Neville that we'd done everything within our ability to save this cow. And his marriage. There was nothing left to do. And he could say the same to Lucy.

We called in a few times in the lead up to the wedding and Belle Star08 was doing well. I heard the odd gut noise which was great news. Her rumen was doing its job.

Lucy was happy. The cow improved. The wedding occurred. Trish went along and she told us that Neville cried like a sook during his speech, which was great because we now had something to hold over him when he inevitably returned to being a smartypants with us.

After the honeymoon, I went out to Neville's to see a different sick cow. I asked him: 'How's Belle Star08?'

'Buried.'

'Shivers, did she make it to the wedding?'

'Yep, got us over the line.' He wandered off into the crush area muttering under his breath, 'Don't know why you'd have an expensive cow. Don't know why you'd ever name a bloody cow. Once you name 'em they're always going to die aren't they. Destined to bloody die.'

PERIPHERAL DROPOFFATHY

Anthony

We've had our fair share of quirky cases, but few have had an impact like Andrina the miracle cat.

Her owner, Eva Bates, was one of our very favourite clients. She was old Berry. Quite eccentric. Along with her husband, Mick, and twin daughters, Sam and Ally, she bred horses and Norwegian forest cats up in the hills. That says a lot about someone. Breeding animals was Eva's and Mick's passion and they put all their energy into their animals.

Neither Eva nor Mick were big on appearances. They typically sported Slazenger-grey trackies and paint-splattered shirts when they came to the clinic. When Eva spoke to you, she was liable at any moment to tilt her head, with its mauve perm (her one concession to fashion) to the side, smile and say something like, 'I like you. You're a really good vet. A really good vet.'

Eva talked a lot, and because a lot of what she was saying wasn't so relevant at that moment, it was easy to fall into the trap of thinking that nothing she said was meaningful, but she was actually a switched-on operator.

They had a tom who was an absolute monster, but he produced lovely kittens so they stuck with him. And they had a Staffie who was prone to serious tumours, so with all that, we expected to see Eva, Sam or Ally in the waiting room at least every fortnight.

It had probably been upwards of a month since they'd last graced our doorway, though, when Trish came in with a message that Sam had rung. They were on their way with a very sick cat. It was an emergency.

Less than five minutes later, Sam came crashing through the door. Unfortunately, she was so focussed on getting in, she forgot to hold the screen open for Eva following just behind with a cat curled in her arms. The door slammed in against her elbows, but Sam realised her mistake and pulled it open again.

'Anthony, I don't think it's good,' Eva said, battling through the screen. 'I think she's already gone. Please try to save her. It's one of our favourites. My dad has just died. We can't have another loss in the family. It's too soon.'

We all knew about Eva's dad because she had talked about him a lot. They'd been close. The atmosphere was heavy with the grief of that recent loss and the urgency of the situation now facing us.

The cat was Andrina, a small, ruddy, young adult, weighing about three and a half kilos. She was one of Eva's favourite breeding queens. I'd seen her a few times for routine procedures after she'd had kittens.

I looked at her now and she appeared dead.

'Trish! Get the crash box ready.' But Trish and James were already on it, preparing the resuscitation gear.

'Okay, what's happened?' I asked as we rushed her out the back.

'She's strangled herself. Got her head wedged under one of the steps in her run. She was moving when we found her and we heard a few breaths on the way here.'

As we moved, I checked Andrina over. There was no heartbeat, no breathing. She was blue in the tongue and motionless, with her eyes open.

'Oh god, she's my champion little darling this one,' Eva said. 'You've really got to save her. She's so special to me. Please. Please. Please save her.'

I suspected Andrina had been dead for quite some time already. Generally the gasps that people report hearing are what's called agonal breathing. It looks and sounds like a breath, but it's just a reflex spasm of the diaphragm muscle after death. About ten per cent of animals and humans do it when they die.

Although I knew it was futile, I really had to go above and beyond to save this cat. Eva would fall to pieces with another death in the family. I took Andrina off her. 'Wait here. There's nothing more you can do. We're going to try to resuscitate her. I'm taking her straight out the back.'

We've got a rigid protocol with resuscitations. All the staff know to go straight for the crash box – a red tool kit in which we have all our resuscitation gear. There are drugs to stimulate breathing, drugs to stimulate the heart, catheters and equipment for getting IV catheters in. The team came from everywhere to do their bit.

One of us got a tube down through Andrina's larynx and into her trachea. She was hooked up to the anaesthetic machine, but it was only running pure oxygen. We had one of the staff trying to oxygenate the body with a manual resuscitator. I was performing cardiac massage on her chest: fingers and thumb lightly gripped around the chest, pumping in a staccato way, imitating a heartbeat. Meanwhile the nurses were trying to get an IV catheter into the arm but were having some difficulty.

'Here Trish, let me have a go. James, can you take over the massage.'

I attempted to glide the catheter in like I'd done a thousand times before but it was impossible. The blood had already congealed in the vein and I couldn't drive the needle in.

'We'd better go for the jugular.'

I got the line in there, which enabled us to give her intravenous adrenaline and atropine which is designed to stimulate the heart if there's any stimulation to be had. It was all futile. The cat was dead. We had to make sure, though. Poor Eva was desperate and she'd asked us to do everything we could.

As I pumped away, I kept checking Andrina's signs, but there was still no pulse. The tongue was still blue and the gums still pale. The pupils were fully dilated. Her body temperature was so low it didn't even read on the digital thermometer. It appeared that Andrina had died a long time earlier.

We got absolutely no response. We worked in a whirlwind for ten minutes, during which time we moved her to the main surgery because we had more monitoring equipment there. We searched for any sign of life but despite all the adrenaline, atropine and Dopram, a drug designed to stimulate breathing, there was nothing.

'It's a waste of time, this IV line,' I said. 'It's probably clotted anyway. The drugs aren't getting to the heart.' I was still committed to giving it everything I had. Eva needed this cat. All I could think of was to get the adrenaline and the atropine straight to where they needed to be. I drew up a couple of millilitres of adrenaline. Silent glances were exchanged between all present, as if to say, 'Here goes. Nothing to lose.' This was the last item in the box of tricks.

I jammed the needle into the heart. Straight out of *Pulp Fiction*.

Nothing happened.

We kept breathing her and giving the CPR. Still nothing.

'Let's give it another one.'

So I drew up the syringe again and gave her that. More breathing. More CPR. James took over the syringe.

'Okay, I'm going to give her one more,' he said. He drew up a final syringe of adrenaline without appearing to pay much attention to the measurement. I surmised that if we did manage to wake this cat, she was never going to sleep again. Andrina was going to have so much adrenaline running through her system she'd have a conservatory's worth of butterflies in her tummy.

But there was nothing. Not a glimmer. Of course there was nothing.

'Okay. This cat's dead. We've done everything we can,' I said.

I had the terrible job of going out to the waiting room and breaking the news to Eva and Sam. It is always difficult, but the gravity of the situation was amplified by Eva's dad's recent passing. I was acutely aware that when you're talking about death to people who have recently been through a situation like theirs, the deaths become intertwined. They don't distinguish between the two. As sad as the pet's death may be of itself, the pain merges into one great amorphous ball of suffering.

I walked into the waiting room and asked them to follow me into the main consult room. I stood on one side of the consult table as they entered, the nerves written on their faces.

'It's not good, Anthony, is it?' Eva said, her head tilted to the side. 'She's dead, isn't she? She's dead.'

'I'm sorry, Eva, but she is. She's passed away. We've been trying to resuscitate her every way possible for the last fifteen minutes and there was just no response. No sign of life, unfortunately. She's gone.'

They were upset, but they weren't blubbering. It was more a vacant kind of disbelief. An absence. Shock will do that. It is often the first reaction.

We stood there in silence while Eva and Sam hugged. Eventually I had to broach a delicate subject. 'I'm really sorry. What would you like to do with the body? You don't need to make a decision right now. You can leave her here and come and get her tomorrow, or we can organise to have her cremated or buried for you.'

'No, we want to take her home now,' Sam said, looking at her mother who was nodding.

'Okay. You go out to the car and I'll bring Andrina to you.'

The two huddled figures left the consult room through the door to the front of the clinic, while I walked out the other door into the back of the clinic. There, I was confronted by the sight of James gesticulating madly towards me from the far end of the room with a cut-throat motion, mouthing, 'No. No. No.'

I whispered, 'It's okay, mate. I've just told them.'

He shook his head even more wildly. I went towards him wondering why he didn't want me out there. I could see he had the cat half into a body bag.

'Don't bring Eva out here,' he said, in a loud, desperate whisper.

'Don't worry she's gone out to the car. She's taking Andrina home,' I said, watching James visibly relax. 'What's happened? Has she emptied her bowels all over the place?'

'Mate, the cat's kind of not dead,' James said.

'What do you mean, kind of not dead?'

'Well, you know how it was dead, completely no sign of life, for about twenty minutes?' I nodded, thinking James may have had some sort of memory failure and forgotten that I'd been there. 'Well, it's not as dead as it was. We were disconnecting everything and about to start putting the cat into the body bag when it twitched. Then it gave a breath, tried to swallow the tube and I picked up a very faint, occasional heartbeat. I restarted cardiac massage and it appears to be working this time.'

I looked at Andrina. Her ruddy body was still flaccid. But I could see an erratic rise and fall of the chest.

'But I just told Eva she was dead.'

'Well, you're going to have to tell her she's not dead.'

Andrina was still as good as dead, though. What we were seeing was probably some vestigial response to the adrenaline. No mammal could come back from being that far gone.

We had a problem, however. Eva and Sam were waiting at their car. I couldn't bring them a cat with a pulse since I'd told them Andrina was dead. We couldn't euthanase her without their permission. If Andrina was in fact still technically alive, she was going to be brain damaged. All she would have left would be the most basic of brain-stem functions. But I was sure that if I just waited a few minutes, the last traces of life would pass gracefully from Andrina's body.

They didn't.

As I hovered over the limp cat, her erratic breathing grew a little more consistent and her pulse got stronger. The nurses, Trish and Kahlia, and our newest vet Hannah were excited and optimistic, willing Andrina to live. James was being the big naysayer.

'It's going to die, guys. You can't be dead for that long and survive.'

They were staring daggers back at him.

'You're such a pessimist. Get over it. It's going to live.'

'Guys, I can count on one finger the number of animals I've seen resuscitated from this level of deadness that have gone on to live a meaningful life. This cat is going to die. But keep going. While there's life there's hope. I just don't want anyone to over-commit to this cat living.'

I must have kept Eva and Sam waiting twenty minutes before I had to face up to the reality: we'd saved the cat. However temporary it proved to be, I had to tell them. I went out to their car where I found Eva in the front seat, curled into the most dejected looking slump.

'Look, um, I don't know how to tell you this, Eva, but, ah, Andrina has started to show some signs of life … way beyond any timeframe we'd consider plausible.'

Her expression didn't change. The lifeless eyes that had cried themselves out weeks ago showed barely a glimmer of light. The flicker of happiness was muted.

'I don't want to get your hopes up. I think the chance of Andrina coming back to life in a meaningful way would be very poor.'

'Yes, I understand. What do we do next?' she asked.

'There's not much we can do. If you give the go ahead, we'll keep her in intensive care and see what happens.'

'Okay, well, that's better than her being dead. You've got to try to keep her alive, Anthony. We'll go home now but can you please keep us informed of everything that happens?'

'Of course.'

For the next five hours, Andrina stayed in intensive care, hooked up to all the machines keeping her alive. She had no gag reflex so we left the tube down her trachea to keep the airway open, running oxygen into her lungs. We had the IV line into her jugular running fluids at 'shock rates' trying to increase perfusion – getting the blood into the tissue. We laid her down on her chest, but she was completely limp.

'This is a disaster,' I said to James as we stood over the wilted, red body. 'She's going to be braindead for sure.'

'And even if she does recover, she's not going to be functional,' he said. 'This is only going to drag the situation out.'

'And all we will have succeeded in doing is raising poor Eva's hopes and messing with her head. '

Nevertheless, we had to push forward and do the best we could for Andrina and Eva. Gradually, the rate and rhythm of her heart and her breathing improved to the point where we thought she might be able to breathe for herself. Later that Thursday afternoon, we had to remove the tube from Andrina's airways because leaving it in for a long time causes irritation and infection. I'd rung Eva about it to explain why we were doing it.

'The thing is though,' I said, 'when we take it out that might be it for Andrina. She might not be able to breathe without the tube down her throat. If that's the case, it kind of tells us that her recovery wasn't going to be viable anyway.'

'She's knows how important she is to me,' Eva said. 'She's not going to leave me … You can't let Andrina die.'

'Well, we're doing everything we can, but ultimately it's not up to us.'

James pulled the tube out, and we watched Andrina with a rising sense of anticipation. But nothing happened. She continued breathing smoothly. This cat was not ready to go. We set her up in an oxygen tent in the cage room, and James divvied up the night-time duties. Andrina got check-ups at 11 p.m., 2 a.m. and 5 a.m. It was just a look-see. We'd promised Eva we'd do it. We expected that one of us would come in and find her dead, in which case we'd promised Eva we would call, regardless of the time.

On these night-time vigils, you crawl out of your winter bed, get dressed, get in the car and drive into town. There's no one around except the bakers at the Berry Bakery. You can see their lights and if you're lucky you can smell their work. The town gets a light coating of fog, so the streetlights give off an eerie glow. You pull in out the back of the clinic and it's pitch black and you have to use your phone or a torch to see your keys to get in through the back door. When I arrived in the wee hours that night, there was Andrina, in the same position we'd left her, still with a pulse, still breathing. So I didn't have to call Eva. I took her temperature, which was steadily rising out of its stony state to be almost normal. I shone the torch in her eyes. There was no reaction. I rearranged her limbs to avoid pressure sores but kept her on her chest, which was best for her lungs.

On Friday morning when I came in at 8 a.m., again expecting to see a dead cat, there was just a heartbeat and a barely discernible rising and falling of the chest. We wondered how long it would continue on like this.

It was getting on towards lunchtime when we got our answer.

Somebody opened a door a bit loudly and Kahlia called out, 'She moved. Did anyone else see it? Her ears moved when the doors opened.'

I went over and clapped near Andrina's head. And sure enough, her ears swung around. Cats' ears are like radar. They can turn them around to get the best sound reception.

'James, come and have a look at this. Am I imagining this?'

We both looked, made little noises, moved around, made more noises. I wasn't imagining it. Her ears were following us.

'I don't get it,' James said. 'That's semi-conscious behaviour.'

'Don't ask me.'

We tried to think it through, to explain it rationally. But instead we just stood there in silence, deep in thought, clapping occasionally and watching the ears move, failing to come up with answers that made sense. Our brain-dead cat was displaying signs of consciousness.

'It's happening but it can't be. I can't believe it,' James said eventually.

'I think it's really happening. I think she's recovering.'

James shone a torch into Andrina's eyes and we both saw a slight flickering of the eyelids. 'No way.'

'Yes way.'

Nevertheless, it was all somewhat academic, since we both knew we were just dealing with degrees of vegetative states. Andrina was hardly going to recover. Hannah, however, became very excited by the prospect. She was getting very close to the cat and was willing it to get better. James, on the other hand, was being the pragmatist.

'If this cat lives, I'll take everyone out to dinner,' James said. It was a throwaway line, but it got picked up on by the nurses.

'Does that include partners?' someone asked. And suddenly James was locked in.

'Yes, of course, because it ain't gunna happen. And if by some miracle it does happen then I'm going to be more than happy to shout you all.'

Late in the afternoon, someone noticed that Andrina had moved. She'd rolled herself off her chest onto her side. Even such small milestones were pretty phenomenal. Maybe there was hope. We remained very cautious, though, in what we told Eva. I was talking to her a lot, but I didn't want to raise her expectations because, in all likelihood, Andrina was still going to die. Eva didn't need her emotions being floated up just to have them dashed against the rocks of reality. I didn't mention the ears or the movement. Just that she was improving.

'We'll need to keep Andrina in hospital over the weekend. She still needs intensive-care support. We'll keep you posted on her progress.'

Not long after I left on Friday afternoon, Hannah rang me.

'Have you been in and moved Andrina?'

'No, why?'

'Well, she's not in the same position she was in when I left her. She's halfway across the cage lying on her side.'

'Well, that's pretty amazing. Put her back on her chest and keep an eye on her.'

The next time Hannah went in to check, Andrina had moved again. Hannah rang me to tell me that Andrina was 'paddling' – lying on her side with her legs moving as if she was walking down an imaginary path. 'Wow. Okay, that is amazing.'

'She's recovering. I just know it,' Hannah said. 'I think she's going to be okay.'

I went in to have a look and by the time I got there, Andrina was making the odd drunken attempt to stand but she didn't get far before face-planting into the blankets lining the cage floor.

I rang James to tell him.

'She might be moving,' he said, 'but what's she got left upstairs?'

'On the evidence, not much.'

As the weekend unfolded, however, Andrina's movements steadied to be, if not feline and graceful, at least stable. We weren't checking her through the night by this time because she was no longer critical, but I was on call so I was in and out of the clinic. When I had a spare moment, I'd pop in to see her if for no other reason than I had to express her bladder. She was unable to go by herself so I'd squeeze her bladder manually through the skin and she'd urinate into a kidney dish.

While I was there, I'd shine my little torch in her eyes, out of habit more than curiosity.

The pupils were maximally dilated and did not move under the glare of the torch like a healthy eye would. If you motioned towards the eye, she did not blink. She didn't even budge. We had figured that Andrina was what we call 'centrally blind', which means the part of her brain that controlled sight had been damaged. There was no coming back from that. She'd be blind forever because the central nervous system doesn't regenerate. Being centrally blind indicated to us that she'd suffered fairly major brain damage. No surprises there.

It was around lunchtime on Sunday that I shone the torch in her eye and her pupil contracted.

So she's not centrally blind?

I rang James.

'I don't know if I'm going mad, but I swear this cat's starting to follow me around with its eyes.'

'No way. Can't happen. I wouldn't think it was possible. It's probably one of those optical illusions like when the eyes in a portrait follow you around.'

'I don't think it is but how would I know. I can't ask her.'

I thought I would put food in the cage to see what happened. I got a tin of Whiskas ocean fish. We use it a lot because it's smelly and highly palatable. Even blind cats will recognise it as food and hoe in.

Andrina appeared to look at it. She could clearly smell it. Then, with jerky head movements, like someone with Parkinson's disease trying to pick up a pen, she almost dived into the bowl and ate it hungrily. And messily.

Andrina had been with us for three days, during which time she had almost regained her bodily functions. And that Sunday night, she voluntarily urinated in the tray. Her recovery was on the fast-track. For a cat that had been dead for so long, I could not believe it. It defied logic.

Holy moly, this cat is moving around the cage. She's eating. She seems able to see. We'd better tell Eva. I called that night.

'We think if she continues to improve like this she can probably go home tomorrow. We really cannot tell you how much brain function she has, but she's got her basic functions back. She may still turn out to be severely brain damaged but only time will tell.'

Eva was always difficult to get off the phone, so every single call to her took half an hour, full of questions I couldn't answer.

'Do you think she's going to be okay? Do you think she's going to have the same personality? Do you think her spirit is still with her?'

'I just don't know.'

The entire idea of a recovery was implausible. Yet here it was happening before our eyes, like a scene from the Oliver Sacks book and the movie *Awakenings*, where patients who were locked in a near-comatose state for thirty years were brought back to life with a new drug. But this was different again. From what we'd seen – the congealed blood in the limbs, the lack of heartbeat for so long, at least fifteen minutes without a pulse in our clinic – this cat shouldn't be doing anything, let alone eating and walking. This was more like Stephen King's novel and the subsequent movie *Pet Sematary*, in which beloved pets are brought back from the dead with dire consequences.

James came back from his weekend away. Trish and Hannah started saying that the restaurant across the road looked nice for that dinner he'd promised.

'Well, let's just define this challenge a little more carefully,' he said. 'It's got to survive of its own accord beyond the end of the month. And it's got to be able to eat and drink and get around on its own.'

Eva, Mick and Sam came in on Monday afternoon to pick up Andrina. Eva was over the moon. In every phone conversation we'd had since she left the clinic on Thursday, and we must have had half a dozen, she had told me how important it was to her that Andrina did not die, and that the cat knew it should not die, so it had come back from the dead to support her. It was destiny. It was fate. It was a higher power at work.

As I put Andrina in their cage, I'm sure the smile on my dial was almost as big as her owners, I carried the miracle cat out into the waiting room. Eva got her out of the cage and had a cuddle. The cat was very affectionate as Mick and Sam gathered around and patted her. She purred and nuzzled into them.

'This is unusual,' Eva said. 'Generally she's quite a bitch to everyone else. She's usually only nice to me.'

'Wow! And I'll tell you what else,' I said. 'That's the first time she's purred since she arrived. This is amazing. She's recognising you guys and is responding appropriately. That's more indication of memory which is a higher brain function. She's really making a full recovery.' I was gobsmacked. What an amazing story. She could see and move and eat and drink. She was going home four days after we'd started putting her in a body bag. The recovery was stupendous.

'You'd better bring her back in tomorrow for a check-up,' I said, as they went through the front door.

The next day, Tuesday, Eva brought Andrina back in a box. She opened it up and Andrina walked out and padded around on the consult table, behaving just like a cat should. A little subdued, perhaps, but friendly and purring, rubbing and nuzzling. I checked her pulse, shone the torch in her eyes and took her temperature. All good, except that when I lifted the tail to get the rectal thermometer in her rear, I noted that the end of the tail was hard, like cardboard.

'Gosh, this is not good,' I said to Eva. 'It looks like the tip of the tail might be dead.'

I took Andrina out the back and got a hypodermic needle and poked the tail on the hard bit. She did not react, nor was there any bleeding. The tail was dead.

James came in the back door and I called him over.

'She's doing great,' I said. 'Isn't it amazing, but it looks like the tip of the tail's died.'

James sized up the patient. 'Hey, I think her ears aren't looking quite right either.'

I felt them and, sure enough, the tips were hard like the tail. I put the needle in at the very tip of her left ear and got the same response, which is to say: no response, no blood. I moved the needle down a little further, same thing, until about one third of the way down, she pulled away and a dot of red appeared. I tried it with the right ear and got the same result. It made sense. The extremities would have been the first areas to lose blood supply and so would have been lacking oxygen and nutrition the longest.

Considering what she'd survived, it wasn't a big deal. I went back to Eva and explained what I'd found.

'We're going to have to remove the tips of the tail and ears because if we don't, they're likely to become gangrenous. But we'd like to wait a day or two to let Andrina more fully recover before we put her through a general anaesthetic.'

'Okay, that's a pity. Is there any way around it?'

'No, there's not. We'll start her on antibiotics right away to stop any infection crossing over from the dead tissue, and we'll send her home with you now.'

So, forty-eight hours later, on the Thursday afternoon, a week since she'd first been rushed in, we crowded around Andrina on the surgery table. It was a big deal to anaesthetise this cat. It was highly risky given her fragile recovery. We didn't want to do it, but I'd spoken to a surgeon, Chris Tan, to find out how urgent the procedure was. He'd been emphatic that if we didn't get the dead bits off, the infection would spread and kill the living bits.

We anxiously anaesthetised Andrina and intubated her again. We were at full alert and took all the precautions available. At least this time she was breathing and had a pulse. The catheter went back into the jugular. Hannah shaved the ears, holding the tip with the thumb and forefinger and shaving upwards, against the grain. I suppose Andrina looked quite funny at the time, like one of those hairless sphynx cats, but our gallows humour had deserted us. I felt a little sick from the gravity and the nerves of the situation.

I trimmed the dead bits off the ears, cutting into the live flesh for a smoother curve. In the end, there wasn't much ear left. I stitched the wounds shut and we moved on to the tail. It had been shaved from the base to the tip, revealing more dead tissue than we'd thought. Andrina's skin was naturally grey but the dead bits were an obvious darker brown/grey/black.

When amputating tails, it's not just a matter of getting a cleaver and chopping. There's a knack to it. You cut the skin above and below in a V shape, so that the Vs are pointing towards the tip. You then lift the skin and peel it off the flesh, revealing the tail bones, which are really just the ends of the vertebrae. You cut through the vertebrae a few notches closer to the body than the tip of the Vs, so that you now have two pointy bits of skin dangling loose over the end. That gives you the spare skin to wrap over the end and stitch shut. If you left the bone tight at the end it would push against the skin and work its way out the back.

So we did that as quickly as we could because we didn't want the cat under anaesthetic any longer than necessary. By now, poor

Andrina looked like Chopper Read with no ears, no tail. But she woke up fine. We kept her in hospital overnight on a drip, with IV fluids running into her to maximise the blood volume and the amount of oxygen reaching the extremities.

The next day, Friday, Andrina was moving around the cage, rubbing on the wires, purring, wanting to be patted and picked up. She was eating. She was great. So we sent her home with instructions for Eva to bring her back the following week for further assessment, which we hoped was just going to be routine.

Eva was back in the waiting room on Monday morning and I could see a worried expression on her face as I ushered her into the consult room.

'She's going really well,' Eva said, 'except that she's lame on her back left leg. Her foot's swollen. Can you have a look at it?'

'Yeah, sure.' I had a look and a feel, and much to my horror, the toes were dead. *Where's this going to end?* I kept my fears to myself. I booked Andrina back into hospital and again I spoke to Chris Tan, the surgeon.

'The foot's dead. It's gone,' he said. 'You've got to remove the bits that are dead. You don't have to remove the entire leg if it's still alive, but you've got to get those dead bits off.'

So we got poor Andrina back into surgery. Before we started doing anything, though, we checked her other limbs. The front right looked a bit dubious to me.

'The other feet feel cold too,' James said.

I thought he was overreacting.

'They're fine,' I said. Blood came out when I pricked them, but it was slow and they did feel a bit cooler than the rest of the body. It was difficult to tell though because they all felt a bit cool.

And I didn't want Andrina's legs to be cold. She couldn't lose many more. I was starting to think like Eva. We could not lose this cat. She was too important.

We proceeded into surgery and amputated Andrina's back left leg, at the ankle. We finished and withdrew the anaesthetic and waited for her to wake.

'Where is this going to end?' I asked again.

'There's a limit to how many limbs can be removed from this cat,' James said. 'A cat with two or less limbs is not a functional cat. I've never seen a case of peripheral dropoffathy like it.'

I laughed. What else could you do? Vets need a bit of gallows humour at times. He was making a pun on the condition 'peripheral neuropathy' where the nerves on the periphery of the body suffer damage causing tingling, numbness and pain.

Andrina woke up fine and I got Eva to take her home.

'Bring her back in a few days and we'll reassess,' I said.

We didn't hear any more from them until they came back for their appointment. I came out to greet Eva, full of nervous anticipation.

'Look, the front right leg is not right,' she said. 'She's limping on that now.'

It wasn't a surprise, but it was upsetting. I'd smelt it before I'd even seen it and so knew that it was dead too. The foot was rotting.

'Look, we're going to have to take that off,' I said.

'How can she survive with only two legs?'

'Good question.' Even though Andrina had a fairly big stump on her back left leg, if she used it for balance, the bone would come out through the skin. It would be like walking on an elbow. It wouldn't take the punishment over time. Euthanasia had been ruled out in my many chats with Eva. It was off the table. So I couldn't even bring it up. We had to keep treating this cat. No matter what. That created its own pressure and now I had to think up a way to make it work.

'We're going to have to try to salvage the limb, which may be possible, but it may not. We've only got one go at it. We'll try to remove the dead tissue around the foot, but we'll leave the living tissue and the bone. Hopefully it will scar over, leaving her with a functional limb. Because you're right. There's no way any animal can survive on two limbs.'

'What are the chances it will work?' Eva asked.

'Very poor, but we don't have much choice. If we do nothing, the dead tissue will kill her.'

Poor Eva, she'd been through the wringer. Andrina, on the other hand, looked happy and healthy. She just had these bits falling off.

And so we prepped for another surgery. I had the unenviable task of peeling the dead flesh off the cat's skeleton, trying to leave as much viable tissue as possible. Dead flesh is hard, like an overcooked steak, whereas live flesh is soft and malleable. It bleeds. So it wasn't hard to distinguish. The dead stuff came away readily because it was brittle and the attachments had broken down. But a cat's foot is a fiddly place to operate with the miniature complexity of the bones.

Andrina's pads had to come off – the digital ones up at the claws and the big one, the metacarpal pad, at the back of her foot. The flesh all around her toes was dead, too, so it had to come off. Once we started, we had to keep going till we got rid of it all. By the end, Andrina looked like Freddy Krueger's cat. Just skeleton and claws. We flooded her foot with a gel-based bandage called SoloSite, then we wrapped it thoroughly because she couldn't walk on a bone.

Eva was out in the waiting room.

'The surgery went well,' I said. 'There's no guarantees, but we just

192

might be able to save her yet. We're going to have to keep Andrina with us in hospital now because she's going to need these bandages changed every couple of days. There's some possibility that maybe the granulation scar tissue will form and maybe one day skin will grow back over. The leg won't be functional, but it might act as a prop. That's the best we can hope for.'

We were coming up to three weeks into the saga now and it was turning for the worse, having looked so good.

Andrina woke up from all the anaesthetic bright and happy. She was friendly and affectionate, eating, drinking. Her temperature and heart rate were all good. Over the next fortnight, we anaesthetised her every second day, removed the bandage, cleaned the wound, dressed it and woke her again. She never missed a beat. Eva and Sam came to visit frequently and she always responded like a healthy, happy cat.

The wound slowly improved, starting to scar up. No new dead bits appeared. The pendulum was swinging back in Andrina's favour. The prospect of long-term survival suddenly started to look very real. She just hadn't taught herself to walk well on her remaining two good limbs. She spent her time lying on her side. She wasn't enjoying life, but we were hopeful that if the front leg could continue healing, she could find her way back to happiness.

So we kept anaesthetising her, cleaning the wound and repackaging her up. We all became increasingly attached to our miracle cat. The first thing that all the staff would do when they came in each morning was to go and give Andrina a pat and a cuddle. She had become a member of the team. It got to the point where we were all spending too much time with her when we should have been out working. People started to remind James about the flippant bet he'd made at the start of this journey.

One day, Chris was cleaning the wound and rebandaging it while I was out the back on the phone to Eva. Those calls were never quick. Suddenly, Chris came belting out the back door with a panicked expression, gesticulating for me to come. I quickly ended the call and raced in. Andrina's heart had stopped while under the anaesthetic.

'What happened?'

'Nothing that I know of,' Chris said. 'One minute she was normal, the next everything just stopped.'

We grabbed the crash box and went through the resuscitation process. She already had a tube down her throat, being under anaesthetic. Trish and Hannah were breathing for her. Chris performed cardiac massage while I drew up a shot of the adrenaline and jammed it straight into the heart. One shot. She didn't respond.

'That's enough,' I said to Chris after a few minutes. 'The cat's been through enough.'

He gave her chest a few more squeezes then slowly pulled away. He didn't need telling twice.

'She's gone.' I said. I could see that Chris was blaming himself. 'It's not your fault. For sure she's thrown a clot and had a major brain embolism. She's been through too much and her body has just called time.'

She had survived so much. She'd been under anaesthetic so many times. She'd suffered all that trauma and not missed a beat. Then, for no apparent reason, five weeks into the ordeal, she just died. Chris was devastated. Hannah was devastated. I was. Trish was. As was James.

'But gee, guys,' he said. 'I would rather have forked out for dinner than have had to go through this.'

It was a real emotional hit. We'd all invested so much into Andrina and had come to see in her an almost supernatural power of survival. Until now.

I called Sam first. I was worried how Eva would take the news so I wanted to test the waters. Ease into it. But Eva overheard Sam speaking and twigged to what had happened. Sam put her on the line. I was surprised how well she took it.

'You did everything you could,' she said. 'We really appreciate everything you did. We gave it a shot. It didn't work out. We're going to come and get the body.'

Hindsight is a wonderful thing. If we'd had a crystal ball and seen the outcome, we'd never have resuscitated Andrina in the first place. But on the other hand, Eva got some precious time with her beloved cat at a time in her life when she needed some hope. As a vet, you have no time to hesitate. You try to save the patient, then deal with complications as they arise. In this case, the complications were insurmountable.

I have never seen or even heard of anything like it. Andrina was a miracle cat. Sure there had been a bit of gallows humour around the clinic. That helps get you through these horrendous situations. But no one was joking any more. A very flat tone permeated the clinic for the next couple of days. Andrina the miracle cat was mortal after all.

BIG BOSS GROOVE

James

As we've come to employ more young vets, we've had to make the transition from employee to employer. From being young James Herriot in *All Creatures Great and Small* to being his grumpy boss, Siegfried. It's a big step. You've got to change the way you think. And it's a big demand on your time. Employing younger vets doesn't solve your workload problems at first because you have to be involved in all their cases. We checked over every job they did, looking for anything we could help them with.

It meant a lot of double handling, or two vets going to one job. But that was good because it introduced the younger vets to the clients as well as training them up.

It was 5.30 p.m., already dark, wet and windy. Everybody was getting into that knock-off time slow-down period, but now there was a problem at a horse agistment place at Terara, a half-hour's drive away on the other side of the Shoalhaven River.

There were probably five vet clinics closer to Terara than us. It's a competitive marketplace. So if a client wants us to get in the car and drive, we'll drive. It's part of the job. And we all love doing horse work.

Just not so much at nearly 6 p.m. in winter when you'd rather be home with the heater on.

So the first thing you do when a job like this comes in is to look for the vet on call. It was Chris's turn this night, so he hopped in the car and away he went.

'Call me when you get there and let me know what you've found,' I said.

I was still at work doing paperwork when he rang.

'It's hiccupping like a lunatic. It's got this crazy spasm going on. I think it might be the thumps.'

'Okay. Listen to its heart,' I said. 'Is the diaphragm spasm happening in time with its heartbeat? The best way to tell that is you put your stethoscope on its heart with your left hand and put your right hand below its ribs. Feel if the two are going together. You'll basically want to look like a faith healer stretched out across the horse. Close your eyes and feel if the spasm and the heartbeat are going together. Once you're there, I want you to repeat after me, "Om ali akbar. Om ali akbar." No, just kidding.'

Chris put down the phone and reported back, 'Yeah, that's what's happening. The spasm is in sync with the heartbeat.'

'Well, you were right then, it is the thumps.'

'Okay. Well, why would it have the thumps?'

The question was logical and I didn't have the answer. The only previous times I'd seen the thumps were at endurance rides. The horses sweat a lot, they lose a lot of minerals and when they get low on calcium that causes the condition known as synchronous diaphragmatic flutter, which is a fancy way of saying hiccups.

But severe cases like this can be very dangerous, and it was distressing for the owner to see their noble pet in that state.

'Have they been working the horse hard?' I asked.

'Nope, hasn't left the paddock in a couple of weeks.'

It was the middle of winter. The horse hadn't been sweating. Its feed hadn't changed. Why would a horse suddenly develop a calcium deficiency?

I pulled down a book and gave Chris a list of some nasty reasons why a horse might get thumps, which is really just a symptom of other problems. It usually occurs in dramatically sick horses as a result of severe dehydration, end-stage tumours, swallowing bizarre materials or severe hormonal imbalance.

Chris gave the owners a few options and they decided to put the horse on a float and drive him up to Berry. We'd recently done a deal with the local show society where we paid for the refurbishment of some run-down old stables in exchange for the use of them as a horse hospital.

I went down to meet them at the showground. Sure enough, the big stock horse came down the ramp hiccupping violently. His name was Romeo and he was owned by a young woman called Emma. He was her passion. They competed together in campdrafting events and she doted over him. His convulsions were causing her a lot of distress.

I went in to have a look. His heart was going at forty beats per minute, so you can imagine the discomfort that was causing with the hiccups going at the same rate, one every second and a half. He wore a light rug, and you could see them pulsing through it.

'Okay, Chris, I'm going to need you to get me a glass of water. When I say go, Emma, can you start rubbing his tummy. I'll try to get him to stand on one leg, and Chris, you try to make him drink the water from the wrong side of the glass.' I'm sure I saw Emma almost crack a smile. 'Or maybe we'll get some IV fluids into him and check his bloods.'

We led Romeo into a small box where we needed to get him onto intravenous fluids. Doing that with horses isn't always the easiest thing. They move around and twist and turn. So you have to get them into a space that is big enough for them to move and stand but not so big as to enable tangles. We hung a five-litre bag from the roof and had the drip on a spiral coil so that when Romeo was standing it concertinaed up and when he lay down, it stretched out.

Horses' necks are so big and the jugular so large you can use a very big catheter and run a lot of fluid into them very quickly. The catheter is so big, you need a little anaesthetic to dull the pain and allow you to ease it in. We didn't want Romeo jumping around. Chris stitched it in place and glued on little tape wings to secure it. Within two or three minutes of the IV fluids starting to flow, the hiccupping had slowed right down, but we were still getting the odd heave.

'I'm sure we would have done just as well with the glass of water,' I said. 'Chris, I reckon we're probably going to have to put some extra calcium in that bag.'

'About 100 mills oughta do it,' Chris said.

'Maybe, but we should figure it out.'

The IV fluid that we'd given Romeo had a little calcium in it, but we needed to understand what his electrolyte levels were like. Luckily enough we had a portable machine that told us just that. Knowing what his levels were, however, was a lot different from knowing how much to give him. And giving an electrolyte intravenously is extremely dangerous. Too much and the heart will just stop.

The difficulty with calculating calcium doses is that they're expressed in millimoles, which is a microscopically small unit of measurement. The different types of calcium that you get also have different levels of availability to the body.

It got very complicated very quickly. Once we'd started figuring it out, I realised it was way too much for my brain to handle on a cold winter night. It was 7.30 p.m. I hadn't eaten for eight hours. But I was now the boss. What kind of example would it set if I started cutting corners just because the going got tough? So we sat there in the stable, illuminated by our head torches, with three different books open, checking and rechecking our conversions from millimoles to micrograms to milligrams, millilitres and back again.

Forty-five minutes of swearing and googling conversion charts, and with four pages of algebra lying in the straw, we had our answer: 102 millilitres. Two mills more than Chris had suggested off the top of his head.

We added the 102 millilitres of calcium on top of the IV bag and all the symptoms ceased.

Chris stayed to monitor the horse through the night. One of the benefits of being the boss, even though it was 9 p.m. and I'd had to come out into the frigid night to do four pages of algebra, was that I could say, 'That's great. You have any trouble, you let me know. See you later.'

Chris stayed with Romeo at first, then checked him hourly, then left him in the wee hours. I went back first thing in the morning and he was doing really well. He made a full recovery and despite our best efforts, we never found the cause of his plummeting calcium.

Back in the early days of my career, I'd look at my boss, Ben Gardner, who knew so much and talked so fast and I'd wonder how on earth you stacked so much information inside one brain. He was so Siegfried. He'd mutter under his breath, rattling stuff off. 'Thumps. Yes, thumps. Bring it in. We'll do ... indecipherable ... give it some ... indecipherable.' I'd bring a dog in for Ben to look at. He'd know nothing about it and wasn't even that interested in small-animal medicine, but he'd walk into the room while I started to tell him about the case. And he'd go, 'Yes, James, that's all very well. It's going to die.' He didn't even know what was wrong with it. He could just look at it and know.

Anthony's old boss Geoff Manning once said to me, 'I can smell a tick over the phone.' It's interesting he should say that because they've done a study that showed that vets who see a lot of tick cases can look at an animal and predict whether it is going to live or die just as effectively as any scientific test. If you see a lot of tick cases, you can wander in and say that one will live, that one will die, and you'll be accurate. It's the vibe.

As you gain more experience, you find yourself saying those sorts of things when you get the call from the younger vets: 'I'm looking at this dog and …'

'Okay, it's really sick, so the first thing you need to get across to the client is that it is probably going to die.'

'Yeah, but it's just coughing and passing a bit of blood.'

'Yes, but it'll have lung abscesses.' Experience teaches you this stuff. You've seen it before. 'You need to tell the client this animal is probably going to die and here are all the things we're going to do to try to stop it. But they need to know this is really bad.'

I now find myself giving definitive diagnoses over the phone with only a skerrick of pertinent info from the new grad. I'll be reeling off information and the grad will be wondering, just as I used to wonder, *How does this guy know all this stuff?*

At other times they'll call up panicking. They'll list just a couple of symptoms and you'll butt in. 'It'll be fine. I'll come out and give you a hand, but tell the client to calm down. She'll make a full recovery.'

Common things occur commonly. So you get to know them really well and then you have to get a few more years behind you before you've seen all the less common things.

One night, Chris rang me to say he had a dog with breathing difficulties.

'I've taken an X-ray and emailed it to you. Can you have a look?'

This is the brilliance of the time we live in. I sat down at my computer at home, still in my pyjamas and Ugg boots, pulled up the pictures, put him on speakerphone.

'Hmmm. It looks like a globoid heart. Can you hear the heart clearly?'

'No. It sounds a bit muffled.'

'What do you reckon?' I said.

'I think it's probably got a bleed around its heart.'

His girlfriend, Sass, was with him in the clinic. She'd been around animals all her life so she held the dog for him while he took an ultrasound of its heart.

'Does it look like the heart's in the middle of a huge sac of fluid?' I asked.

'Yep.'

'Well then you're right. It's got a bleed into the sac around its heart.'

The dog needed that sac drained. The sac won't stretch so the fluid fills up that sac and it sort of squeezes the heart in so it can't beat, which was what was causing the dog so much trouble.

I got out of my pyjamas and came in to the clinic. I manned the ultrasound and used it as a navigational tool so Chris could steer the needle into the space between the heart and that sac. He sucked out about a coffee mug's worth of blood from the narrow space.

When we finished, the dog went from being near dead to trotting back to its cage. For Chris to be able to do that – only six months out of uni – was great. All I did was offer reassurance and a few directions to guide the needle.

I might also have told him about the time when I were a lad, at a similar stage in my career, when a retired greyhound came into the little clinic where I worked in Manilla.

'Stop me if you've heard this before ...'

The greyhound had the same thing – a very rapid, weak pulse. I took an X-ray and whereas now we've got instant digital pictures, back then in the dark ages of the early twenty-first century, I had to drive five kilometres to the local hospital, introduce myself to the nurses, sneak out to the X-ray department, feed my X-rays through the film processor and get my pictures. I took them out and had a quick look at them in the sunlight of the car park before driving to the clinic for a better look. The greyhound's heart looked enormously enlarged.

Like Chris, I diagnosed a pericardial effusion. I told the owners that fifty per cent of pericardial effusions happen for no known reason. The other fifty per cent happen because the dog has got a nasty tumour that's bleeding. I knew they had no money to pay for a specialist, so I said, 'If you're willing, I'll have a go at draining it.' There was nothing to lose.

I didn't have an ultrasound machine but I read the book and it gave directions: 'Insert the needle at the fourth rib on the right and aim for the point of the left elbow.' So I had the dog on its side on the table. It was awake because a general anaesthetic would likely kill it in its fragile state. Having said that, it was so sick it wasn't going to get up and try to play fetch. All it had to deaden the pain was a local around the heart. I pulled its left arm upwards, counted down to the fourth rib space and drove the needle in, pointing at the other elbow which was lying under the torso. I guided the needle in until I struck blood. Eureka!

So I had this dying dog, a needle, a book and a fabulous nurse, Suzanne Barton, holding him down. No ultrasounds to guide us in them days. No sir. The book said that as I drained the fluid, my needle might touch the heart. 'When it touches the heart, you cause an arrhythmia.' And it did too. The needle disturbs the electrical currents and the heart goes into atrial fibrillation. The needle was like a little phone alarm. *Ding-a-ling.* Vibrating away. I backed off and kept draining, but the more I emptied, the less space there was to drain from and so the needle touched again. *Ding-a-ling.*

I did this a few times until I figured I wasn't going to get any more out. I finished the op and, with the patient being awake, it was like a miracle cure. We lifted him off the table and he was instantly a tail-wagging, tongue-out, happy greyhound. His cardio output had gone from near zero to normal in a couple of minutes and there were no nasty scars to deal with. The owners came in to find their hound up and nuzzling its big, wet nose into their thighs. They hugged me and thanked me and thought I was a genius. I didn't feel like one, but I might have allowed myself to bask in the warm glow that emanated from them. I might not have mentioned that I did it with the textbook open beside me. But I did warn them that there was a fifty-fifty chance the problem would return and that would be the last race for their lovely old dishlicker.

That's what did happen, unfortunately. The heart sac filled up the very next day and we put him to sleep. I did a post-mortem and confirmed that he did have a malignant tumour. It also revealed scratch marks on the heart surface. *Pretty sure I know what they are.*

On this happier occasion, with Sass holding the dog and me on the ultrasound probe and Chris holding the needle, we were able to drain the sac around the heart very effectively. I could say 'go deeper', 'back up' and 'you're getting very close to the heart'. So they didn't get to see the *ding-a-ling* vibrations. But they did get to see the dog go from death's door to miracle cure, dancing up out of its proverbial wheelchair. By the time the owners got back, they had Chris right up there on that genius pedestal and I was at least able to bask in his reflected glory. It was great to see Chris have this sort of moment and develop as a vet. Mentoring younger vets can be difficult, but it can also be a hugely rewarding experience.

FORTY WINKS

Anthony

I was a little bit cranky at Trish. 'You've got to get as much information as possible off the client so we know what we're dealing with,' I said, with my finger on the appointment book, trying to stay civil.

'I tried,' she said, 'but I just couldn't. All she'd tell me was that the cat was unwell.'

'Look, we just need to persist. "Unwell" isn't good enough. I'm sure with a few well-thought questions you could have got something more.'

'Well, I asked her how long it had been unwell for and what symptoms it had. Is it eating and drinking? She just didn't answer.'

'Okay, sorry,' I said, perhaps a little begrudgingly.

The cat arrived at the appointed hour in the arms of a woman in her late thirties who was wearing a leather skirt and cashmere sweater, perhaps just a little better dressed than we'd normally see of people bringing their cat to the vet. She was bear-hugging the cat, which is a dangerous thing to do because in the dash from the car to the clinic, an unexpected noise or a dog coming out the door can cause the cat to freak out and bolt. Cat people usually know better than to bring cats in without cages.

'Hi, Dianne. Come quickly into the consult room,' I said. 'The last thing we need is for the cat to panic out here.'

'It's pronounced Dee-AHN,' she corrected me as we rushed in and closed the door.

'Sorry Dee-AHN. Okay, so what's up with the cat?'

'I think he's unwell.'

'All right, let's start from the beginning here,' I said, noticing that the owner had a funny expression on her face. Was it a smirk? I couldn't tell.

'What's the cat's name?'

There was a pause. 'Forty,' she said.

'Okay. How old is Forty?'

'Ohhhh, about five.'

'Okay. About five. Now, in what way is he unwell?'

'He's just not himself.'

'Okay, great. In what way is he not himself?'

'I can't really put my finger on it.'

'Okay, you don't have to name a disease. Explain the symptoms. What are you seeing?'

'I don't know.'

'Let me try to help. Is he eating normally?

'Yes. Maybe. I think so.'

Dee-AHN was open and friendly and despite the emptiness of her answers, she talked in a way that seemed to indicate intelligence. She was giving me nothing, though, and I realised that more information was not going to be forthcoming. I made a note to myself to apologise more wholeheartedly to Trish. From a professional point of view, I was frustrated that there was a mystery illness here which I was not getting to the bottom of. I had to find a way through.

'Is he going to the toilet?'

'Yes.'

'Urine and poo?'

'Yep, it's all fine.'

'Has he had any medications lately?'

'No. I don't think so.'

'Has he got any diseases that you know of?'

'No.'

'Is he on any treatment of any sort?'

'No.'

'Okay.' They say you get ninety per cent of your advice from listening and looking and ten per cent from knowing. By talking to the client, getting a good history then making a thorough physical examination you're going to garner a lot more, and get the diagnosis right more often, than the really smart textbook vet who just takes a quick look and decides they know what the problem is.

Unfortunately in this case, there wasn't much pertinent information forthcoming, so I went to the physical examination. I ran through Forty's temperature, his heartbeat. I felt around his limbs and his body, looking for sore spots, lumps or any sort of abnormality. I looked into his mouth and checked his teeth.

The cat appeared to be the epitome of good health.

'He hasn't escaped recently?' I asked. 'He hasn't been hit by a car? Not dropped by a child?'

She shook her head with a sorry kind of smile.

He was five years old and his name was Forty. That's all I had. I started to wonder if I was having my leg pulled. *Why would you bother bringing an animal in for an examination if there was nothing wrong with it? Why is Dee-AHN here?* 'Well, I'm sorry. I can't find anything wrong with your cat,' I said. That's difficult to say to a client. They're saying it's sick and you're saying it's not. You worry that they're going to think you're a dope.

'I'm stumped,' I said. 'I need more information about what's wrong with Forty so I can focus my testing.'

'No, never mind. I'm happy with that. I'm glad that you've looked and if you haven't been able to find anything that's probably all we need to do. I was probably just being over-concerned.'

'So you're happy with these findings?' I asked, a little surprised. Over-concerned owners tend to stay over-concerned.

'Yes, I'm very happy. Thank you, Anthony.'

'Okay. But I want you to take Forty home and look carefully and try to specify exactly what it is that is making you think he's not right.'

'Okay, I'll do that. I'll watch him like a hawk.'

'Great. Now if you can just see Trish on the way out that'd be great.'

'Actually, can I call you back and pay over the phone?'

Trish knew the family. 'That's fine, you can do that. Here, wait a moment. I'll lend you a cat cage. It'll be safer.'

The next day, I came through the back door after a farm visit and Trish came over to see me. Her brow was furrowed and her lips pursed; she looked confused and angry at the same time. I was scared.

'I just got a call from Dianne or Dee-AHN or whatever to pay the bill for Forty.'

'Oh yeah,' I said, anticipating there might have been a problem. 'Was everything okay?'

'Yes, no problem there, but as I was waiting for the payment to go through I was making small talk and I said, "Forty's an interesting name. Why's he called that?"'

'"Well, I don't know its real name," she said. "It's actually the neighbour's cat that I grabbed. I called it Forty because that's how much it was going to cost to see Anthony."'

'I said, "I beg your pardon."'

'She said, "I called it Forty because that's how much it costs to see him for fifteen minutes."'

'I didn't know what to make of her. So I just said, "Oh, right". I must have done it a bit haughtily because she started to panic.'

'She said, "Oh. He's not your partner is he?"'

'I said, "Do you think I'd still be speaking to you if I was?"'

'I can't believe she stole a pet to just to see you. Whatever happened to buying someone a drink?'

We cracked up.

SOCK GUY

James

Every time Anthony tells that story about the cat called Forty, I see it as my cue to roll out the one about a case I had when I was working in London, a couple of years before I came to Berry.

It was a quiet morning when I saw in the book that there was a bird in the waiting room. I went out to usher the client through. It was a guy sitting in an unusually rigid, upright posture with a bird in a cage beside him. His hands were in fists on his knees, like he was in the front row of a school photo – back straight, staring ahead, but just not saying cheese. He was wearing bone-coloured pants, pressed flat, brown leather brogues and a brown leather belt. His shirt was bright pink, buttoned to the throat and at the cuffs.

He presented such an extraordinary sight that I almost stopped just to take it all in. He was maybe late twenties, with his hair shaved at the sides, short and spikey on top. Everything was perfectly in place. He looked like Forrest Gump.

'Hi, there. Do you want to come through? We'll take a look at your bird.'

He stood, rigid and jerky, picked up the tiny cage with a yellow budgie in it and walked stiffly to the door.

'My name's James, anyway,' I said, mentally admonishing myself for adding the 'anyway'. I could hear the voice of the other vet I worked with, Kate, saying, 'Nice to meet you, James Anyway,' as she was wont to do from her adjoining consult room.

I went to shake his hand and I could see him awkwardly shuffling the cage about so he could shake. He tucked it under his left arm, reached out with his right and shook my hand in a rapid, up-and-down, machine-like motion. He tilted his head. 'Bernard,' he said in a high-pitched voice.

'Okay, what seems to be the problem with the little guy?'

'Yes. Well. The bird. Very worried. Yes. He's unwell.'

'In what way?'

'Well, he's extending his neck up and down. He looks uncomfortable in his throat. There is seed around his mouth. Worried he's choking.'

Before coming out to greet Bernard, I'd checked on his files and seen that about a year earlier the bird had had an impacted crop. The crop is a diversion of the bird's oesophagus which they fill with food that can then get packed down so firmly it won't move. My colleague had treated it with an oily antibiotic substance and the bird had rapidly improved.

'Yes, well this looks very similar to what he had a year ago,' I said.

'It's exactly the same. Yes. Exactly the same.'

'Okay. Let's have a little look at him. What's his name, by the way?'

'Socks.'

'Okay. Would you be able to catch Socks for me?'

Bernard did it proficiently. Catching a bird in a cage is not an easy thing. As daft as it sounds, it's difficult to do with minimum fussing and flapping. Bernard held Socks with a firm confidence while I examined him. I couldn't see anything else wrong with him so I got hold of the same antibiotic oil we'd given him last time, gave him some more, then asked Bernard to put Socks back in the cage.

You have to be careful with these tiny birds. Over-handling them is dangerous. They can just drop dead from the stress, so you don't want to mess about with them too much.

Within minutes Socks looked more comfortable and it was obvious the obstruction had passed. He started screeching and chattering like a happy budgie should.

'Let me get you some medicine to give to Socks over the next few days,' I said. 'Should sort him right out. Keep an eye on him though and see how he goes.'

I was making my notes and making small talk, patting myself on the back for another mission accomplished, when Bernard spoke.

'I take it you're from Australia.'

'Yes, you noticed.'

'I had a very dear friend from Australia. He's from Brisbane.'

'Oh, yeah, I was born in Brisbane but lived all over.'

'Do you play football?' he asked.

'No, no. I'm retired. I've long given it away because I'm no good at it and the last time I played I broke my arm.'

'Do you play any other sports?'

'Don't mind a game of cricket. Actually, I play across the road here.'

I could hear him considering what he was going to say next, shifting awkwardly.

'I hope you don't mind me asking, but I have this thing. It's only for certain people. Certain men. You remind me of my friend. I was wondering if I might be able to purchase some of your socks.'

I looked at him blankly.

'I don't want you to wash them,' he said, as though me washing my socks might be the big impediment to this transaction taking place.

I was taken aback, but I tried to hide behind my best poker face.

'As it turns out, I've only just moved here and I've only got a couple of pairs of socks and I need them all. I'm living out of a backpack.'

'I will pay, of course.'

'No, sorry. I don't have any to spare.'

He didn't seem to carry any resentment at my miserliness, and we finished the consult.

'The nurse will bring the medications through in a moment,' I said.

Bernard exited through one door into a corridor and I exited into a parallel corridor that the staff used on the other side. As soon as I got through the door I burst into a silent kind of chest-hugging laughter. The nurse, Sarah, was looking at me strangely and I put my finger to my lips in a shushing gesture as I retreated to a distant, dark faraway corner of the clinic to tell her what had happened.

Sarah was absolutely skint at the time.

'I know where your dirty socks are,' she said. 'You've got loads. They're out the back in the washing pile. I'm going to flog 'em off to this geezer.'

'Do Not Do That. I am *not* cool with that.'

Sarah went and dispensed the medication to Bernard, although he would henceforth only ever be referred to as Sock Guy. Two or three days later Sock Guy called up. We always asked clients to let us know how the patient was going. A different nurse took the call.

'I'm just phoning to let James know that Socks is much, much better,' Sock Guy said. 'He's completely back to normal, I'm really happy.'

'Oh, okay, who is calling, please?'

'It's Bernard Billingsworth. I'm pretty sure James will remember me.'

She came out the back. 'Someone called Bernard rang to say his budgie, Socks, is much better and he's very thankful and that he can't wait to see you again … What's wrong? Sarah, James, are you okay?'

HIGH ANXIETY

Anthony

Timothy Chatfield was very proud of his role as an aged-care volunteer. That's how he first came to be a client of ours. A senior gent himself, Timothy brought in an older lady, Mrs Newton, whose Cavalier King Charles Spaniel had a problem with itchy skin. Mrs Newton had been going to see another vet about it for years, but they hadn't made any progress with the chronic scratching so she'd decided to give us a try to see if we could come up with anything different.

We managed the Cavalier King Charles's chronic itch with modest success, so Timothy started coming in to see us with his lovely little long-legged terrier, Lukie, who looked like a miniature Old English Sheepdog, with similar colours and the big flopping fringe.

Lukie was a rescue dog so we didn't know what he might have lived through with his first owners, but he was certainly a hard one to win over. The main thing that was stopping him from being your friend was that he was so scared of you. I tried giving him a liver treat but he wouldn't even take it from my hand. He just shrank into the corner, into Timothy's grip, tail hooked between his legs, head bowed. Food was the last thing on his mind while he was dealing with this stranger who wanted to touch him on this weird metal table. He clung to Timothy and tried to climb up onto him. I had to get the stethoscope on him while he clambered up over Timothy's shoulder and around Timothy's portly frame. I heard more of Timothy's heartbeat than I did Lukie's. Timothy thought it was hilarious.

Lukie Chatfield was a great little feller who checked out to be in perfect health, but it was obvious that he was quite anxious. So after I gave him his vaccination, I thought I'd better have a chat about anxiety and the unwanted behaviours it can lead to.

Timothy was very on-song with this. 'I think you're right. It all makes a lot of sense. Sometimes when I come home he will have urinated inside and I think he does it as soon as I leave because I don't have to be gone long for there to be a puddle in the house. When I get home he's incredibly excited to see me and he just will not let me out of his sight.'

We talked about how he handled the dog day to day. Timothy had acquired Lukie after the unexpected demise of Lukie's former owner. Being Timothy's first dog and given Lukie's sudden relocation, some adoption issues were only to be expected. He let Lukie sleep on his bed and he fed him before he fed himself. All those little things that allow the dog to think that it's a human and higher up the pecking order. Then when Timothy left to do his day's charity work, Lukie got left on his own and couldn't cope, adding to his cycle of fear and insecurity.

'When I'm in the shower, he breaks into the bathroom and sits on the bath mat staring at me, licking his lips. And I can tell you, it's been a long while since anybody looked at me that way in the nude.'

'Okay, yes, lip-smacking is a general sign of anxiety,' I said, playing it straight.

'Are you saying my naked form makes him anxious?' Timothy let out an uproarious laugh. 'What has it all come to? No, seriously, is there anything we can do for this?'

'Well, you can actually put them on medications to reduce anxiety. I feel that the behaviours you're talking about are based out of anxiety and if we can control and suppress that to some extent, then we can probably get some behavioural training done. We've got an excellent dog trainer in the area who can come out and make an assessment.'

'That sounds great. What medications are we talking about?'

'Actually it's Prozac and Xanax.'

'Really?'

'And it's the human stuff that we use. There are doggie versions of the same drugs with different names, but they're three times the cost so we just use the human stuff.'

I remember that when these antidepressants first started getting used for pets – and it's only been in the last decade – I thought I was going to get slapped or at least ridiculed for bringing up the topic: 'Don't be bloody ridiculous. I'm not putting my dog on Xanax.' But it's amazing how many people go, 'Oh yeah, I'm taking Prozac,' or 'Mum's on it and the kids are on it, so why not Fido?'

All this was unheard of when we left uni in 2004, but it has become totally normal in the last few years. The more you know about problems – and the more ability you've got to treat them – the more you look for them, so the more commonly you'll diagnose them. If you don't know about anxiety in dogs and the problems it causes, when somebody tells you how their dog constantly follows them around, you'll say, 'Well, tell it to stop.' Or, 'What's the problem? Isn't that why you've got a dog?'

It's not all about drugging the dog. If the dog's weeing on the carpet, it's about looking at the situation and saying the dog's weeing on the carpet because it's left inside too long, or it's left at home alone, or it's marking its territory because it is jealous of the new baby.

Unfortunately, with the way that animals have been bred as companions, a lot of the traits that humans find desirable in a friend are behaviours that, when exhibited by animals, are signs of anxiety, like the friendly neediness of Lukie. Everyone who owns a dog likes the fact that when they arrive home, Rover is glad to see them. That's not necessarily anxiety. But if Rover barks all day, he's got separation anxiety. He is overly anxious.

There is an enormous number of drugs that have been developed for humans that animal behaviourists have taken to with gusto to address these underlying problems. And once you ease the anxiety, the dog becomes easier to train out of its barking or urinating or aggression.

Pets are often an extension of their owners' personality. And anxious pets will often have anxious owners. I didn't know about Timothy. He didn't seem such a nervy type, but he had no reluctance in putting Lukie on antidepressants. So we put Lukie on Prozac and Xanax. I told Timothy not to expect an instant response but maybe things would start to change in a few weeks. I booked them in for a repeat consult in three weeks.

They turned up right on time with Lukie freshly bathed and smelling sweetly. Timothy – well presented in a green polo shirt with the volunteer carers' logo – came in gushing.

'Hello Doctor. My goodness, haven't you made a difference to my little Lukie Chatfield.'

'That's great. What's he been doing?'

'You see, I have my little routines that I follow quite strictly. I get up in the morning, put my dressing gown and slippers on, and go out to the kitchen. Lukie jumps off the bed and follows me out while

I put the kettle on, then I go back and have my shower and a shave. Lukie follows me into the bathroom and just sits there watching me. It's most remarkable because yesterday morning I did all that and for the first time ever, Lukie didn't even get off the bed. I thought, *Once he hears the shower running he'll come running in and take up his position.* And sure enough he jumped off the bed and came walking down. But he went straight past the bathroom, into the kitchen and sat out there on his own. It's extraordinary. He's still the same dog. He's as affectionate as ever, but he's not following me around like a shadow all the time.'

I wasn't sure if there was a note of disappointment in Timothy's voice that Lukie wasn't quite so devoted, but certainly on the surface Timothy knew that it was a healthy improvement. As time went by, we weaned Lukie off the Xanax and just kept him on the Prozac and that was adequate. We had a behaviourist go out to train him and give Timothy some tips to further reduce the anxiety. And it all went well. They've continued to pop in regularly to get Lukie's medications and Timothy still thinks it's a hoot that his dog is on them – the urbane sophisticate that Lukie is.

Mrs Newton became a regular client too. We never quite cured her Spaniel's itch. But we did manage to control the symptoms. We had to explain to her that the problem would never be cured without desensitisation vaccines and that she had to keep feeding him his tablets. It was a communication thing as much as anything, which wasn't easy because she was quite hard of hearing. Over time, the Spaniel developed congestive heart failure with the additional complication of pulmonary hypertension – high blood pressure in the arteries and veins of the lungs. The Cavalier King Charles breed is particularly prone to the condition which causes all sorts of problems.

The treatment of choice for pulmonary hypertension happens to be a drug called Viagra. In fact, this condition is what Viagra was originally intended to treat. When they were experimenting with it in the early stages of development, it cured hypertension in rats, but when they came to the first human trials, they noticed that the male patients came back with some very positive reviews and hard evidence of certain side effects.

It doesn't have the same side effect in dogs, but it still took a long while before it came into use in the veterinary world. Most of the dogs getting it are castrated, anyway, so they're not sexually minded or active. We pick up our Viagra from the chemist in Berry. The first time we sent our lovely, innocent nurse Kahlia to get it for us, she turned bright red with embarrassment. So now we make sure she always gets that job. Sometimes we ask her to pick up some KY jelly while she's there. We use that for sterile procedures like passing urinary catheters in dogs or lubricating their eyes during surgery.

Her attitude is, 'Not again.' But ever the diligent employee, off she trudges.

The staff at the pharmacy think it's very interesting that the vet clinic is buying so much Viagra. *What's going on over there?* Everyone has a laugh about it.

But Kahlia has taken matters into her own hands. One of the chemist staff told me recently that she now says the Viagra is for James: 'He's getting on a bit, you know.'

A MYSTERY

James

Figuring out what's wrong with the animal in front of us is mostly pretty straightforward. If we don't know as soon as we arrive at a farm or as soon as Fido comes into the consult room, we can usually figure it out with a few probing questions and a couple more well-considered tests.

When a mystery comes along, it is frustrating. I don't like to be puzzled. It can be a little bit interesting to be stretched, but you don't want to be baffled when it's a beloved pet or an animal owned by one of your biggest clients. And so it was when I got a call late one afternoon to go and see a crook cow at one of the biggest beef farms in the district, Wonga Park.

I dealt with the acting manager, a young bloke in Hi-Viz and a wide hat. He said they'd had a few cows get sick in the last week.

'We had one that went staggery in the hind legs. It was real cranky for a day, then went down and died.'

He drove me out to the paddocks where I saw a thick, black shape protruding out of the flat expanse of green. I got out and the earth squelched beneath my feet as I walked over to the big, black heifer. She was down on her side. The grass all around her was pounded down into a muddy circle where she'd clearly been spinning herself round and round with legs that were going through the motions of walking but were too weak to lift her. On closer inspection, I saw she'd taken a lot of skin off her face on the downward side and her downward eye was badly inflamed from pushing into the mud and grass.

I took her pulse. It was elevated and her temperature was high. I looked at the grass in the paddock. About a week earlier we'd had a big flood and all these paddocks had been underwater. The Shoalhaven flats might be super fertile but when the waters come down, they're nothing but a glorified swamp. The water can sit there for days, even weeks. The grass around her was quite rank. It goes stale with age and had clearly been affected by being submerged. But new green growth was starting to shoot through.

It looked like she might have a condition called hypomagnesaemia, or grass tetany. It occurs when cattle eat rapidly growing grass and there's no older roughage-type grass around. The younger grass has no magnesium in it, so the cow's metabolisms get all out of whack. The traditional name for this condition is 'grass staggers', because of the way affected animals go all wobbly in the legs.

Looking around at the rank grass damaged in the flood, I figured it probably wasn't going to be very palatable to the cattle so they would have ignored it and just eaten the flush of new shoots which wouldn't have enough magnesium.

This heifer had all the classic symptoms for grass tetany. She was weak and she was down. According to the farm hand, she had been very angry before, but she was beyond that now and could barely raise her head to snort at us as we approached. So I treated her with subcutaneous injections of a magnesium-rich solution with some calcium phosphorous and glucose in it. Her chest was rasping too, so I gave her antibiotics for that. I also took blood so I could test my diagnosis.

'They don't always respond to the treatment for hypomagnesaemia,' I told the acting manager. 'So she may well still die.'

'Well, we've got a few more out in the paddock that aren't as sick as this one but they look like they might have the same thing.'

'Well, you've got your magnesium lick blocks out so you're probably a fair way ahead of the game in terms of protecting the rest of your herd. Maybe you need to feed out some more roughage and spread it out a bit more.' Animals lower down the pecking order will often get pushed off the hay bales and won't get to eat any. 'I think that'll sort your problem, but I'll test my blood sample here to confirm this diagnosis.'

I had a final look at the sick heifer. 'Look, if she dies overnight, we should post-mortem her because we'll need to know why she died. There's 4000 animals at risk here. This could be a big problem.'

I got back to the clinic about 7 p.m. Chris was working back, so I got him to run the blood samples for me while I went and discharged a dog. I came back in.

'How'd that test go? Was the magnesium low?'

'No, it's actually high.'

'High magnesium?' That stumped me. 'You don't see high magnesium very often. That's a bit weird.'

I ran through the mental checklists I'd been building and renovating ever since uni and I couldn't come up with anything. It made it all the more worrying for the other sick cows at Wonga Park. This could be some sort of an epidemic and if it swept through the whole herd, thousands of animals could be affected. But there was nothing else I could do about it that night.

I realised that the magnesium injections I'd given the sick heifer were now irrelevant. She had looked so crook and now I held out even less hope for her survival. I was left scratching my head so I did a bit of reading at home, which left me none the wiser.

In the morning, I talked to Anthony about my mystery and headed off back to Wonga Park, expecting that the sick heifer was going to be dead and I'd have to do an autopsy on her.

I was in the yards, going over everything a second time, trying to see what I'd missed when the phone rang. It was Anthony.

'I think I know what's wrong with your cow,' he said.

THINKING TIME

Anthony

James had approached me in the early evening.

'Gee, I don't really know what's going on with this cow I just saw at Wonga Park.' He told me about what he'd seen – an almost semi-comatose animal along with signs that it had been seizuring and fitting earlier. 'I don't have any genius ideas,' he said. 'You got any?'

I didn't.

Soon after, I was sitting where a lot of the best thinking gets done, on the toilet, when I received a text message from one of our young dairy farmer clients, Todd Bushnell, who's also a good mate.

'Got a few sick cows,' the message said. 'Could you come down and have a look in the morning?'

I rang back a few minutes later to ask if he wanted me to come straight away.

'No. They're not that sick. They're shivering and they've got diarrhoea. But they don't look too bad.'

Todd had only recently taken the place over from his dad, from whom he'd inherited freckles and a super-relaxed manner. The Bushnells were warm, welcoming people. Todd was more progressive than his dad, always keen on trying to improve the genetics in the herd and improve their farm management techniques.

I booked in to see him in the morning. When I hung up, a thought struck me. *The Bushnells' place adjoins Wonga Park.* Todd's cows weren't dying like at Wonga Park. There wasn't an obvious parallel between the symptoms, but the proximity made me wonder.

Next morning, James had booked in to go back out to Wonga Park. He was expecting that if his cow hadn't come good overnight, he'd have to put it down, then do a post-mortem and some further disease investigation. He was hoping I'd go with him to help. But I was booked in to see Todd who'd not long before had a disaster when a number of his cows had died from a poisoning that was not his fault.

I arrived at the dairy and Todd, with his farmer's tan over the red freckly complexion, came out to meet me with a friendly handshake.

'Some are a bit worse than others,' he said. 'They've all gone off their milk. But some of them are shivering as well as having the diarrhoea.'

I had a look at the cows that Todd had got up into the race for me. None looked very sick, but none of them were right either. Some were pooing through the eye of a needle. Their faeces was like water, shooting out more than a metre behind them. I got the stethoscope out to take their heart rates. But it was difficult to examine them because every time I put the disk on their chest to listen, they'd start snorting, bucking, kicking and bellowing and their heart rate would go up correspondingly. I realised they were all hyperaesthetic – super-sensitive to external stimuli. They were feeling the touch of the stethoscope, hearing the sounds and seeing the sights far more sensitively than usual. So they jumped every time I touched them or made a noise.

227

I had to work out whether the elevated heart rate was caused by the stress of the stimuli or whether it was more systemic. Some of the sicker ones were tremoring. That's what Todd had described when he'd said they were shivering, but their body temperatures were normal so it wasn't cold that was doing it.

Despite all this, they were standing there looking relatively healthy. I had no idea what was going on.

'Well, let's treat the symptoms that we know,' I said. 'They're uncomfortable and they've got diarrhoea. I'll give them fluids and painkillers and take some samples to see if we can get to the underlying cause.'

I needed to fill some buckets with water to pour down their throats with electrolytes to replace the fluids they were losing. I walked from the crush to the side of the dairy where there was a tap on the outside corner. The buckets were large and it took a while to fill them, so I stood there looking at the view. The dairy was built on a rise, giving it a beautiful vista across the fertile flats to the paddocks of their neighbour, Wonga Park. *What could the connection be?* I wondered. I looked across to the Wonga Park yards, two or three kilometres away, knowing I was expected to be over there to help James and that he was desperate for an extra pair of hands. With my mind wandering, I squinted at the horizon trying to see the ocean. I couldn't make it out, but I knew it wasn't far away. I looked for the property of another client who I'd seen about two weeks earlier. She had a horse that, ultimately, I'd had to put down in her yards which were right next door to Wonga Park's. My mind drifted to a phone call I'd had with her where she'd ask me to send the bill by post.

'I might not get it for a few days, though,' she said, 'because the flood waters are coming up and we're not going to be able to get out for a couple of days. It's so flat here that when the river comes up, the water just sits there. We've got high tide in a few hours. This is when we get the big ones.'

'I can't send you a bill if you're flooded in,' I'd said.

'Well, email it to me then.'

'I didn't mean that. I don't want to send you a bill with all this going on. We'll talk in a week or so when the water's settled.'

I began mentally sifting through all the information I had. *Okay, so I know it flooded severely last week. And the river is affected by seawater because she told me about the influence of the tides. I wonder if the saltwater's got anything to do with this. What does salt toxicity look like in a cow?* I had no idea. I'd never dealt with salt toxicity before because we live in a wet area and the problem was more associated with droughts. I'd heard about it in other animals in other districts, and I saw no reason why a cow couldn't suffer from it too.

Salt toxicity occurs when animals that have been very thirsty get access to a lot of water and guzzle it. It also gets called 'water poisoning'.

It was time to get back to the job at hand which was to rehydrate these cows. I had to fill the buckets and pump the water into them through a tube. Cows need a lot of fluid. Their rumen capacity is about 180 litres.

I grabbed some blood samples from the worst-affected cows and gave them some painkillers. Then we let them out of the crush to rejoin the herd.

'As it turns out,' I said to Todd, 'your neighbour's having a problem as well. It doesn't sound like they're related but you never know. Where have you been grazing your cows?'

'That's interesting because I've had them down on that Wonga Park fenceline for the last couple of days. They go down there for the day, then come back here to get milked in the afternoon.'

'What sort of fresh water do you have down there?'

'They pass water troughs on the way up to be milked. Then they go to another paddock overnight which has got those big troughs. Then they go back to the bottom during the day.'

'Okay. Interesting. I'm going to duck over there now and see what's going on.'

I jumped in the car and straightaway called the associate professor of bovine medicine at Sydney Uni, John House. Even though the properties adjoined each other, it was a fifteen-minute drive from one gate to the next so I knew I had time.

'John, what does salt toxicity look like in a cow?'

'Why?'

I told him what I was seeing and what James had told me he'd seen.

'Absolutely,' John said. 'What you're seeing is a mild case where they get a bit of gastric irritation. They can tremor. Usually they'll recover. With the worst cases, their brains swell and they become comatose and can seizure and die. That sounds like what James is seeing.'

'What's the treatment?'

'Depends how badly affected they are. If they're very profoundly affected, the treatment is salty solutions in decreasing concentrations. The real risk is if they're incredibly loaded with salt, their brains will shrink and then if you give them a whole heap of fresh water the brain quickly swells to a great size and the pressure in the brain will cause the seizuring and death. They don't die from the salt toxicity, they die from the consequent drinking of fresh water when they get access to it.'

'Right. That's perfect. That fits. Todd's cows had been down on the salty flats for half the day. So they might be loaded up with salt but they were getting more access to fresh water.'

'Yes,' John said 'that's going to nullify the problem.'

Wonga Park, on the other hand, had the cows out in the paddock all day because they weren't milking. And they might have been cut off from the water troughs by the flood and so had nothing to drink but the briny water surrounding them.

I called James.

'I think I know what's wrong with your cow.'

YEAH, WELL THAT MAKES SENSE

James

When Anthony told me he thought it was salt toxicity, I was dubious. For a start, he was up at the dairy on a hill next door, but when I looked over, I saw that the back of Todd's place came down onto the flats adjacent to Wonga Park. *Okay, there might be something in this.*

Salt toxicity and water toxicity are the same thing. I'd only seen it once before: when I was fresh out of uni, working at Barraba in northern New South Wales. The owners of one of the best merino ram producing properties in Australia had rung to say sixty of their sheep had just dropped dead. This was a place that often sold rams for $5000, so it was a big deal.

Whenever you get a call to go out and see multiple deaths in a herd or flock, it's a scary phone call. All that's going through your head is, *Why are they dying?* There are so many possibilities. And you know that it's all up to you to find the cause. Your success or failure can affect the very survival of a farm.

To digress a bit further, I had one guy who came home late one night to find eighteen dead cows in a paddock. He rang at 2 a.m.

'Can you come and have a look?'

I went and did a post-mortem but was none the wiser by 3 a.m. when I found myself helping him herd the remaining cows out of the paddock in case they'd eaten some toxic weed or picked up a killer virus from sniffing around the dead bodies. So I went to bed dumbfounded and worried. Next morning, the farmer called me at 7 a.m.

'Don't worry. I've figured it out.'

'What was it?'

'It's arsenic.'

In the cold light of day, he saw that the cows had pushed out the corrugated iron on the side of the shearing shed and got in under it where some old drums of arsenic had leaked out. I tested the blood samples I'd taken the previous night and they were sky high with the poison.

Case closed.

But whenever you get these calls, you worry.

So I rocked up to the home of this prize-merino stud and said, 'What's the problem?'

The owner pointed over towards two troughs about 100 metres away. The dead bodies were littered around the troughs in two rough circles. It was as though the troughs had been filled with arsenic.

I could see that there were also a lot of other sheep on the far side of the paddock that looked okay, plus a few that looked wobbly.

My mind was racing. I was packing death. So much was at stake. I examined the sheep but could see no obvious cause. The owner told me that there'd been some trouble with the troughs earlier in the day so the sheep had been without water, but they'd got it back on before any of them started to show any sign of trouble.

I had nothing.

I rang the district vet. It was his job to investigate disease outbreaks in production animals. He picked up, thankfully.

'Ah, I've got sixty dead sheep around some troughs that had been off, then turned back on. They'd also had some salt blocks put out for them. They're just piled up around the troughs. Dead. Could it be something wrong with the water?'

'Nup, I'll tell you exactly what it is.'

This is good, I thought. Is this guy magic or something?

'Water toxicity,' he said.

'What?'

'They've got sky-high salt levels, they get super-duper thirsty, so they've gorged themselves on water when the trough's been turned back on and their brains have swollen and they've died.'

It was one of those great times when you call the right person at the right time and they just give you the answer.

But here at Wonga Park, I didn't initially see the connection between this dry-country problem and our post-flood lush, green paddocks. Fortunately, I'd anticipated needing some help, so I'd thrown the cattle textbook into the car in the morning. I pulled it out and read up on salt toxicity and everything started to correlate.

Anthony was like the district vet all over again. This one phone call had the answer. We still had to prove it, though. I phoned Chris back at the clinic and got him to test last night's blood sample for sodium.

He got back to me soon after. The sodium levels were sky high. It was walking and quacking like a duck. The acting manager had, by this time, got the other affected cows into the yard and I tested those. Some had high salt levels, but most didn't. The manager took us for a drive on the back of the Gator, a farm vehicle that's like an all-terrain golf buggy. It was like riding on a hovercraft. Even paddocks that looked dry from a distance were sodden once the Gator got into them, sending out a little bow wave as we slipped and slid about, dodging the detritus – branches, trees, old footballs and tyres – that had been dropped by the falling waters.

Crucially, what we also saw was salt encrusted on the high-water marks, indicating quite clearly that sodium chloride was at play in this case.

The acting manager confirmed that the ten sick cows were the ones that had been stuck away from the feed pad and had the least access to fresh water. It was all fitting together.

We got Chris to come and pick up the blood samples so they could test the sodium levels back at the clinic. Anthony had a lot of samples from the dairy next door so we gave him those too. They would prove that the illnesses were linked across the two farms. When Chris rang back, however, it didn't quite go to plan.

'Don't know what you were expecting to see, but the sodium levels in these samples are normal,' he said.

It was time to speak to Associate Professor House again.

'The sodium is normal in most of these animals. Do you have any other ideas what's making them sick?'

'No, that's all to be expected. It's still going to be salt toxicity. Once they've drunk fresh water their blood sodium equilibrates quickly. The salt drives the thirst but the water gets absorbed into the blood very quickly. You're only going to see the elevated levels in the animals that have not had access to fresh water.' So we knew we were still on the money.

This brought us back to that very first very sick cow. She was on her side. Her eyes were rolled back. Her legs were 'paddling' like she was walking quickly in an imaginary field. I had treated her with fluids and painkillers, but she hadn't responded.

By this time we knew that she wasn't going to get better because once her brain had swollen and been compressed inside the skull, she had almost certainly suffered profound damage. It was unlikely she would recover, but it would also take days for her to die if we let nature take its course. So we had to euthanase her with a lethal injection.

Despite the fact we were pretty certain of what was wrong with her, we still needed to do a post-mortem to confirm it. For that, we had to rule out other causes of death and we had to collect brain samples to send away for analysis. For most farms we wouldn't have gone to such lengths. We would have said that the symptoms fitted the diagnosis and the evidence of the salt on the flats. And that the same thing had happened to the neighbour. But because the ramifications of the diagnosis are so large in an operation of this size, we had to go to all lengths to prove it. Plus the blokes who were riding around with us in the Gator were not the owners. They needed reports and a piece of paper saying definitively what it was and how to prevent it in future.

A cow post-mortem is relatively easy once you know the technique. You always open the chest first because it's the most sterile cavity. You cut the ribs with those long-armed secateurs you use for pruning the garden. You follow the line of that cut with a knife, cutting the flesh and a few more ribs. Once you know what you're doing, you can open an animal very quickly.

Then you open the abdomen. It's smelly and foul. The rumen is full of putrid bacteria so you leave that bit to the end. The most dreaded bit in most vets' minds, however, is getting the brain out of the animal, because in cattle it is encased in an enormous bony shell, a bit like a safe. They don't have particularly large brains. You can't blast them out with dynamite. Well you could, but it wouldn't be much good for analysis. You've got to be delicate. Every time you do a post-mortem, you think, 'Do we really need the brain for this one?' And we knew in this case the answer was yes. So we opted for an angle grinder to cut the skull. It sounds barbaric, but it's actually quite a good way to cut the casing, lift it off and get to the brain.

The farm manager had been keen to hang around and watch the post-mortem. He was a country guy who'd seen most things. He had plenty of intelligent questions to ask about what we were doing, but once it came to cutting the cow's brain out with an angle grinder, he excused himself and went and had a smoke.

Once you've got the brain out, you cut it into sections because you need a one-to-three ratio of tissue to the preservative formalin to make sure it preserves. But we didn't need an awful lot. The lab just needed to look at the cells to see if they'd swollen.

After Anthony's very busy morning, he rang Todd to tell him all about our detective work. He explained that we'd nailed the problem down to salt toxicity and so he shouldn't be having too much trouble from here on in.

'Yeah, well that makes sense, doesn't it,' he said.

ENDURANCE RIDES

Anthony

The race began at midnight and it was my job to watch the horses go out the gate, shooting white mist from their nostrils as they trotted into the winter night all charged up and fizzy from their extra rations of oats and barley. It was the NSW championship endurance ride at Woodstock, in central western NSW, and I was one of four vets whose job over the next twenty-four hours was to look after the horses' welfare. They had to travel 160 kilometres consisting of four legs of forty kilometres in a kind of clover-leaf-shaped course. They were to return to the central point after each leg to rest and for us vets to determine whether they were fit to continue.

It was bitterly cold at the witching hour when I saw the horses off and afterwards there was nothing left for me to do but to return to my tent and the warmth of my sleeping bag, still with my beanie and gloves on. The first horses were due back sometime after 3 a.m., so sleep was a somewhat pointless exercise, which was just as well because I was too cold to sleep. I lay there wondering how I'd ever let myself get dragged into this sport.

It was my old boss Geoff Scarlet's fault. He'd vetted many endurance rides over the years, but by 2005 when he was asked to do a small ride at Wandandian, thirty kilometres south of Berry, he'd had enough and passed the torch to me. In endurance rides, the role of the vet has been formalised into the process, like the umpire in a cricket game. Horses have to be checked before, during and after the race and they have to pass a set of criteria before they can be allowed to continue or, indeed, to be declared winner.

For example, if a horse crosses the line first but its heart rate is over sixty beats per minute after thirty minutes of rest (a sign of physiological stress), that horse is declared unfit to continue and ruled out of the race, even when it's already finished. If the vet has listened to the horse's gut and heard none of the healthy sounds of digestion, it will also be ruled out. Same if it is limping. They have to finish fit and well enough to be considered capable of going back out there to do it all again.

This is great for the horses, but it puts the vet under pressure because the fitness of a horse can be a grey area. Some owners and riders will disagree with the vet's call, leading to tensions that the vets just don't need. They're out there giving up their weekends to facilitate other people's fun, and they get burnt by the process.

So that's how Geoff came to tip me into the Wandandian ride, but it was small, local and fun. I found that the owners were just as concerned with the horses' welfare as I was. If anything, if I started to question a horse's fitness, they would withdraw it before I ruled it out. They just didn't want to take any risks with their beloved pets. I grew to love the people and their animals and getting out into the bush on my weekends off, even though I didn't have many to spare. So I kept putting my hand up to vet more rides.

I'd find myself in a clearing in a forest sloping down to a river or up against an escarpment protected from the winds in these unbelievably beautiful spots. You'd see the horses off all bristling and frisky and they'd return forty kilometres later all flat and docile. They'd pretty much let you cut their legs off by that point, but they were sound and fit to continue after a rest.

Most horse sports involve a lot of money. From thoroughbred racing to equestrian and polo, there aren't a lot of battlers involved. But endurance riders could pick up a good horse for $5000. I found it refreshing to hear people tell me how they'd bought a horse for next to nothing and had worked it up over six months. The riders were in tune with their animals and very knowledgeable. At the higher end of the sport, there's more on the line and people get antsy, as I learned when I started to go further afield to do bigger rides. I found myself in a few nasty arguments. But on the whole, I just loved the people, their integrity and their full-of-beans horses.

So here I was in my sleeping bag at Woodstock. At 3 a.m., it was almost a relief to have to get up and get active. With this event, the horses came off the track and had to pass the vetting before they went for a rest. In other rides, they get a thirty-minute break before vetting. So as those first horses came through, we were seeing horses that were more tired than usual. The riders were tired too. And we were vetting on the same criteria as if they'd had a thirty-minute rest.

I was busy but it all went smoothly. As always, a few horses got ruled out with limps or overly elevated heart rates, but the riders took it well. By the time the last horses came through, the first horses only had an hour or so before they were due back from their second leg, so there was barely enough time to grab a coffee.

The sun rose to burn off the frost, and we gradually shed our layers until by the middle of the day we were down to short sleeves and the horses were lathered and thirsty.

The leading horses were coming back from their third leg when one of the older riders, a woman in brown riding pants and a checked shirt, came through leading a bay mare.

'This horse is not right,' she said. 'I don't know what it is, but there's something wrong with her.'

I had a quick look at the horse, an Arab-thoroughbred cross, seventeen hands, which was a big horse for endurance rides.

'What have you noticed?' I asked.

'She's not performing. Her name's Cleopatra, and she's a great horse. But she won't respond to my commands like she normally does, will you, Cleo?' The rider, whose name I would later learn was Sue, gave the mare a gentle rub on the jowls. 'She'll only walk and she won't drink on track. She usually loves a drink on track. She's not eating either. It's not right.'

I knew that the riders tended to be highly attuned to their animal's performance. Sue was wiry and fit, with the look of someone who'd been around horses all her life. I had no reason to doubt her assessment so I expected the horse to fail my test.

I listened to Cleopatra's heart. The standing heart rate of a fit horse is around thirty to thirty-five beats per minute. This one was forty-four, which was well below the cut-off point for the event. I also listened for irregularities in the pulse, which could be a sign of trouble, but Cleopatra's heart was beating like a metronome. I listened to her chest for rasping lungs but they were all clear. I pressed my finger into her jugular and watched how quickly the vein filled. If it was slow, I'd know the horse was dehydrated. But the vessel filled with a bulging certainty. I listened to Cleo's gut for the tinkling, gurgling noises of the stomach. You want to hear a good strong gurgle in the background with the occasional loud tinkling on top. If you hear nothing, it indicates a serious problem. While this horse had reduced noise, it was still within an acceptable range. I looked at Cleopatra's skin tone, I took her temperature and lastly I had Sue walk her out and back so I could check her gait, but there was no sign of a limp.

Cleopatra was clearly tired, but all the horses were tired and that's not a criteria for ruling them out.

'The good news is she's fit to continue,' I announced. 'The bad news is I can't tell you what's causing the problem you suspect. But if you think she's not right, you should consider not going back out.'

'Yeah,' Sue said, 'I'll take her back for my thirty-minute break and I'll make a decision then.'

'That's a good idea. She might just need a rest and a feed.'

One of the rules of endurance riding is that the riders are not allowed to administer any veterinary assistance themselves. No needles, no tubes, no IV lines. But there's always the suspicion among the vets that there are home remedies going on out of view of everybody. One of the most common problems is colic (severe gut pain), mainly because in endurance riding, blood that would normally be used for powering digestion gets diverted to the muscles. Also, horses are designed to trickle feed – to eat constantly through the day and not go for long spells without eating – but they are ridden for so long in these races that they barely get a chance to pick at anything and their guts begin to slow down. When they get back into camp they might be exhausted and just stand around doing nothing, so they get a very high incidence of colic. Their guts basically shut down, causing a lot of pain, sometimes leading to death. So there are a lot of remedies surrounding this problem, none of which make much scientific sense. One guy who was one of the big personalities of the sport – very opinionated but very nice – told me that the best treatment for colic was marijuana.

'I have no training in that field,' I said. 'I don't know why it would be any good.'

'Mate, trust me. It works,' he said.

'Even if it does, how do you feed it to a horse that's not eating? I doubt they'd like the taste.'

'It's simple. You just roll a joint, breathe it in and cover one of the horse's nostrils, then you blow it out into the other nostril.'

This guy did not strike me as a pothead type. He was a serious contender. I could see how his delivery method could work, though, because horses can't breathe through their mouths. They are what we call obligate nose breathers.

'Don't you get stoned yourself?' I asked.

'Oh, no, I'm like Bill Clinton. I don't inhale.'

I never saw it happen. All these things are done on the lowdown. Anybody caught doing such a thing would be expelled from the ride and face further suspensions from the sport. But you never knew exactly what went on in the float or at night.

Anyway, I digress, because there was never any suggestion that such a thing might have happened here. About fifteen minutes after I'd passed Cleopatra as sound, Sue's husband, Richard, came belting up to the vet station. The first thing I noticed was the worry on his face.

'Someone better get over here quickly. Cleopatra's gone down. She's rolling around in pain. Sue is trying to get her up,' he said. 'But she almost got kicked. I can't get her to come away from the horse. She loves it so much. You'd better bring a Valium for her as well.'

Crikey, what's going on? I wondered. *Have I missed something?*

Before going to see Cleopatra, I went back to the book because hundreds of horses had gone through already that morning and they all tended to blur very quickly in your mind. I checked the book and read my notes: *heart rate normal, hydration normal, gut sounds reduced but okay.* All right. So another vet, Darien Feary, and I took off at a jog to Sue's little camp on the flank of the base station.

Sure enough, Cleopatra was rolling around in the little electric-fence yard, sweating and in obvious distress. I took her by the halter and coaxed her back to her feet to start examining her. She was agitated and unsettled. Usually, after a hard morning's work like she'd just been through, a horse would be head down and quiet. But she was moving about, with her head dropping down and around as she looked at her belly trying to figure out what was hurting so much down there.

It wasn't hard to pinpoint the problem. In the twenty minutes since I'd examined her last, Cleopatra's gut sounds had completely stopped, and her heart rate had shot up to sixty, indicating that she was in a lot of pain.

'Look, she's obviously got colic,' I told Sue. 'We need to treat her and it's going to have ramifications for her down the track.' Once a horse has had an interventional treatment, there's a mandatory rest period of around six weeks. So you have to tell the owners because it's going to influence how they proceed.

'We don't care,' Sue said, the strain marked in her furrowed forehead. 'We want the best for her. Whatever she needs. We don't care if we never ride her again.'

With that permission, I put my thumb on Cleopatra's jugular groove until the vein swelled as big as my thumb. I jammed a needle into it and quickly put my thumb over it before too much blood squirted out. I attached a syringe and injected a sedative with pain relieving properties directly into the vein.

'Okay, we'll see what happens,' I said. 'That should make her comfortable at least for the next forty minutes to an hour. The hope is that we'll make her comfortable until the pain passes and after she's had a bit of a rest the gut will get itself going again.'

Cleopatra calmed down pretty fast. I stood there chatting to the owners, trying to keep them calm too. Unfortunately, I wasn't able to give them the sedative they clearly needed. The other vet, Darien, went back to her normal vetting while I stayed to observe Cleo. I took her heart rate again and it had steadied back into the forties.

Sue chatted about the ride and how bright Cleopatra had been through the morning, but, fifteen minutes after I administered the painkiller that should have lasted forty minutes to an hour, the horse started to appear weak at the knees again. She was looking at the ground, which is what they do before they get down and roll around. They want to check out the landing spot. And she was looking at her belly again too. It was an indication that the pain was back.

We call it 'breakthrough' – where you've given them what should be adequate relief but the pain is so strong it breaks through that barrier. It's a really bad sign.

'I'm going to have to take Cleopatra over to the hospital to do some more treatment,' I said. 'The painkiller hasn't worked and that's a problem.'

We took her over to our little hospital yard but Cleo was in all sorts of distress, trying to collapse. It's a bit of a truism in the vet world that when a horse wants to go down, it's ready to die. We gave her more IV painkillers straight into the jugular.

Her heart rate was back up into the sixties and she was sweating – as were the owners and I. We all knew Cleopatra's life was in the balance now. And while we knew it was colic, we didn't know what was actually causing the problem. A diagnosis of colic doesn't tell you any more than a diagnosis of 'gut ache' would in a human.

For now though, I just had to manage the symptoms and nurse this horse through the crisis. I threaded a tube through her nose down to her stomach. Horses can't vomit so if they get a build-up of fluid or gas it can burst the stomach. But if you push a tube down through the sphincter in their stomach, it can relieve the pressure. When I got the tube through, however, nothing much came back out of it. But that was okay; at least it meant the stomach wasn't about to burst.

With the tube in place, I put a funnel on the end and got Sue to pour in six litres of electrolyte fluids to rehydrate her. Cleopatra needed anti-inflammatory painkillers but they're risky with endurance horses because they can damage their kidneys. You've got to be very judicious with them, so I gave her half the normal dose. Earlier, Darien had got a catheter into her neck so we rigged up IV fluids to that. We'd done just about all we could. Cleopatra appeared a little calmer and her heart rate dropped. All we could do was hope.

I remained with her, though, making sure she stayed on her feet. All looked good for a while, but twenty-five minutes after the second dose of painkillers, she started pawing at the ground trying to collapse, looking weak at the knees again. Sue was with me, a firm grip on the halter, walking her round the yard, patting her jowls.

'Come on girl. Stay up.' She jerked the halter around while Cleo looked at her with sad drooping eyes.

I was on her flanks slapping her a bit harder. 'Come on. Get up! Get up!'

As we harassed poor Cleo around the yard, I explained to Sue that horses' stomachs and intestines are very loosely organised in their abdomen. 'So if they go down and roll when they're in this inflamed state, it can all twist up on itself and, bang, that's it. Dead horse. The act of walking them doesn't do anything therapeutic. It just stops them doing further damage.' What I omitted to say was that walking the horse also keeps the owner occupied.

Cleopatra wanted to lie down so badly. She wanted to die. She was trying to switch off to the world. Horses are flight animals. They don't stand and fight. They run, and they run some more. That's why they're so good at racing. When an animal that is hard-wired like that says, 'You know what, I'm just going to sit down with all these strange people around,' they're saying they'd rather be dead. 'Let the wolves come and get me.'

I was mindful that the pain relief we had given her was only masking the pain and even then it was failing. It certainly wasn't fixing whatever the problem was. A horse's stomach has an unusually high number of nerves going to it. So if there's pain there, they feel it ten times worse than a human or a dog would.

Cleopatra was in so much pain we suspected something catastrophic had happened deep inside her. Perhaps she'd torn or twisted some of her bowel. We ramped up the pain relief even more to a dose that in a normal situation would last three or four hours. We increased the rate of flow of the IV fluids till they were running at emergency rates. We put a second catheter in the other side of her neck so we could run fluid in as fast as possible. I put another tube back down her nose and gave her more fluid and electrolytes that way. Then I put on the long glove and lube and put my hand in her rear end to feel around for something out of place there: a piece of gut or bowel full of gas; a hard blockage somewhere; or a knot. I groped around in the warm slipperiness of the abdomen but could feel nothing out of place. The only unusual thing I could come up with was a lack of faecal balls. There was no poo waiting to come out. I feared there might be an obstruction further upstream.

My examination, though, was limited by the size of the horse relative to the length of my arm. There was only so far that I could reach. In cases like these, there is always a feeling that we are flying blind and just hoping for the best. We were limited in what we could do out in the field and it was coming to the point where, if this horse was going to survive, it had to go to hospital. Often, the only way to find out what is wrong is to open the horse up to look inside.

You have to be careful when and how you start discussing referral to a hospital. It can freak clients out. They'll say, 'Why are you referring us? Why can't you fix it? This must be so serious, she's going to die.' And once the client is thinking that, it's just a step away from them thinking that you're thinking, *It's so bad we want you to go off and die somewhere else.* Emotions come into play and spiral out of control. I've seen it happen a lot, but luckily Sue and Richard were an older, sensible couple and they understood what was going on. The closest hospital was Canberra Equine, about two and a half hours away. The concern was that Cleopatra would go down in the float and writhe around, damaging not just her guts, but also her legs and joints.

I didn't see that we had much choice, however.

'If she stays here she's going to die. We've done what we can do.'

'Whatever you think is best,' Sue said to my relief. 'You've got to consider it's going to cost $10,000 minimum for surgery,' I said. 'And they're going to expect that money up front. They're not going to cut your horse open without that money being paid. And it's a long weekend. We don't like to talk about money, but if you go there, that's what you've got to be prepared to do. And if you're not prepared to go through with that, there's not a lot of point getting on the float and risking the horse on the road.'

So they had a little confab and came back quickly.

'That's fine,' Sue said. 'If it's $10,000 or $15,000 we can deal with it. Cleo is worth it. But first, let's just see what happens with this last lot of treatment you've given her.'

'Okay, we'll see what happens,' I said. 'Fingers crossed.'

So we stood and watched poor Cleopatra. There were catheters sticking out of her, tubes down her nose. She'd had hands up her bum. She'd been stabbed many times. She was looking understandably sorry for herself. She was still on her feet, but if we weren't there giving encouragement, she would have been down and writhing long ago.

With nothing left to be done, I went back to my normal vetting duties until, about forty minutes after the last big round of painkillers, Richard came running back to the vetting ring.

'She's down again,' he said. 'Her knees just buckled and there wasn't anything we could do about it.'

It's always confronting to walk into a stable to see a horse sitting on its front legs like a dog, just looking at you with its head extended. It's a vastly abnormal way for a horse to behave. And that's what Cleopatra was doing. She was going to die, I was sure.

'I think you'd better go,' I said. 'I think she probably won't make it but if you're going to have any chance of saving her, you've got to get there as quickly as you can because something major is happening.'

'Right. Let's go,' Richard said.

All the stops were pulled out. They had to pack up their camp, including pulling down yards, dismantling the tent and loading all their gear. In a whirlwind of activity people pitched in to help while Sue and I and a few others worked to get Cleopatra back on her feet and onto the float.

Just before they left, I handed Sue some more painkillers.

'If she goes down in the float, inject this into the muscle. It's not the ideal route but it's better than nothing. Then just go. Don't stop again. Get there as quickly as you can. If they have to drag her off with a crane, so be it.'

As they pulled away down the rutted track in their battered Landcruiser, which had clearly done a lot of miles, I called ahead to notify Canberra Equine that a horse was on its way, telling them what we'd seen, what we'd done, and that we thought the horse needed urgent surgery just to diagnose what was happening.

I went back to my normal duties. I had been on this mad emotional roller coaster trying to fix Cleopatra and failing, followed by the rush to package her up on the float while all the other competitors and spectators wanted to know what was going on. And while all that was happening, the race was hotting up and the other competitors were dealing with their own dramas, vying for the state championship. They weren't tolerant of a vet being off their game so I had to get my head back into gear.

There were 150 horses in the ride, all staggered out by now, but horses like to run in packs so they bunched up. Ten horses would come in at once and there'd be a rush to get everyone through. When there was a break in the traffic, I pulled my phone out to call Sue.

'She's still standing. I can see her in my sun-visor mirror,' she reported.

'Excellent. Let us know if anything happens.'

I called her a few more times and it was almost surprising each time she told me the same thing – Cleopatra was still on her feet.

About three hours after they left, my phone rang and I could see it was Sue.

Here we go, I thought. *This is bad. She should be in Canberra by now. She must be calling to tell us the horse is dead.*

'You're not going to believe this,' she said, 'but Cleo has just walked off the float, done a huge crap and hoed into her hay, hungry as a church mouse.'

'Huh?'

I couldn't say anything more. I was stunned into silence. Sue filled the void.

'The vets had a quick look at her and said everything was fine. They're keeping her in for observation, but they're not worried.'

It was the classic case of the therapeutic car ride to the vet. We often get calls about animals in great distress at home, but by the time they get to the clinic there's nothing wrong.

The movement on the float had kept Cleopatra alert and on her feet which gave her enough time for her system to get itself working again. The defecation indicated that things had started moving again. We'd hoped that would happen while we were treating her several hours earlier back at base camp, but the extra two hours of stimulation on the float did the trick. There's every possibility that if we hadn't put her on the float, she would have stayed down and died.

Nevertheless, I felt like an idiot getting everyone on high alert: the owners, the vets in Canberra. They'd called in nurses on the long weekend, all sharpening scalpels ready to dive in for this big emergency only to be greeted by a strapping, shining, pooing mare getting off the float.

I apologised to Sue and Richard.

'Don't be stupid,' Sue said. 'It was amazing what you did and we're very happy.'

A new bunch of horses was coming in to finish the race, lathered in sweat, puffing in the warmth of the afternoon sun. I said goodbye to Sue and went back to vetting. As I waved another through, I realised that I had a great big smile on my face.

RAMMING IT HOME

James

Coming to Berry meant that I took over Geoff Manning's slot at the Easter Show, and wasn't that a great eye opener. I loved the privilege of hanging out with some of the best vets in the country and seeing all the prestigious livestock. Not to mention the lively conversation of the Members' Bar after the animals were put to bed.

I was treating up to thirty or forty beef cows and bulls with another vet until the beef events finished and they all got put on trucks and left. There was a day and a half before the dairy cattle turned up. As the cattle vet, you have to look after all the other animals for which there is not a specific vet – sheep, goats, alpacas, pigs – and if the poultry vet or the horse vet is missing, they call the cattle vet. Cattle vets are usually from a mixed-practice background so we tend to have the most adaptable skills.

In that day between the beef and the dairy, there was only one cattle vet rostered on. Me. There were still a few cows around the place, in the display dairy and a few other parts, but not many. So I was looking forward to using the quiet time to have a look around the show, see the district display, maybe even go on a roller coaster. Early in the morning, though, I got a call to see a sheep.

I put on my coat with its badge saying I was a vet, my hat and my tie. I doubt that an item more impractical for a vet than a tie has ever been invented. It's a beacon for any faecal material, urine, blood, guts and cats' paws. But you have to wear the full rural-gentleman clobber at the show whenever you're on display.

So I trotted off on my rounds thinking how I couldn't wait to get out and look at all the other pavilions. I'd been locked in the confines of the cattle vet's office and the cattle pavilion for the whole time I'd been there in conditions that are much like a prison. You feel like you're on day release when you get out. I reported in to the head vet.

'No cows today. I've just got the one sheep to see. So I'll be off to see that. If anyone needs me, I'll probably be in the sheep pavilion all day.'

That was a joke.

Sheep people don't tend to call vets. At the show there are a stack of sheep and I'm sure they get sick and have little problems but you wouldn't know about it because their owners just don't call vets. It's ingrained in sheep people – like my father – to do all their own doctoring. An individual sheep is worth far less than a visit to the vet so it's just not worth it for them. When a sheep is cut, it is stitched up by the shearer. When it is unwell, the farmer will try to fix it and if that doesn't work, the sheep dies. And sheep are famous for their enthusiasm for dying. All this permeates the graziers' thinking even when they're dealing with their most prized animals.

In the cattle pavilion, on the other hand, some of the cows are only worth a few thousand dollars, but their owners call the vet at the first cough. The cost of a consultation is only $30 so it's a bargain compared to the cost of getting a vet out at home.

So off I trotted into the unfamiliar world of the sheep pavilion and I was conscious of the stares from the sheep people tending their animals. I wouldn't say it was quite like the whole saloon going quiet as I walked through the swinging doors, the piano player stopping and all that, but it was heading in that direction as I wandered around, clearly identifiable as a practitioner of the veterinary sciences – crumpled linen jacket, stained tie, Akubra and bag.

'I'm looking for a guy called Simon,' I said to a young guy in moleskins and tweed.

I was pointed towards a tall, angular young bloke. Checked shirt, white pants, RM Williams boots. The proper uniform.

'G'day, Simon. How's it going?'

'Yeah, not too bad,' he said, looking me up and down. 'Do you know anything about bloody sheep? Where are you from?'

'Berry.'

'Don't reckon you'd see too many bloody sheep there. Ever seen one?'

'We see plenty of sheep. We probably see more sheep than the vets out your way, because all the sheep around Berry are treated like pets so the owners call us all the time.' Berry isn't known as a sheep area. It is too wet for serious wool production and the humidity contributes to worms, but the sheep that we do have are very well looked after.

I might have mentioned that I'd treated a stack of sheep when I worked in Wales and also a few when I'd worked at Barraba. Forgetfully, I neglected to mention the HC Belschner Prize for Wool and Sheep that I won at university (strange, because I rarely forget to mention that) but I did throw in that Mum and Dad ran sheep on their property at Bundarra, in northern NSW, so I'd seen a few in my time.

Simon started looking at me a little less scornfully when he realised I was a better-than-even-money chance of telling a sheep from a goat.

'So what seems to be the problem?'

'My ram over here is pissing blood.'

Simon showed me over to this animal and he was enormous – 110 kilograms. Possibly the biggest ram I'd ever seen. Rams are more commonly about seventy kilograms. The first thing I thought of was bladder stones, a fairly common problem of sheep and goats, particularly show animals, when they're fed a lot of rich feed. I could see the ram peeing, its discoloured urine dribbling to the floor like a slow leak. So I had a feel around his penis but couldn't find any stones lodged in there blocking up the works.

I gave him some anti-inflammatory pain relief and some relaxation – Valium. If you relax the spasm in the penis, you can often get the stones to pass. He looked more comfortable and he peed a better stream.

'This is good,' I said. 'Let's keep an eye on him. I'll come back and check him in half an hour.'

Simon was one of the premier exhibitors of the sheep world so anything he did was going to be of interest to his friends and competitors scattered about. While I was attending the ram, a small crowd had floated in, sceptically watching this vet character from the coast. As I readied to leave there were about a dozen of them circled about. One of them pulled me aside, almost on the quiet.

'I've got a problem with a ram over here. It's got a cut in its leg. You reckon you could have a look at that too?'

'No worries. I'm here.'

So I went over, had a look at the gash and told the farmer I was going to give it some antibiotics.

'I've already given it some of those.'

'Okay, what one did you give it?'

'Dunno. Got it from that feller over there and he's one of the best sheep blokes in Australia, so it'll be a good one.'

I tried to hide my horror as I flushed the wound. The farmer went off to survey his oracle on the other side of the shed and came back.

'It's oxytetrasomethingorother,' he said.

'Yeah, that's okay. I would have given it penicillin but that'll do the job. You should've just called. It's only thirty bucks for a consult.'

'Is it? That's bloody cheap. Woulda come and got you if I'd known that.'

'How much is this feller worth?' I asked.

'Oooh, dunno. Maybe two and half grand.'

'Two and a half grand! Makes thirty bucks sound pretty reasonable. You should just call us.'

'Yeah, I'll do that in the future.'

By this stage a new peanut gallery of about fifteen graziers had gathered around and I could see them all looking at each other. Thirty dollars. Who knew? There were some wrinkled leather faces and plenty of grey hairs among them and it was pretty apparent that none of them had ever bothered a vet at the show before.

I could see them calculating that maybe it'd be worth trucking in a few more animals to the next show for the vet to see. Thirty dollars was a showstopper.

I went back to check on Simon's enormous ram and it was still weeing the blood.

'I might get some of that urine and have a look at it,' I said. So I collected a sample and had a closer inspection. 'Hmmm. I'm not so sure about my bladder stones theory,' I said. 'I think this is actually myoglobin in the urine and not blood.'

This caused much rumbling from the gallery.

'What's myoglobin?' Simon asked.

'It's a protein found in muscle tissue and when it breaks down it gets peed out in the urine. A number of things can cause that. Poisons, being crushed in transit, problems of the muscle due to feed, water toxicity, salt toxicity. I think the most likely thing with this feller is that he's gone down in transit, or maybe there's been something in his feed.'

'What do we do about it?'

'Look, I'm pretty worried about his kidneys. I'd like to have a look at his bladder with an ultrasound and get that urine looked at in a laboratory.'

I made a phone call to Derek Major who is one of Australia's premier horse vets and was working at the show.

'Derek, have you got an ultrasound machine?'

'Yeah, I do.'

I flagged down a golf buggy being driven by a show staff member and jumped in it. Would have put the siren on if only we'd had one. We got Derek's ultrasound from his vehicle on the other side of the enormous showground and got it back to the sheep.

Simon tipped this 110-kilogram ram on its bum and I gave it an ultrasound. Its bladder looked normal. I couldn't see any stones.

'Okay, he's not obstructed,' I said. 'I think it's the myoglobin.'

It was a Sunday. No laboratory was open, but there was a small-animal hospital in a nearby suburb so I called them and asked if they'd look at this sample for me.

'No, sorry,' the person who picked up the phone said. 'We don't know anything about sheep. We can't do it.'

'But I just need you to run a urine dipstick and spin down some urine.'

'No, sorry, we don't know anything about sheep.'

'Can I speak to the vet, please?'

The vet came on and I explained to her that I just wanted a urine analysis.

'It'll take five minutes and it's very basic. Doesn't matter if it's a sheep, dog or cat.'

'Yeah, yeah. No problems.'

So I packed Simon's mother off with the sheep urine. The clinic was only a few kilometres away from where we were, but it was quite a convoluted route to get there.

The results came back and I found Simon again.

'Yeah, it is myoglobin in his urine. That's not good. It's going to damage his kidneys. We can do some stuff for him, but I guess it comes down to how much is he worth?'

Simon looked around and made sure that the peanut gallery were out of earshot. 'Put it this way,' he said on the quiet, 'his brother was the most expensive ram ever sold in Australia.'

'Holy shit! What did you get for him?'

'Forty thousand dollars.'

I almost fainted. 'So what's this one worth?' I said, gesturing towards our pinot-pissing friend.

'Not very much right now. Yesterday he was probably worth twenty-five.'

The attitude was so different from what it would have been in the cattle pavilion if an animal of that value had got sick. There's a fatalism about sheep people. 'What are you gunna do? Sheep die.'

Well, what I was gunna do was set up a little makeshift hospital between two shipping containers out next to the skate park behind the showground. We put the ram in a little pen and I had to climb up the skate ramp to hang the bags of IV fluids from the top of the shipping container, running an extension lead down to reach him. The fluids were to help flush his kidneys from the damage the myoglobin would be doing. He was in the makeshift hospital for a few hours before Simon got special dispensation to leave the show early and take him back home, out near Dunedoo.

I heard that the local vet came out to continue the treatment and the ram made a full recovery.

After people had seen me treat this famous ram and word had got around about the $30 consult fee, they started lining up. It became a sheep consultathon. I spent the whole day in the sheep pavilion. I kept having to dispense the drugs for them to take home

I'd say things like, 'You can just go into your vet at home and pick that up.'

'Don't have a vet. Never seen one.' Or, 'Our nearest vet's 400 kilometres away. I'm probably not going to call him out for some ointment. Have you got any in your truck?'

The following year I went back into the sheep pavilion and saw all the same people again. There are graziers who live 500 kilometres away from me but for whom I am now their vet. The only one they've ever seen.

FATSO

Anthony

The big bloke came to the door in well-worn fancy riding boots, a roll-your-own cigarette dangling from his lips. His big, wide hat was tilted forward like he was coming in to transact some serious business. Or star in a Marlboro cigarettes commercial.

'Fatso's crook,' he said, in a rugged country drawl.

This was big. I'd probably never treated a horse as famous as Fatso before.

'What's up with him?'

'He just wants to lie down. He's off his food.'

'Okay, we'd better go take a look.'

I was at the Berry Show, where, for the last twenty odd years, Fatso had established himself as an institution, albeit a tiny one. He was a thigh-high miniature horse with a long white mane that hung almost to the ground and a distinctive black and white spotty coat. Without the spots he would have been Julian Assange the horse. He was the most delightful animal. Bulletproof. You could tickle him under the chin and he'd just about roll over and play dead. A year or two earlier, when he was deemed too old to take kids for rides any more, his owners decided to keep him at home when they did the round of shows throughout our region. There was such a huge number of complaints and queries about his absence that the following year they brought him along as his own attraction. You couldn't ride him any more but you could pat him and have your photo taken with him.

So could your kids.

It had been a quiet day at the show. The biggest drama had been dealing with horses getting mascara in their eyes. (Some horse events are exhibitions of athleticism but others are beauty contests, and like all beauty contestants, the horses wear makeup.) So it was almost a relief to be dealing with the Marlboro man – whose name was Lachlan Sheldon – and a serious medical case. I checked Fatso over. There was no noise coming from his belly like there should be. His guts had stopped working. It was colic. Everything was just sitting there inside him. We moved him into the treatment stables, out of the way of the crowds, and I realised pretty quickly that Fatso was in trouble. His heart rate wasn't that high, which was good, but the zero gut sounds was a really bad sign. The gut had stopped working, but the fluids would still be secreting into his stomach and the bacteria in his gut would still be producing gas. So he was blowing up like a balloon. Nothing could move. He couldn't fart. Horses can't vomit.

Some horses get this stagnation in the gut following some sort of insult: an infection, stress, injury or overwork. Minis and Clydesdales – the smallest and the largest of horse breeds – are particularly prone to getting solid impacted balls in their guts. They could be calcified or just plain compressed balls of food and hair.

My first thought was of dread. *I hope this is not a repeat of Toby the miniature horse.* We'd had to put Toby down because of colic – on national television – only a month earlier.

There were no other vets there, so I was on my own. Just me and the film crew. I put Fatso on a drip, gave him IV fluids and pain relief, then tried to get a tube down his throat in the hope that it might get things moving.

It didn't.

I had the ultrasound with me so I was able to get a look into his gut and it was all incredibly dilated. All his bowel loops were expanded, which tended to back up my fears that there was a blockage in there.

'Mate, this looks very severe,' I said to Lachlan. 'I think he could die without an operation.'

He didn't say much at all to that. I was under the false impression that being a pragmatic country type, he would most likely want the horse put down, and probably wouldn't give it a lot of thought. But it appeared that while I knew this horse was a local celebrity, I was the only person in the shed who didn't appreciate just how huge little Fatso was.

Colic surgery is a big deal. It's fraught with danger, it's incredibly expensive and it takes a lot of effort. We don't do it at Berry and always refer the patients up to Sydney where only a few specialist surgeons will take it on. And they insist on the $10,000 fee up front. Otherwise they don't proceed.

The film crew had filmed the initial examination of Fatso but they'd finished their day and the producer, Tim, said, 'Let us know if anything transpires because we're going to head off.'

'Yeah, that's fine. Nothing's gunna happen with Fatso. The only thing we could do for him would be to operate and I can't do that here. And I'm going out to dinner with some old uni friends who've come down for the weekend.'

An hour later, one of those friends, Monique Haan, turned up with her husband, Fabio Pelosi, who happened to be a specialist horse surgeon. I walked him over to Fatso to see what he thought. While we were there, Andy Stewart, another university friend, who was now an equine medicine specialist, arrived. We'd barely had time to say hello to her when another of our classmates, Giselle Rousseau, now a highly regarded horse surgeon, entered the office.

The cavalry had arrived. It went from me running around wiping mascara off horses' faces, to a panel of vets of a calibre you wouldn't expect to find at a university. They all had a poke and a prod at sad old Fatso, and they all agreed he was in dire straits and was probably going to die unless we could pull something out of the bag.

We now happened to have two surgeons who'd spent their careers mending this problem.

'I've done four colic surgeries this week,' Giselle said. 'One per night. Wouldn't it be great if I could do another one tonight and that'd be five nights in a row. A record for me.'

But there was nothing the cavalry could do. It wouldn't be possible to operate at the show. We didn't have the gear. Fatso was stable on the IV fluids and pain relief. So off we went to dinner. Andy, the medicine specialist, was sitting next to me. She was tall, with a voice that was surprisingly quiet for someone with her level of experience. She worked at a university, and she dealt all the time with students, other specialists and ordinary vets like me who needed advice.

'We should just treat him medically,' she said. 'You've got to make sure you explore all the possibilities before diving into surgery.'

The two surgeon sat opposite us. Being surgeons, they had an attitude which sometimes got mocked within the profession – 'A chance to cut is a chance to cure.' Giselle, a brunette with dark brown skin, dark eyes and a strong will, was a very busy person. Always busy. Whenever you saw her, she was doing something purposefully.

Fabio was the funniest. He was tall, dark and Italian. 'I am a Tuscan first, an Italian second,' he would say with an accent that made women's hearts melt. Fabio was laid-back, yet incredibly accomplished. He graduated in Rome, but did his specialist study in Britain. So his English was very good but his accent was still strong.

'Yeah, we cut the horse. Is fine. Huh. Is good. Don't worry about it. It'll be okay. I'll fix it. Cut, cut.'

So the plight of Fatso dominated the conversation. Everybody was quite certain he was going to die. The surgeons were urging surgery and the medical specialist was urging patience along with more intensive medical therapy.

'It's all very well that we all know what's going to happen,' I said, 'but Lachlan and his family can't afford to send this horse off for colic surgery because they're going to be hit for $10,000.'

'Then we should do it here,' Fabio said.

I pointed out the lack of a surgery and the lack of rules permitting such a thing. It was out of the question.

'Is okay. Cut cut. We save the horse.'

'He's just not going to get better,' Giselle said. 'We have seen this so many times.'

'I just think we should give it a bit more time,' Andy said. 'It's incredibly risky. And how do you do it here? You don't have any equipment.'

'Come on. We cut, we save it,' Fabio said. 'We do it here. Cut, cut. Is done. Anthony has some scalpels, some anaesthetic, no.'

I tried to be the middle man. Fatso was my patient, but I was stuck between the rock of my friends' surgical abilities and the hard place of Andy's enormous medical knowledge.

'You have to remember that you could kill this horse with surgery,' I said.

'I will not kill this horse with surgery,' Giselle said, clearly insulted. 'I've done this hundreds of times. It's going to die anyway. And if it dies during surgery, it won't be because of anything we've done.'

'If you had a proper surgery it would be different, but you don't,' Andy said. 'It's madness to even be talking about doing it here.'

The conversation ping-ponged back and forth throughout dinner. But by the time the apple pie arrived the surgeons had gained the upper hand and by the time we left, the decision had almost been made.

We went back to the showground where we found Lachlan sitting quietly with Fatso in the treatment stables. Our voices automatically went quieter as we each explained our fears to him and that he needed to go to a university hospital. He saw no hint of the intense debate that had been raging just minutes earlier. It would have been unprofessional to discuss it in front of the client. They let me do the talking since I was the treating vet.

'Unfortunately, without surgery, the likelihood is he's going to die,' I said. 'We can maintain him on medical management overnight, fluids and pain relief, but it's not going anywhere good.'

Lachlan was in his late forties, a very experienced, quietly spoken horseman. He'd seen it all before and knew what we were saying was true.

'Okay, let me go and talk to Mum.'

It seemed strange hearing a bloke of that age, with his enormous physical presence, going and talking to Mum but his parents still owned all the animals and still had control of the purse strings. He went off and returned soon after.

'Look, I understand what's going on,' he said, seeming to take an eternity to get each word out, 'but we simply can't afford that kind of money on this horse. He doesn't work for us any more. You know, he's not a working horse. We can't justify it. I think we're going to have to think about putting him down. We're really upset. He means a lot to us. If we had the money, we'd spend it. But we don't.'

At that point I noticed movement at the station between the ears of my surgeon colleagues.

'If you're going to put him down, why don't we have a go at fixing him here,' Giselle said.

Once a client has said to you that they're electing to euthanase, it can be a green light to try something different. We could never have offered to operate on Fatso at the show. It wasn't set up for it. There were no facilities. No tables, no gear, nothing. But if you're standing around after dinner with a bunch of Australia's leading equine surgeons, why not give it a crack. We really wanted to save Fatso. He was a beautiful horse.

Andy already knew Lachlan from having treated his animals before, so they had a good relationship, but she showed professional restraint by not using that influence to lobby hard against the surgery. So I needed to put that to him.

'Mate, we're not set up for surgery here. Even in the best theatres there'd still be a fifty–fifty chance of him dying.'

I expected him to say that the odds didn't seem too good, but much to my surprise he said he'd go talk to Mum again. He came back soon after.

'Okay,' he said. 'Let's give it a crack. Fatso is real important to us. We trust you guys and if you're willing to do that for us, we'd really appreciate it.'

I looked behind me to take in the sick horse and … the stall was empty. Fatso had disappeared. Vanished. Momentarily it seemed like some sort of miraculous recovery and escape. Like he'd heard the talk of euthanasia and scarpered.

'Look. There he is,' Fabio said. We turned to see Andy disappearing into the darkness with Fatso on a lead. She'd taken the drip out and it looked to us like she was doing a runner to get poor Fatso out of the clutches of these crazy surgeons.

So the surgeons and I took off after them like the Keystone Cops.

'What's the go? You trying to save him from the evil surgeons?'

'No, no, look, I heard the way you guys were talking all gung-ho about diving in and cutting him open when we really don't have the set-up for it and I just thought we should trot him out and see if we could unblock him before we went down that road.'

'I think we have to cut,' Giselle said.

'So do I, Andy,' Fabio said.

'Well, I don't think we should just yet. I think we should explore our other options first,' Andy said.

They all turned to me.

'Well, what do you think, Anthony?' I knew that what Andy was saying was right. In some cases you can unblock the horse by taking them for a walk, or, like in my case at the endurance ride, putting them on a truck. But the surgeons were right too. It was time to act.

'What does it matter what I think?' I said. 'Crikey, you're the top guns. I'm just the local vet. But Andy, I've recently had a case just like this where the horse died and it probably would've survived with surgery, so if these guys think we should do it, I'd go with them.'

It was 11.30 p.m. We really shouldn't have been doing it. But we had to give it a go, because the alternative was to sit around and watch Fatso die.

The only equipment on hand was what I had in my ute.

'Okay, well, what have we got?' Giselle asked.

Because of the breadth of work we do as a country mixed practice, we keep a fair store of things in our cars. I had drip lines and anaesthetic, but only injectable anaesthetic which is not appropriate to put an animal out for longer than forty-five minutes. I had antibiotics and stitching material. I had sterile surgery kits, but not ones you'd do major surgery with, more the type you'd use to treat animals with cut legs. There was a good array of sterile gloves. We were missing some gear, but we had a lot of know-how. What could go wrong?

Fabio disappeared out into the show ring. He came back with one of the thick, blue pads from the side of the ring. The sort that stops riders being crushed against the wall by rampant bulls.

'Can you find two hay bales, Anthony?' Giselle said.

So I went and got some and Fabio placed them a little over a horse-width apart and put the rodeo padding on top of them. This was to be the operating table.

Fabio went searching for a couple of garden hoses which he connected together and ran from the nearest tap, which was out in the area where all the show people and carnies were camped.

'We might need flowing water,' he said. It didn't have a nozzle so he crimped the end before turning it on at the tap.

Giselle got a garbage bin and lined it with a fresh black garbage bag.

I went out and got a pallet, put it on its side and used it to hang up our drip bags and medications. Then we got all our kit sorted out. I had clippers to shave him. I had iodine and methylated spirits for sterilising the skin. What we didn't have enough of was sterile drapes to put over him. So the skin and hair were more exposed than in a normal surgery.

'Here goes nothing.'

It was 11.45 p.m. when we walked Fatso from his stable to what we were now calling the surgery room. He had his catheter in his neck, so we gave him the sedative and the anaesthetic and he promptly fell to the ground. The clock was now ticking. The anaesthetic was only good for forty-five minutes. And we weren't even sure it was going to have him out for that long.

We took a hold of one leg each and lifted his 150-kilogram body onto the rodeo padding with his feet in the air. The padding then sank between the two hay bales, acting as supports on either side of him to keep him on his back.

'Anthony, can you get me four of those long preg-testing gloves?' Giselle asked. I ran and got them and she put them over each of Fatso's feet to stop the dirt falling into the sterile zone. So there was the celebrity horse on his back with these four hands waving to us. I had to laugh, despite the urgency.

Andy ran the anaesthetic and I ran the surgery room. The surgeons prepared themselves for surgery while I clipped his abdomen, sterilised it and rummaged around for everything because I was the only one who knew where everything was.

They were soon ready to go and Fabio made a huge, lightning-fast incision down Fatso's belly. Good surgeons don't muck around. There's no 'little bit here, little bit there'. They're confident. They know how hard to push. How big the cut has to be.

With the abdomen now opened, they both plunged their gloved hands in, feeling up to their elbows, swirling the innards about like washerwomen scooping deep into a tub. 'Where's the problem? Where's the problem?' It only took about ten seconds to find.

'Okay, I've got it,' Giselle said. 'It's the caecum.' The caecum is a pouch between the large and small intestines, towards the back of the bus. Its primary job is to absorb water.

Fabio reached over and had a feel. Together they lifted the whole caecum out of the horse and laid it on the side. It was the width of rugby ball, perhaps even wider, and about three times the length. I thought we were looking for something the size of a rockmelon, not this almost-metre-long megalith.

'Right, get the garbage bin over here now, and the hose,' Fabio said.

'What's going on?' I wondered. 'What are they going to do? They can't chop it out. It'll take an enormous cut.'

The caecum is a blind passageway, like a dead-end alley off the bowel. The ingested food comes down the bowel into the caecum, the water gets absorbed and the dried food matter gets pushed out through the same hole it came in, like if you drove into a dead-end street in the left lane, did a U-turn then exited from the left lane going the other way. It's only pushed out by peristalsis, the natural squeezing of the gut. But because Fatso had no peristalsis, there was no emptying occurring. No U-turns were being made and all the traffic had just piled up in there till it was squashed in like it had been through one of those wrecking-yard crushers.

Fabio lifted the blind end of the caecum into the garbage bin and before I knew it, he'd slashed the end of it with a deft stroke of the scalpel.

'Get the hose. Stick it in that hole in the caecum and turn it on.'

'What are we doing?'

'We're flushing it out.'

I turned on the hose while Giselle massaged the caecum. Dark green matter started to come away. Grass, hay and hair. It was incredibly

270

contaminated with bacteria so we had to direct it away from Fatso's open abdomen. Before long, the garbage bin was full and overflowing. The dark green mat of goop spread across the floor until eventually the caecum started running clear.

All the while, Andy was worrying about the anaesthetic.

'How long is this going to be? This is not good. I think he's too deep…. I think he's too shallow.'

We knew we were racing the clock and we were going as fast as we could. Periodically, we'd hear little worried sighs coming from her up at the horse's head, letting us know of her concerns.

Fabio quickly stitched the caecum with an overlapping watertight pattern. The outside of the caecum was washed off with the tap water. Totally inappropriate for the job, but it was all we had. Fabio and Giselle then stitched like human sewing machines, each starting at different ends and meeting in the middle as they pulled the muscle layer, the subcutaneous layer and the skin back together.

With the stitching done, Fatso got pumped full of antibiotics to try to negate the contaminated surgery. We had tried to be as sterile as possible, but it just wasn't possible.

'It is done,' Fabio said at last.

'Okay, if we each grab a foot, we'll lift on three,' I said. Next thing, we were carrying Fatso by the feet in the most undignified manner over to the stable and attaching him to his drip. We applied a special bandage designed to support the wound. When a human has had their guts opened and they stand up, everything falls downwards away from the cut, but when a horse stands up, all the weight of those internal organs pushes down on the stitches so the risk of the whole thing falling apart is enormous. The weight of their guts is ten times that of a carnivore's. So we put a special roll of sterile cotton along the line of the wound, then a whole lot of reinforcing tape all the way around his body.

Fatso woke up unremarkably. He sat on his chest with his legs underneath. The crazy white-and-pink bandage was a dramatic contrast to his body of white with black spots. He sat up and gave one of those breathy, burring horse exhalations.

'He's alive!' Andy cried.

That was kind of amazing in itself. He'd survived the anaesthetic. I looked at my watch. It was 12.15 a.m. The whole thing had taken just thirty minutes.

It had felt so much longer. Your mind speeds up in that incredibly focussed state. Like the slow-mo of an accident or when that family-heirloom vase teeters on the edge of a wobbling table.

'Well, that's all we can do,' Fabio said.

Having seen that enormous caecum, I had no doubt that Fatso would have died within a day or two. It was so apparent that there was no need for anyone to say anything. There was also relief on the part of Giselle, Fabio and me, because Andy's comment that we were being gung-ho had been left hanging in the air. There was no gloating. But we all knew we'd done the right thing. Everything remained professional and convivial. While the surgeons *had* been keen to cut, it wasn't bravado. It was just that they felt all along that this was what needed to happen.

We went outside and there was Lachlan, sitting quietly smoking a roll-your-own. We thought he'd gone back to his camp but he'd hovered out there the whole time while we raced about, swearing and carrying on.

'The operation was a success,' Andy said. 'He's up and awake.'

I could see a tear in the corner of Lachlan's eye.

'My family and I are incredibly grateful for what you've done and it will never be forgotten.'

We showed him in, like the old-fashioned father in the waiting room of the maternity ward. He gave the little spotted horse a smooch, his leathery skin up against the long, white mane, which was now a lot messier than the public would ever see.

Fatso was by no means out of the woods, but he was alive. There was a strong possibility he still might die from infection. Horses would normally just have to think about a procedure like that to drop dead from contamination, if the shock hadn't killed them first.

But we hoped.

I had to get up before dawn the next day and I dropped in on Fatso before heading off. I peaked over the top of the stable door, and he was standing there, awake. He looked at me and nickered – that little noise they make, the equivalent of a cat meowing. I took it as a big thank you.

It was either that or, 'Don't you come near me, you butcher.'

Andy called about ten days later after she took the stitches out. She said Fatso had never looked back. He came in later to have his teeth filed down. Having over-sharp teeth and therefore not chewing properly leads to impactions because the food clumps up and doesn't pass through.

At the next Berry Show, Fatso took pride of place in his own little enclosure, as unaware of his massive drama as the kids and parents who gathered around him for photographs. Andy, Giselle, Fabio and I met up for a big roast dinner at my place. And as we looked at the beautiful leg of lamb, sizzling out of the oven, Andy insisted that Giselle and Fabio cut it.

THE SHOW MUST GO ON

James

Life was continuing at an amazing pace. The growth of the business seemed exponential, and we struggled to keep pace with employing enough people to keep up with the growth. What had been a small clinic of two vets and one nurse a few years ago was now a practice with five vets, five nurses and three locations. Anthony and I worked as hard as ever, but with more staff on the ground we spent a little less time doing basic hands-on stuff and a bit more time helping out junior staff members and running our business. There were some new demands on our time that were pretty strange, media commitments that we would never have dreamed of doing. These were all kept outside work hours so that we could continue to focus on the job at hand, but it meant that our days were as long as ever.

One of the perks of this was that we did less on call, only one in sixteen weekends where we were directly on call. This sounds like a dream, but the devil was in the detail. We actually worked and backed up a junior employee every second weekend, so basically we worked twelve days straight then got two days off – kind of. On those two days off we often had work commitments, talks to do at local community events, special information and procedure days and the ever-present serious emergency calls that could suck either of us in at any time. Add on top of this your personal and family life, and it was a crazy and exhausting time. But being busy is a great problem to have as a small business owner, and both of us enjoyed the challenge and the joy of watching our baby grow up and make its way in the world.

One such weekend Anthony was on call. He'd been super busy all week with 5 a.m. starts for large animal calls and had another full week ahead. We caught up for lunch at a mutual friend's birthday party on the Sunday and Anthony looked buggered.

'Mate, I'll take the phones this arvo and give you a break,' I offered, optimistically envisaging a lovely afternoon of blissful, job-free on-call relaxing and hanging out with my kids.

'No mate, that's okay, I'll be fine,' was his reply. One thing that I don't think either of us have been accused of is being lazy, and neither of us wants to shirk our responsibilities. I left it at that, but later on I received a text, saying he'd like to take me up on the offer. Not a problem – I flicked the phones to me.

It started innocently enough; a farmer called and needed a drug. Ralph Simpson was a good client so I said I'd meet him at the clinic. Charlie was super keen to tag along and have a look at the animals, so I threw him in the car and told him we could feed the hospital patients and clean their cages – a job I'm sure he won't be so enthusiastic about later in life. We got in to the clinic and Charlie was thrilled to tick off his tally of goat, kitten and dog and he was pleased as punch to give the medicine to Ralph. While we were there the phone rang – Murphy's law at work. A dog had suffered a nasty wound and the owner was bringing it straight in. I thought about trying to drop Charlie home but he seemed happy and I could put something on the computer for him to watch while I admitted the dog, a bounding Kelpie came with a wound to the side of the face. I admitted him and administered the pre-med, and was getting in the car to drop Charlie home before coming back to do the surgery when the phone rang again. This time it was a true emergency.

'There's a horse down in a truck, it can't get up and it's freaking out,' urged Simone, a small-animal client of ours who as far as I knew didn't have horses and lived in the middle of town, so I was a little confused. Sensing this, she added, 'It's on a truck travelling through town and it's gone down. They've pulled over out the front of my house.'

Okay, this is making a bit more sense. Not wanting to waste a second, I diverted, Charlie in tow. I was there 30 seconds after receiving the call. As I turned on to the street I looked up the hill and saw a horse truck with a horse lying prone on its side, not moving at all.

I parked a little distance away so as not to startle the horse and jumped out of the car, telling Charlie to stay there for a minute. 'I'll be back.'

There was quite a scene. Obviously the horse lying on its side was the dramatic centrepiece, but to the left were the people who were transporting the horses, one of them with a swollen lip and a cracked tooth. A ladder was pressed up against the truck, with the fly screen cut out and a rope dangling, evidence of where the young lady had scampered up the hastily borrowed ladder and used a kitchen knife to cut through the flyscreen and cut the horse loose moments earlier. To the right were groups of huddled onlookers, gathered at the front of each house. One of them I recognised: our vet nurse, Michelle.

'What can I do?' she offered.

'Well first, could you please get Charlie out of the car for me, then could you call Anthony and ask him to get here and give me a hand, then call Ronnie and get her to come and get Charlie,' I said urgently before turning my attention to the horse.

'Okay, how old is this horse and how quiet is it?' I asked after briefly introducing myself.

'She's a yearling called Stella who we just bought from the national sales, worth a bit too. She's unbroken but she's been prepped for sale and she's pretty quiet,' came the reply from Alannah, the young lady with the swollen face.

Luckily, after initially panicking and thrashing about after going down in the truck, Stella had realised that there was no point in continuing to struggle and had gone into freeze mode to deal with her fear. She was in the middle of the truck so they had managed to get the two horses behind her off to give us access and keep her from being trodden on. There were two horses in front of her, the nearest a big quarter horse called Ted, who was very quiet – which was lucky for Stella as her head was right next to Ted's left hind leg.

Horses need a bit of room to get themselves up off the ground. They need to swing their head upwards and extend their legs forwards, before rocking themselves up on the front legs and bringing their back legs under them. If they don't have enough room, they simply can't do it and we refer to it as being cast. This horse was stuck solid. The big thing to consider here is safety, both of the horse and of the humans involved – Alannah's busted lip was a reminder of how easy it is to get hurt. She had been hit by a gate while getting the other two horses off the truck.

'Can you get me a lunge whip?' I enquired as I doubled back to the car to grab some ropes. Charlie looked on, jabbering away to anyone who would listen and looking lovingly at the horse that had been unloaded.

I eased my way up the loading ramp and approached the rump of the horse. Everyone looked on in silence, wondering if I would be the next person hurt. I touched Stella gently with the lunge whip, using it like a long extension of my arm and letting her know that I was there. She jerked initially but then relaxed once she got used to me.

'Good girl, good girl,' I soothed as I approached and started rubbing her legs, staying in a relatively safe spot. I had a treasure trove of sedatives and syringes in the pockets of my vest. I assembled the needle and syringe and drew up a dose that I thought would heavily sedate Stella and make everything a little safer. I ran my hands along her legs feeling for a blood vessel I could access. There was a large superficial vessel on the inside of her right hind leg which was lying on the bottom of the truck. I rested my body on her rump, leant over her hindquarters and got my hand on the inside of her right leg. All the time I was poised, coiled ready to jump backwards and get the hell out of danger.

Luckily, Stella was as quiet as promised and my luck held. I was able to inject a combination of sedatives that relaxed her and left her practically motionless, though still capable of moving if she panicked. The danger was lessened, but by no means gone.

Anthony arrived moments later. It was great to see him and very handy to have someone to help manage the growing crowd. He got the lunge whip and passed it to me and I tried to pass it under the horse's back and through to the belly so we could attach the rope to it and pull it back under the horse. We were attempting to do something called a backwards assist, where we place a loop around the hind end of the horse. You pass the rope between the hind legs, over the back in front of the pelvis, down the other side and back between the legs. This way you can pull on the ropes without any knots or tightening on the horse. It's beautifully simple, safe and effective.

I couldn't get a great angle because Stella's back was almost pressed against one side of the truck. As I tried to pass the whip underneath the horse I heard a sudden cracking sound: it had snapped in two. Luckily, Alannah had another lunge whip, but despite all the grunting and groaning, we weren't able to thread the lunge whip to allow us to safely pass the rope.

Suggestions were coming thick and fast from the gallery of onlookers, but Anthony and I were the only people who had done this before, and we were the ones who were in danger of getting hurt, so his was the only voice I was listening to. We concocted a plan that involved placing the rope underneath the horse at the back and pulling both ends forward to get it under the horse. This meant me clambering like a monkey along the inside of the truck and sitting on the divider that separated Ted and Stella. Once I got up there I had to pull the rope forwards while Anthony tried to lift her hind end.

Luckily Ted was very amenable. I practically ended up sitting on him to heave this rope forwards. Anthony used all his strength to lift the hind end of Stella, and we managed to get the rope threaded without anyone getting hurt.

Now we had to anaesthetise Stella so that we could drag her out of the truck. Once again I injected into the only blood vessel I could safely access, but I couldn't get it all in. I had to scurry forwards and inject into her jugular vein, before wrapping her head in blankets. We thought we'd need the ute to pull her out but we were able to get four people on the ropes and gently ease her backwards and slide her down the ramp to the safety of terra firma. The truck was moved away and the other horses were taken to the showground for an overnight stay. The relief was palpable in everyone, and to most of the onlookers this signalled the end of the show. But we now had another tricky problem: managing the recovery of a young anaesthetised horse on a public street in the middle of town. To make matters worse, dusk was upon us.

Amateur traffic control was instituted to keep the cars away, and Stella snoozed for some time. At some stage while I was focussing on the horse, Ronnie had come and collected Charlie, and as I stood around waiting for Stella to wake up I called her to check everything was okay. Charlie asked after the horse and insisted on photos to see that she was okay.

We filled Stella with anti-inflammatories and antibiotics, and after what felt like an eternity she sat up, and groggily got to her feet. She was still very wobbly and it took four people to keep her standing. We zigged and zagged and started edging our way to the showground on foot, some 700 metres away. By this stage it was dark and we had head torches lighting the way. We tried to take the quietest route possible, and it took the best part of an hour to get Stella back to a stable for the night. You could sense everyone exhale and relax – we'd gotten the job done.

While we watched her slowly normalise in her box, Anthony's attention was drawn to his phone. There was an email from Screentime saying the second series of *Village Vets* had got the green light to go ahead. We grinned and high fived.

Where was the bloody camera today though? That would have been amazing!'

So here we are, ready to embark on a new series with a full cast of furry, feathery, scaly and woolly companions lined up. Who would've thought? One thing's for sure, with our dedicated team of staff gearing up, and our families cheering us on, we are thrilled to tackle the veterinary challenges and adventures that tomorrow will surely bring.

ACKNOWLEDGEMENTS

It is with great pride and a sense of wonder that we have completed our second book! Life has been a whirlwind of activity. With so many things happening in parallel, it's hard to believe that we've squeezed in this process.

An enormous thank you to Mark Whittaker. Without his enthusiasm and dedication this book would not have happened. We're sure Mark avoids us at dinner parties now, as he's already heard most of our stories! We really enjoyed the process of getting these experiences down on paper and Mark's efforts crafted them into the final polished product.

The team at ABC Books HarperCollins have been wonderful believers in this project. Lachlan McLaine has been an amazing editor to work with and has made this process incredibly smooth. I'm sure his day trip to Berry gave him a little insight into the practice and how we're constantly being pulled in different directions. Brigitta Doyle has been a great advocate for us from day one, and her enthusiasm for this project has never wavered. Thank you for all the support, and here's to another successful book.

Our families have been an amazing support, both in our lives to get us to this point, and on an enduring basis. Family (and the extended group of people bunched under that umbrella) is an incredibly important part of our lives and at the end of the day the reason behind everything we do.

A big thanks also to our long-suffering manager, Simone Landes at the Lifestyle Suite. It's safe to say that Simone has probably had as many stupid conference calls with us about this book and other projects to last a lifetime. Well, we think we are funny, Simone.

Our clients and their animals are the lifeblood of our practice and our lives. It's a privilege and a pleasure to have them in our practice and they make all the hard work worthwhile and fulfilling.

The nurses and vets who work in our practices deserve spectacular praise for their hard work and enthusiasm in the face of the challenges of our work. While it is difficult sometimes, the reflection required to write the book has given us time to pause and admire the extraordinary work we do as a team and how important each and every one of you is in that process. Now get back to work and stop scanning this book looking for the nice things we've said about you!

We hope you, the readers, enjoy this book, and that it gives you an insight into the action of a busy mixed veterinary practice. Our jobs provide us with a rich tapestry of life experience and it's a pleasure to have the opportunity to share it with you.